Human
Rights
& Human
Wrongs

John R. W. Stott has an international ministry as a scholar, pastor, and author. For many years rector of All Souls Church, London, he is now director of the London Institute for Contemporary Christianity.

Human Rights & Human Wrongs

Major Issues for a New Century

JOHN R. W. STOTT

Baker Books

A Division of Baker Book House Co
Grand Rapids, Michigan 49516

© 1984, 1990, 1999 by John R. W. Stott

Published by Baker Books
a division of Baker Book House Company
P.O. Box 6287, Grand Rapids, MI 49516-6287

Printed in the United States of America

First published in Great Britain in 1984 by Marshall Morgan and Scott. Second edition published in Great Britain in 1990 by Marshall Pickering. Third edition published in Great Britain in 1999 by Harper Collins Publishers.

Library of Congress Cataloging-in-Publication Data

Stott, John R. W.
    Human rights & human wrongs : major issues for a new century / John R. W. Stott.
        p.   cm.
    Rev. ed. of: Decisive issues facing Christians today. c1990.
    ISBN 0-8010-6094-X (pbk.)
    1. Church and social problems. I. Stott, John R. W. Decisive issues facing Christians today. II. Title. III. Title: Human rights and human wrongs.
HN31.S838   1999
261.8'3—dc21   99-37517

All the royalties from this book have been irrevocably assigned to the Evangelical Literature Trust (UK), which distributes evangelical books to pastors, theological teachers and students, and seminary libraries in the developing world. Further information may be obtained from, and tax-deductible donations sent to, the evangelical literature program of John Stott Ministries, 871 Pinegrove Court, Wheaton, Illinois 60187.

A companion volume by John Stott is *Our Social and Sexual Revolution: Major Issues for a New Century*.

For current information about all releases from Baker Book House, visit our web site:
http://www.bakerbooks.com

Contents

Abbreviations   7
Preface to the First Edition (1984)   9
Preface to the Second Edition (1990)   11
Preface to the Third Edition (1999)   13

Part 1   Christians in a Non-Christian Society

1. Involvement: Is It Our Concern?   17
   The Evangelical Heritage of Social Concern
   Reasons for "The Great Reversal"
   The Church and Politics
   The Biblical Basis for Social Concern
   Practical Action

2. Complexity: Can We Think Straight?   45
   A Christian Mind
   The Reality of God
   The Paradox of Our Humanness
   The Future of Society
   An Appendix on Postmodernity

3. Pluralism: Should We Impose Our Views?   63
   Imposition
   Laissez-Faire
   Persuasion
   Examples of Persuasion by Argument
   Political Systems

4. Alienation: Have We Any Influence?   79
   Salt and Light
   Prayer and Evangelism
   Witness and Protest
   Example and Groups

Part 2　Global Issues

5. Wars and Rumors of Wars　99
   Contemporary Realities
   Theological and Moral Reflections
   The Call for Nuclear Disarmament
   Questions and Qualifications
   Christian Peace-Making

6. Our Human Environment　127
   Reasons for Environmental Concern
   The Biblical Perspective
   The Conservation Debate
   Contemporary Awareness

7. North–South Economic Inequality　145
   The Brandt Commission Reports
   Debt and Development
   The Principle of Unity
   The Principle of Equality
   Personal and Economic Deductions

8. Human Rights　165
   Human Rights Violations
   Concern for Human Rights
   Human Dignity
   Human Equality
   Human Responsibility

Notes　180

Abbreviations

The biblical text quoted is normally that of the New International Version. If another text is used, this is stated.

Arndt-
Gingrich   *A Greek-English Lexicon of the New Testament and Other Early Christian Literature* by William F. Arndt and F. Wilbur Gingrich (University of Chicago Press and Cambridge University Press, 1957).

AV   The Authorized (King James') Version of the Bible, 1611.

JB   The Jerusalem Bible (Darton, Longman and Todd, 1966).

NASB   The New American Standard Bible (Moody Press, Chicago, 1960).

NEB   The New English Bible (NT 1961, 2nd edition 1970; OT 1970).

NIV   The New International Version of the Bible (Hodder & Stoughton, NT 1974; OT 1979; revised edition 1984).

RSV   The Revised Standard Version of the Bible (NT 1946, 2nd edition 1971; OT 1952).

Preface to the First Edition (1984)

One of the most notable features of the worldwide evangelical movement during the past ten to fifteen years has been the recovery of our temporarily mislaid social conscience. For approximately fifty years (c. 1920–70)
evangelical Christians were preoccupied with the task of defending the historic biblical faith against the attacks of theological liberalism, and reacting
against its "social gospel." But now we are convinced that God has given
us social as well as evangelistic responsibilities in his world. Yet the half
century of neglect has put us far behind in this area. We have a long way
to go to catch up.

This book is my own contribution to the catching up process. Its source
may be traced to 1978–79, when Michael Baughen, now bishop of Chester,
but then rector of All Souls Church, invited me to preach a series of occasional sermons under the title *Issues Facing Britain Today.* Several of these
chapters began their life in the pulpit, and subsequently grew into lectures
at the London Institute for Contemporary Christianity, whose raison d'être
is to help people develop a Christian perspective on the complexities of the
modern world.

I confess that several times in the course of writing I have been tempted
to give up. I have felt now foolish and now presumptuous to attempt such
an undertaking. For I am in no sense a specialist in moral theology or social
ethics, and I have no particular expertise or experience in some of the fields
into which I trespass. Moreover, each topic is complex, has attracted an
extensive literature, only some of which I have been able to read, and is
potentially divisive, even in a few cases explosive. Yet I have persevered,
mainly because what I am venturing to offer the public is not a polished
professional piece but the rough-hewn amateur work of an ordinary Christian who is struggling to think Christianly, that is, to apply the biblical revelation to the pressing issues of the day.

For this is my concern. I begin with a commitment to the Bible as "God's
Word written," which is how it is described in the Anglican Articles and
has been received by nearly all churches until comparatively recent times.
Such is the basic presupposition of this book; it is not part of my present

purpose to argue it. But we Christians have a second commitment, namely, to the world in which God has placed us. And our two commitments often seem to be in conflict. Being a collection of documents that relate to particular and distant events, the Bible has an archaic feel. It seems incompatible with our Western culture, with its space probes and micro-processors. Like every other Christian I feel myself caught in the painful tension between these two worlds. They are centuries apart. Yet I have sought to resist the temptation to withdraw from either world by capitulation to the other.

Some Christians, anxious above all to be faithful to the revelation of God without compromise, ignore the challenges of the modern world and live in the past. Others, anxious to respond to the world around them, trim and twist God's revelation in their search for relevance. I have struggled to avoid both traps. For the Christian is at liberty to surrender neither to antiquity nor to modernity. Instead, I have sought with integrity to submit to the revelation of yesterday within the realities of today. It is not easy to combine loyalty to the past with sensitivity to the present. Yet this is our Christian calling: to live under the Word in the world.

Many people have helped me develop my thinking. I thank the "apostolic succession" of my study assistants—Roy McCloughry, Tom Cooper, Mark Labberton, Steve Ingraham, and Bob Wismer—who have compiled bibliographies, assembled groups for the discussion of sermon topics, gathered information, and checked references. Bob Wismer has been specially helpful in the final stages, reading the MS twice and making valuable suggestions. So has Frances Whitehead, my secretary for twenty-eight years. She and Vivienne Curry typed the MS. Steve Andrews, my present study assistant, has been meticulous in proof correcting. I also thank friends who have read different chapters and given me the benefit of their comments— Oliver Barclay, Raymond Johnston, John Gladwin, Mark Stephens, Roy McCloughry, Myra Chave-Jones, and my colleagues at the London Institute, Andrew Kirk (associate director) and Martyn Eden (dean). I am particularly grateful to Jim Houston, founding principal and now chancellor of Regent College, Vancouver, whose vision of the need for Christians to have an integrated worldview has stimulated both my own thinking and the founding of the London Institute.

Preface to the Second Edition (1990)

Six years have passed since the publication of *Issues Facing Christians Today*, and in this brief period the world has witnessed many changes. Detente between the superpowers has dawned, and disarmament has begun. Freedom and democracy, undreamed of only a year ago, have taken root in Eastern Europe and the Soviet Union, even while brutal repression has trampled on these tender plants in China. Old debates (like the nuclear threat) have moved on, while new debates (like the AIDS epidemic) have arisen.

Hence the need for a second and revised edition of this book. The statistics on armaments, human rights violations, other religions, unemployment, divorce, and abortion have all been brought up to date. It has been necessary to read and reflect on newly published books on almost every issue. A number of these have been written by evangelical authors, which is an encouraging sign of our developing social conscience. Another sign of this is the merger of the London Institute for Contemporary Christianity with the Shaftesbury Project for Christian Involvement in Society in order to form "Christian Impact," and so combine research, education, and thought with action. Yet other signs are the stronger commitment to social action explicit in the *Manila Manifesto,* which was adopted at the conclusion of the second Lausanne Congress on World Evangelization (1989), and the "Salt and Light" project sponsored by the British Evangelical Alliance.

This second edition of *Issues Facing Christians Today* also incorporates new material on many topics—on the rapid growth of the green movement and its warnings about ozone layer depletion and the greenhouse effect; on the Brundtland Report, *Our Common Future,* and its concept of "sustainable development"; on the burdens of debt borne by many nuclear families in the West and—to a crippling degree—by Third World countries; on three important Christian documents recently published in South Africa; on further thinking by evangelical Christians about the role, ministry, and leadership of women; on human fertilization and modern reproductive technologies; on the theological, moral, pastoral, and educational aspects of AIDS; and on the effectiveness of Christian social protest and witness.

11

I express my cordial thanks to Toby Howarth and Todd Shy, my former and present study assistants, for painstakingly rereading the whole book and making numerous suggestions; to Marty Eden, Elaine Storkey, Roy McCloughry, Maurice Hobbs, John Wyatt, and Stephen Rand for perusing individual sections or chapters and proposing changes; and to Frances Whitehead for much retyping and some really skilful "scissor-and-paste" editing.

In conclusion, I feel the need to restate what I wrote in the Preface to the first edition, namely, that *Issues* represents the struggles of a person who lays no claim to infallibility, who is anxious to go on increasing his Christian integrity over against the pressures of a largely secular society, and who to that end is continuously seeking fresh light from Scripture.

Preface to the Third Edition (1999)

This book was first published in 1984, and its second, updated edition appeared in 1990. Since then eight more years have passed, and a third, revised edition is already overdue. It is extraordinary that in the topic of every chapter the debate has moved on, and in some cases the situation has changed significantly.

With the collapse of Euro-Marxism, following the demolition of the Berlin Wall, much of the map of Europe has had to be redrawn. The end of the cold war has made possible some international disarmament treaties. The "Earth Summit" at Rio in 1992 both mirrored and stimulated growing public alarm over ozone layer depletion and global warming. New policies of development and proposals for debt cancellation have brought realistic hope to the poorest nations. The conciliatory leadership of President Mandela and the dismantling of apartheid shine brightly against the increase of racially motivated violence and the reemergence of nationalism in Europe. Christians are also disturbed by the influences which undermine marriage and the family (especially cohabitation and same-sex partnerships) and which challenge the sanctity of human life (especially abortion and euthanasia).

Ten consultants, each a specialist in his own field, have been kind enough to read the chapter covering their area of expertise and then to recommend changes to make, books to read, and new issues to consider. I am most grateful for their criticisms and suggestions. They are (in alphabetical order) Sir Fred Catherwood, Martyn Eden, Dr. David Green, Gary Haugen, Sir John Houghton, Roy McCloughry, Dr. Alan Storkey, Pradip Sudra, Dr. Neil Summerton, and Professor John Wyatt.

I reserve my special gratitude for John Yates, my current study assistant. Not only has he given himself the chore of reading the book's second edition several times over, made his own insightful suggestions, and updated the statistics, but he has also followed up our consultants' proposals, done some redrafting himself and advised me which books and articles I needed to read and ponder myself. I cannot speak too highly of his conscientious work.

PART 1

Christians in a Non-Christian Society

1

Involvement:
Is It Our Concern?

It is exceedingly strange that any followers of Jesus Christ should ever have needed to ask whether social involvement was their concern, and that controversy should have blown up over the relationship between evangelism and social responsibility. For it is evident that in his public ministry Jesus both "went about . . . teaching . . . and preaching" (Matthew 4:23; 9:35 RSV) and "went about doing good and healing" (Acts 10:38 RSV). In consequence, "evangelism and social concern have been intimately related to one another throughout the history of the Church. . . . Christian people have often engaged in both activities quite unselfconsciously, without feeling any need to define what they were doing or why."[1]

The Evangelical Heritage of Social Concern[2]

There were some remarkable examples of this in eighteenth-century Europe and America. The Evangelical Revival, which stirred both continents, is not to be thought of only in terms of the preaching of the gospel and the converting of sinners to Christ; it also led to widespread philanthropy and profoundly affected society on both sides of the Atlantic. John Wesley remains the most striking instance. He is mainly remembered as the itinerant evangelist and open-air preacher. And so he was. But the gospel he preached inspired people to take up social causes in the name of Christ. Historians have attributed to Wesley's influence rather than to any other

17

the fact that Britain was spared the horrors of a bloody revolution like France's.[3]

The change which came over Britain during this period was well documented in J. Wesley Bready's remarkable book, *England Before and After Wesley,* subtitled "The Evangelical Revival and Social Reform." His research forced him to conclude that "the true nursing-mother of the spirit and character values that have created and sustained Free Institutions throughout the English-speaking world," indeed "the moral watershed of Anglo-Saxon history," was "the much-neglected and oft-lampooned Evangelical Revival."[4]

Bready described "the deep savagery of much of the 18th century,"[5] which was characterized by "the wanton torture of animals for sport, the bestial drunkenness of the populace, the inhuman traffic in African negroes, the kidnapping of fellow-countrymen for exportation and sale as slaves, the mortality of parish children, the universal gambling obsession, the savagery of the prison system and penal code, the welter of immorality, the prostitution of the theatre, the growing prevalence of lawlessness, superstition and lewdness; the political bribery and corruption, the ecclesiastical arrogance and truculence, the shallow pretensions of Deism, the insincerity and debasement rampant in Church and State—such manifestations suggest that the British people were then perhaps as deeply degraded and debauched as any people in Christendom."[6]

But then things began to change. And in the nineteenth century slavery and the slave trade were abolished, the prison system was humanized, conditions in factory and mine were improved, education became available to the poor, trade unions began, and so on.

"Whence, then, this pronounced humanity?—this passion for social justice, and sensitivity to human wrongs? There is but one answer commensurate with stubborn historical truth. It derived from a new social conscience. And if that social conscience, admittedly, was the offspring of more than one progenitor, it nonetheless was mothered and nurtured by the Evangelical Revival of vital, practical Christianity—a revival which illumined the central postulates of the New Testament ethic, which made real the Fatherhood of God and the Brotherhood of men, which pointed the priority of personality over property, and which directed heart, soul and mind, towards the establishment of the Kingdom of Righteousness on earth."[7]

The Evangelical Revival "did more to transfigure the moral character of the general populace, than any other movement British history can record."[8] For Wesley was both a preacher of the gospel and a prophet of social righteousness. He was "the man who restored to a nation its soul."[9]

The evangelical leaders of the next generation were committed with equal enthusiasm to evangelism and social action. The most famous among them were Granville Sharp, Thomas Clarkson, James Stephen, Zachary Macaulay,

Charles Grant, John Shore (Lord Teignmouth), Thomas Babington, Henry Thornton, and, of course, their guiding light, William Wilberforce. Because several of them lived in Clapham, at that time a village three miles south of London, and belonged to Clapham Parish Church, whose Rector John Venn was one of them, they came to be known as "the Clapham Sect," although in Parliament and in the press they were mocked as "the Saints."

It was their concern over the plight of the African slaves which first brought them together. Three days before his death in 1791, John Wesley wrote to Wilberforce to assure him that God had raised him up for his "glorious enterprise" and to urge him not to be weary of welldoing. It is largely to the Clapham Sect (under Wilberforce's leadership) that the credit belongs for the first settlement of freed slaves in Sierra Leone (1787), the abolition of the trade (1807), the registration of slaves in the colonies (1820), which put an end to slave smuggling, and finally their emancipation (1833). It is true that "the Saints" were wealthy aristocrats who shared some of the social blindspots of their time, but they were extremely generous in their philanthropy and the range of their concerns was extraordinary. In addition to the slavery question, they involved themselves in penal and parliamentary reform, popular education (Sunday schools, tracts, and the *Christian Observer* newspaper), Britain's obligation to her colonies (especially India), the spread of the gospel (they were instrumental in the founding of both the Bible Society and the Church Missionary Society), and factory legislation. They also campaigned against dueling, gambling, drunkenness, immorality, and cruel animal sports. And throughout they were directed and motivated by their strong evangelical faith. Ernest Marshall Howse has written of them: "This group of Clapham friends gradually became knit together in an astonishing intimacy and solidarity. They planned and laboured like a committee that never was dissolved. At the Clapham mansions they congregated by common impulse in what they chose to call their 'Cabinet Councils' wherein they discussed the wrongs and injustices which were a reproach to their country, and the battles which would need to be fought to establish righteousness. And thereafter, in Parliament and out, they moved as one body, delegating to each man the work he could do best, that the common principles might be maintained and their common purposes be realized."[10]

Reginald Coupland in his biography of Wilberforce justly commented: "It was, indeed, a unique phenomenon—this brotherhood of Christian politicians. There has never been anything like it since in British public life."[11]

Anthony Ashley Cooper was elected to the British Parliament in 1826, age 25. First in the House of Commons, and then in the House of Lords as the seventh Earl of Shaftesbury, he concerned himself successively with the plight of lunatics, child workers in the factories and mills, "climbing boys" or chimney sweeps, women and children in the mines, and the children of the slums, more than 30,000 of whom in London were without a home and more than a million of whom in the whole country were without schooling. His biographer Georgina Battiscombe, who is often sharply critical of him, nevertheless concludes her account of his life with this generous tribute: "No man has in fact ever done more to lessen the extent of human misery, or to add to the sum total of human happiness."[12] And he himself felt able to claim that "most of the great philanthropic movements of the century have sprung from the Evangelicals."[13]

The same story can be told of the United States in the nineteenth century. Social involvement was both the child of evangelical religion and the twin sister of evangelism. This is clearly seen in Charles G. Finney, who is best known as the lawyer turned evangelist and author of *Lectures on Revivals of Religion* (1835). Through his preaching of the gospel large numbers were brought to faith in Christ. What is not as well known is that he was concerned for "reforms" as well as "revivals." He was convinced, as Donald W. Dayton has shown in his *Discovering an Evangelical Heritage,* both that the gospel "releases a mighty impulse toward social reform" and that the Church's neglect of social reform grieved the Holy Spirit and hindered revival. It is astonishing to read Finney's statement in his 23rd Lecture on Revival that "the great business of the Church is to reform the world. . . . The Church of Christ was originally organized to be a body of reformers. The very profession of Christianity implies the profession and virtually an oath to do all that can be done for the universal reformation of the world."[14]

It is hardly surprising to learn, therefore, that through Finney's evangelism God raised up "an army of young converts who became the troops of the reform movement of his age." In particular, "the anti-slavery forces . . . were drawn largely from the converts of Finney's revivals." Chief among these was Theodore Weld, who gave his whole life to the anti-slavery struggle. He was converted under Finney's ministry and worked for a time as his assistant.[15] Not that Weld was the American equivalent of Wilberforce, however, for he was not a parliamentarian. In fact, "the agitation [that is, the anti-slavery agitation in America] was accomplished not so much by heroes of reform as by very numerous obscure persons, prompted by an impulse religious in character and evangelical in spirit, which began the Great Revival of 1830."[16]

The nineteenth century is also known for the enormous expansion of Christian missions which it witnessed. It must not be imagined, however, that the missionaries concentrated exclusively on preaching, or indeed that their social concern was restricted to aid and relief, to the neglect of development and even sociopolitical activity. It is doubtful if these distinctions have ever been neatly drawn in practice. The American missiologist Dr. R. Pierce Beaver has written:

Social action in mission can be traced from the time of the apostles. . . . Concern was never limited to relief. The itinerating missionary carried with him a bag of medicines, new or better seeds and plants, and improved livestock. Nevius introduced the modern orchard industry into Shantung. The Basel missionaries revolutionized the economy of Ghana by introducing coffee and cocoa grown by families and individuals on their own land. James McKean transformed the life of Northern Thailand by eliminating its three major curses—smallpox, malaria, and leprosy. Wells and pure water often came through the help of missionaries. Industrial schools were stressed through the nineteenth century, and industries were established. In addition, the missionaries were constantly the protectors of the native peoples against exploitation and injustice by government and commercial companies. . . . They played a very important part in the abolishing of forced labour in the Congo. They resisted blackbirding in the South Pacific. They fought fiercely for human rights in combating opium, foot-binding, and exposure of girl babies in China. They waged war against widow-burning, infanticide, and temple prostitution in India, and above all broke the social and economic slavery of the caste system for the low and outcaste peoples.[17]

Reasons for "The Great Reversal"

It seems, therefore, to be an established fact that at least during the nineteenth century, not only in Britain and America but also through the agency of missionaries in Africa and Asia, the gospel of Jesus Christ produced the good fruit of social reform. But then something happened, especially among evangelical Christians. At some point during the first thirty years of the twentieth century, and especially during the decade following World War I, a major shift took place which the American historian Timothy L. Smith has termed "The Great Reversal," and which David O. Moberg investigates in his book with that title.[18] Although Dr. Moberg does not attempt a thorough analysis of the origins of the evangelical renunciation of social responsibility, they seem to have included the following.

The first cause was the fight against theological liberalism, which at the turn of the century was seeping into the churches of Europe and America. Michael Cassidy has called this "The Great Betrayal" (the liberal neglect of the gospel); it occasioned "The Great Reversal" (the evangelical neglect of social responsibility). Evangelicals felt they had their backs to the wall.[19] Understandably, they became preoccupied with the defense and proclamation of the gospel, for nobody else seemed to be championing historic biblical Christianity. This was the period (actually 1910–15) when the series of twelve small books entitled *The Fundamentals* was published in the United States, from which the term "fundamentalism" arose. When evangelicals were busy seeking to vindicate the fundamentals of the faith, they felt they had no time for social concerns.

Second, evangelicals reacted against the so-called social gospel which theological liberals were developing at this time. Its most popular spokesman was Walter Rauschenbusch, who was Professor of Church History at Rochester Seminary, New York, from 1897 to 1917. He had come face to face with oppressive poverty during his twelve-year Baptist pastorate in New York City (1886–97), and this experience shaped his message. In his first book, *Christianity and the Social Crisis* (1907),[20] after tracing the social compassion of the Hebrew prophets, Jesus, and the early Church, he criticized capitalism and advocated a simple kind of "communism" or Christian socialism.[21] He also contrasted "the old evangel of the saved soul" with "the new evangel of the Kingdom of God."[22] "It is not a matter of getting individuals into heaven," he wrote, "but of transforming the life on earth into the harmony of heaven."[23] Again, the "essential purpose of Christianity" is to "transform human society into the Kingdom of God by regenerating all human relationships."[24] These quotations are enough to disclose his two errors, which led evangelicals to condemn the "social gospel" and so hindered the development of an evangelical social program. First, he identified the Kingdom of God with "a reconstruction of society on a Christian basis."[25] Second, he implied that human beings can establish the divine Kingdom by themselves (whereas Jesus always spoke of it as a gift of God). Though he said he cherished "no Utopian delusion,"[26] he nevertheless believed that "it rests upon us to decide if a new era is to dawn in the transformation of the world into the Kingdom of God."[27] The "common aim" of church and state, he affirmed, "is to transform humanity into the Kingdom of God."[28]

It will be clear from this unguarded language that Christianity and the social crisis was not a work of serious theology. Nor was Rauschenbusch's second book, with its misleading title, *Christianizing the Social Order* (1912). His third book gave the game away, however: *A Theology for the Social Gospel* (1917).[29] He began it with these ingenious words: "We have a social gospel. We need a systematic theology large enough to match it and vital enough to back it." Indeed, a "readjustment and expansion of theology" is necessary in order to "furnish an adequate intellectual basis for the social gospel."[30] Thus Rauschenbusch betrayed himself. First, we formulate our social gospel, and only then do we hunt around for an intellectual or theological justification for it! He finds it in the Kingdom of God. "This doctrine is itself the social gospel."[31] For "the Kingdom of God is humanity organized according to the will of God."[32] "The Kingdom of God is the Christian transfiguration of the social order."[33]

But the Kingdom of God is not Christianized society. It is the divine rule in the lives of those who acknowledge Christ. It has to be "received," "entered," or "inherited," he said, by humble and penitent faith in him. And without a new birth it is impossible to see it, let alone enter it. Those who do receive it like a child, however, find themselves members of the new community of the Messiah, which is called to exhibit the ideals of his rule in the world and so to present the world with an alternative social reality. This social challenge of the gospel of the Kingdom is quite different from the "social gospel." When Rauschenbusch politicized the Kingdom of God, it is understandable (if regrettable) that, in reaction to him, evangelicals concentrated on evangelism and personal philanthropy, and steered clear of sociopolitical action.

The third reason for the evangelical neglect of social responsibility was the widespread disillusion and pessimism which followed World War I, because of its exposure of human evil. Earlier social programs had failed. Human beings and human society appeared to be irreformable. Attempts at reform were useless. To be sure, because of the biblical doctrines of original sin and human depravity, evangelicals should not have been taken by surprise. But between the Wars there was no evangelical leader to articulate the providence and common grace of God as grounds for persevering hope. Historic reformed Christianity was in eclipse.

Fourth, there was the spread (especially through J. N. Darby's teaching and its popularization in the Scofield Bible) of the premillennial scheme. This portrays the present evil world as beyond improvement or redemption, and predicts instead that it will deteriorate steadily until the coming of Jesus, who will then set up his millennial reign on earth. If the world is getting worse, and if only Jesus at his coming will put it right, the argument runs, there seems no point in trying to reform it meanwhile. Adopting political programs is "like cleaning the staterooms on the Titanic after it has hit the iceberg. . . . It is far more important simply to preach the Gospel and to rescue souls for the next life."[34]

The fifth reason for evangelical alienation from social concern was probably the spread of Christianity among middle-class people, who tended to dilute it by identifying it with their own culture. This is without a doubt one of the factors underlying the American sociological findings reported by Milton Rokeach in 1969 and summarized by David O. Moberg. These were highly critical of the negative social influences of organized religion.

> The general picture that emerges from the results presented . . . is that those who place a high value on *salvation* are conservative, anxious to maintain the *status quo*, and unsympathetic or indifferent to the plight of the black and the poor. . . . Considered all together, the data suggest a portrait of the religious-minded as a person having a self-centred preoccupation with saving his own soul, an other-worldly orientation, coupled with an indifference toward or

23

even a tacit endorsement of a social system that would perpetuate social inequality and injustice.

David Moberg tells how this report brought a storm of protest on the ground that the research methodology was faulty, but he adds that altogether to ignore these findings and conclusions "would be a serious mistake."[35] Though I have been able earlier to mention some fine examples of social action in the eighteenth and nineteenth centuries, there have certainly been other situations in which the Church has acquiesced in oppression and exploitation, and has taken no action against these evils, nor even protested against them.

This "Great Reversal" is explicable for these five reasons. We do not blame our evangelical forebears; in their place we would probably have reacted to contemporary pressures as they did. Not that all evangelicals mislaid their social conscience at the beginning of the twentieth century and between the Wars. Some soldiered on, deeply involved in social as well as evangelical ministries, and thus retained this indispensable outworking of the gospel, without which evangelicalism loses part of its authenticity. But most turned away. Then during the 1960s, the decade of protest, when young people were rebelling against the materialism, superficiality, and hypocrisy of the adult world they had inherited, the evangelical mainstream recovered its morale, and the process of "Reversing the Great Reversal" (as David Moberg entitles his final chapter) got under way.

Probably the first voice to recall the evangelical constituency to its social responsibilities was that of the American Christian scholar Carl F. H. Henry, the founding editor of *Christianity Today*, in his book, *The Uneasy Conscience of Modern Fundamentalism* (1947). Not many seemed to listen. But gradually the message caught on. And in 1966, at the conclusion of an American conference on world missions, the participants unanimously adopted the "Wheaton Declaration," which firmly bracketed "the primacy of preaching the gospel to every creature" and "a verbal witness to Jesus Christ" with "evangelical social action," and urged "all evangelicals to stand openly and firmly for racial equality, human freedom, and all forms of social justice throughout the world."

In Britain in the 1960s a number of evangelical leaders began to grapple with the social application of the gospel. Most of them were laymen in professional and business life, and prominent among them were George Goyder (*The Responsible Company*, 1961), Fred Catherwood (*The Christian in Industrial Society*, 1964) and Professor Norman Anderson (*Into the World*, 1968). This incipient groundswell of social concern found public expression at the first National Evangelical Anglican Congress at Keele University in 1967. There Anglican evangelicals publicly repented of their tendency to withdraw from both the secular world and the wider Church, and committed themselves to conscientious involvement in both. As for the scope of mission, the Report produced by the Congress said that "evangelism and compassionate service belong together in the mission of God."[36]

The turning-point for the worldwide evangelical constituency was doubtless the International Congress on World Evangelization held in July 1974 at Lausanne, Switzerland. Some 2,700 participants gathered from more than 150 nations under the slogan "Let the Earth Hear His Voice," and at the conclusion of the Congress endorsed the Lausanne Covenant. After three introductory sections on the purpose of God, the authority of the Bible, and the uniqueness of Christ, its fourth is entitled "The Nature of Evangelism" and its fifth "Christian Social Responsibility." The latter declares that "evangelism and socio-political involvement are both part of our Christian duty." But the two paragraphs stand side by side in the Covenant, with no attempt to relate them, except for the statement in paragraph 6 that "in the church's mission of sacrificial service evangelism is primary."

During the years which followed the Lausanne Congress, there was a certain amount of tension within the evangelical movement, as some emphasized evangelism, others social activity, and all of us wondered how according to Scripture we should spell out the relationship between the two. So in June 1982, under the joint sponsorship of the Lausanne Committee and the World Evangelical Fellowship, the "Consultation on the Relationship between Evangelism and Social Responsibility" (CRESR) was held in Grand Rapids, and issued its report entitled *Evangelism and Social Responsibility: An Evangelical Commitment.* Although we did not see eye to eye on every point, God led us to a remarkable degree of consensus. Social activity was said to be both a consequence of and a bridge to evangelism, and indeed the two were declared to be partners. Besides, they are united by the gospel. "For the gospel is the root, of which both evangelism and social responsibility are the fruits."[37] The Report also has a chapter on "History and Eschatology" and a final, more practical chapter entitled "Guidelines for Action."

A significant consultation was held in Britain in November 1988 entitled "Salt and Light." Jointly sponsored by the Evangelical Alliance, Tearfund, and the Evangelical Missionary Alliance, it brought over 300 people together from a wide variety of backgrounds in church, culture, and experience. Twenty-one specialist groups reviewed the major contemporary issues of social ethics. In spite of participants" different theological and political perspectives, they expressed a common commitment to the integration of evangelistic and social concerns and to promoting this holistic vision among Christians.

Eight years later, in November 1996, the National Assembly of Evangelicals brought 2,700 evangelical leaders together. The Bournemouth Declaration, endorsed at its conclusion, included the following unambiguous statements: "We recognize that no area of life is outside God's sovereign rule. We take the incarnation and transforming work of Christ as our model for engagement. We affirm our commitment to releasing Christian people for involvement at all levels of society." Moreover, these are no mere pious aspirations. For example, "UK Action" (a joint initiative of Tearfund and the Evangelical Alliance) is enabling an increasing number of local British churches to develop holistic ministries among the urban poor. In order to encourage more informed prayer and political action, the Evangelical Alliance now produces *Westminster Watch,* a bulletin of news and Christian comment from the Palace of Westminster. And a number of evangelical Christian leaders and organizations were involved in the founding in 1990 of "The Movement for Christian Democracy." Its ideals are given a fine biblical expression in its Westminster Declaration. Its purpose is "to further Christian understanding of social and political matters, to initiate appropriate forms of action, to stimulate informed discussion, and to influence policy-making."

The Church and Politics

It will have been noted that the Lausanne Covenant speaks not just of "social responsibility" but of "socio-political involvement." It is the use of the word "political" which causes red warning lights to flash in the minds of many evangelicals. They have always engaged in humanitarian work, especially in medical and educational programs; it is political activity of which they have often fought shy. Indeed, opposition to it is much wider than the evangelical constituency. Whenever the Church (or any branch of it) becomes politically embroiled, a howl of protest can be expected from both within its membership and from outside. "The Church should steer clear of politics," people cry. "Religion and politics don't mix."

Several different issues are involved in this controversy, and the waters of the debate are muddied by a failure to distinguish between them. The first is the definition of the word "politics." The second concerns the relationship between the social and the political, and why they cannot be kept apart. Third, we need to consider the reasons why some people oppose the Church's involvement in politics, and what they are trying to safeguard. Then, fourth, we need to ask to whom Christian political responsibility belongs.

First, we must define our terms. The words "politics" and "political" may be given either a broad or a narrow definition. Broadly speaking, "politics" denotes the life of the city (*polis*) and the responsibilities of the citizen (*polites*). It is concerned therefore with the whole of our life in human society. Politics is the art of living together in a community. According to its narrow definition, however, politics is the science of government. It is concerned with the development and adoption of specific policies with a view to their being enshrined in legislation. It is about gaining power for social change.

Once this distinction is clear, we may ask whether Jesus was involved in politics. In the latter and narrower sense, he clearly was not. He never formed a political party, adopted a political program, or organized a political protest. He took no steps to influence the policies of Caesar, Pilate, or Herod. On the contrary, he renounced a political career. In the other and broader sense of the word, however, his whole ministry was political. For he had himself come into the world in order to share in the life of the human community, and he sent his followers into the world to do the same. Moreover, the Kingdom of God he proclaimed and inaugurated was a radically new and different social organization, whose values and standards challenged those of the old and fallen community. In this way his teaching had "political" implications. It offered an alternative to the status quo. His kingship, moreover, was perceived as a challenge to Caesar's, and he was therefore accused of sedition.

Second, we need to consider the relation between the "social" and the "political," now using this word in its narrower sense. In its final chapter the Grand Rapids Report addressed itself to this question. It distinguished between "social service" and "social action," and helpfully drew up the following table:

Social Service	Social Action
• Relieving human need	• Removing the causes of human need
• Philanthropic activity	• Political and economic activity
• Seeking to minister to individuals and families	• Seeking to transform the structures of society
• Works of mercy	• The quest for justice[38]

The Report went on to delineate sociopolitical action in these terms: "It looks beyond persons to structures, beyond the rehabilitation of prison inmates to the reform of the prison system, beyond improving factory conditions to securing a more participatory role for the workers, beyond caring for the poor to improving—and when necessary transforming—the economic system (whatever it may be) and the political system (again, whatever it may be), until it facilitates their liberation from poverty and oppression."[39]

It seems clear, then, that genuine Christian social concern will embrace both social service and social action. It would be very artificial to divorce them. Some cases of need cannot be relieved at all without political action (the harsh treatment of slaves could have been ameliorated, but not slavery itself; it had to be abolished). To go on relieving other needs, though necessary, may condone the situation which causes them. If travelers on the Jerusalem–Jericho road were habitually beaten up and habitually cared for by Good Samaritans, the need for better laws to eliminate armed robbery might well be overlooked. If road accidents keep occurring at a particular crossroads, it is not more ambulances that are needed but the installation of traffic lights to prevent accidents. It is always good to feed the hungry; it is better if possible to eradicate the causes of hunger. So if we truly love our neighbors, and want to serve them, our service may oblige us to take (or solicit) political action on their behalf.

Why, then, is there so much hostility to the idea of the Church becoming politically involved? This is our third question. An articulate criticism was made by Dr. Edward Norman in his 1978 Reith Lectures, *Christianity and the World Order*.[40] He was not actually denying either that "biblical teachings have social consequences" ("they obviously do," he said, p. 74), or that the love of God will involve Christians in "corporate social and political action" (p. 79). His concern was rather over "the politicization of Christianity," by which he meant "the internal transformation of the faith itself, so that it comes to be defined in terms of political values" (p. 2). Dr. Norman was surely right that Christianity cannot be reduced to or identified with a political program. But it seems to me that he overreacted to this tendency and so gave many people the impression that he thought the Church should be entirely apolitical.

Yet the 1978 Reith Lectures contained at least four warnings, to which we will be wise to give heed, albeit critically. I will collate them in my own way:

1. The contemporary Church's political emphasis, that is, its frequent preoccupation with political issues, tends to eclipse what should be its central concerns, namely, the individual ("personal redemption," p. 78), the inward ("the indwelling Christ," pp. 72–85), and the eternal ("the ethereal qualities of immortality," p. 2). Dr. Norman is right that some churches have lost these dimensions altogether. Yet in retaining them, the Church must not overlook its corporate, external, and temporal responsibilities. Christians are citizens of two kingdoms and have responsibilities in both. To love God with all our being is indeed the "first and greatest" commandment; but to love

28

our neighbor as ourselves is "similar." Each is askew without the other.

2. The contemporary Church's political opinions are nothing but "the moral and political idealism of the surrounding culture" (p. 32), whether this is Western bourgeois liberalism or Marxism. All the Church does is "tag along, offering a religious gloss" to borrowed ideas (p. 4). It conforms instead of criticizing.
3. The contemporary Church's political contribution is amateurish; it lacks the necessary expertise to participate.
4. The contemporary Church's political expectations are naive, because it tends to forget human fallibility and sin.

It will be observed that all four criticisms are leveled at the particular behavior of some churches (though Dr. Norman tends to generalize), and not at the concept itself that the Christian Church does have sociopolitical responsibilities.

To whom do these responsibilities belong? That is our fourth and final question. Failure to ask and answer it is one of the main reasons for the current confusion over Christian political involvement. We need to distinguish among Christian individuals, groups, and churches. All individual Christians should be politically active in the sense that, as conscientious citizens, they will vote in elections, inform themselves about contemporary issues, share in the public debate, and perhaps write to a newspaper, lobby their member of Parliament, or take part in a demonstration. Further, some individuals are called by God to give their lives to political service, in either local or national government. Christians who share particular moral and social concerns should be encouraged to form or join groups which will study issues at a deeper level and take appropriate action. In some cases these will be exclusively Christian groups; in others Christians will want to contribute their biblical perspective to mixed groups, whether in a political party, a trade union, or a professional association.

Granted the propriety of political thought and action by Christian individuals and groups, however, should the Church as church involve itself in politics? Certainly the Church must teach both the law and the gospel of God. This is the duty of the Church's pastors, teachers, and other leaders. And "when the church concludes that biblical faith or righteousness requires it to take a public stand on some issue, then it must obey God's Word and trust him with the consequences."[41] Whether we think the Church should go beyond teaching and take corporate political action of some kind is likely to depend on whether we adhere to the Lutheran, Reformed, or Anabaptist traditions within Protestantism in relation to church and state. At least we can agree that the Church should not enter this field without the necessary expertise. But when church leaders do their homework thoroughly, and take the time and trouble to study a topic together in order to reach a common Christian mind and recommend common Christian action, their informed and united stand is extremely influential.

The Biblical Basis for Social Concern

What, then, is the biblical basis for social concern? Why should Christians get involved? In the end there are only two possible attitudes which Christians can adopt toward the world. One is escape and the other engagement. (You could say that there is a third option, namely, accommodation. But then Christians become indistinguishable from the world and on that account are no longer able to develop a distinctive attitude to it. They simply become part of it.) "Escape" means turning our backs on the world in rejection, washing our hands of it (though finding with Pontius Pilate that the responsibility does not come off in the wash), and steeling our hearts against its agonized cries for help. In contrast, "engagement" means turning our faces toward the world in compassion, getting our hands dirty, sore, and worn in its service, and feeling deep within us the stirring of the love of God which cannot be contained.

Too many of us evangelicals either have been, or maybe still are, irresponsible escapists. Fellowship with each other in the Church is much more congenial than service in an apathetic and even hostile environment outside. Of course, we make occasional evangelistic raids into enemy territory (that is our evangelical speciality); but then we withdraw again, across the moat, into our Christian castle (the security of our own evangelical fellowship), pull up the drawbridge, and even close our ears to the pleas of those who batter on the gate. As for social activity, we have tended to say it is largely a waste of time in view of the imminent return of the Lord. After all, when the house is on fire, what is the point of hanging new curtains or rearranging the furniture? The only thing that matters is to rescue the perishing. Thus we have tried to salve our conscience with a bogus theology.

"Do you realize," a student asked Tom Sine during one of his futurology seminars in the United States, "if we start feeding hungry people, things won't get worse, and if things don't get worse, Jesus won't come?" She was utterly sincere, writes Tom Sine. He continues: "The response of the (student) . . . reflects what I call the Great Escape view of the future. . . . The irony of (this) approach to the future is that, while it claims to take God seriously, it unwittingly moves God outside history, insisting that even he is powerless 'in these last days.' . . . It unintentionally fashions him into an impotent absentee landlord, who has lost control of his world and of human history. . . . The Great Escape becomes an incredible copout from all Christ called us to be and to do."[42]

Instead of seeking to evade our social responsibility, we need to open our ears and listen to the voice of him who calls his people in every age to go out into the lost and lonely world (as he did), in order to live and love, to witness and serve, like him and for him. For that is "mission." Mission is our human response to the divine commission. It is a whole Christian lifestyle, including both evangelism and social responsibility, dominated by the conviction that Christ sends us out into the world as the Father sent him into the world, and that into the world we must therefore go—to live and work for him.

Still, however, we come back to the question "why?" Why should Christians get involved in this world and its social problems? In reply, I propose to marshal five great doctrines of the Bible, which all of us already believe in theory, but which we tend to cut and trim in order to make them fit our escapist theology. My plea is that we have the courage to hold these doctrines in their biblical fullness. Any one of them should be sufficient to convince us of our Christian social responsibility; the five together leave us without excuse.

(1) A Fuller Doctrine of God

To begin with, we need a fuller doctrine of God. For we tend to forget that he is concerned for the whole of humankind and for the whole of human life in all its color and complexity. These universals have important consequences for our thinking.

First, the living God is the God of nature as well as of religion, of the "secular" as well as of the "sacred." In fact, Christians are always uncomfortable about this distinction. For everything is "sacred" in the sense that it belongs to God, and nothing is "secular" in the sense that God is excluded from it. God made the physical universe, sustains it, and still pronounces it good (Genesis 1:31). Indeed, "everything God created is good, and nothing is to be rejected if it is received with thanksgiving" (1 Timothy 4:4). We should be more grateful than we usually are for the good gifts of a good Creator—for sex, marriage, and the family, for the beauty and order of the natural world, for work and leisure, for friendships and the experience of interracial, intercultural community, and for music and other kinds of creative art which enrich the quality of human life. Our God is often too small because he is too religious. We imagine that he is chiefly interested in religion—in religious buildings (churches and chapels), religious activities (worship and ritual), and religious books (Bibles and prayer books). Of course, he is concerned about these things, but only if they are related to the whole of life.

31

According to the Old Testament prophets and the teaching of Jesus, God is very critical of "religion," if by that is meant religious services divorced from real life, loving service, and the moral obedience of the heart. "Religion that God our Father accepts as pure and faultless is this: to look after orphans and widows in their distress and to keep oneself from being polluted by the world" (James 1:27). The only value of religious services is that they concentrate into an hour or so of public, vocal, congregational activity the devotion of our whole life. If they do not do this, if instead we say and sing things in church which have no corollary in our everyday life outside church, at home, and at work, they are worse than worthless; their hypocrisy is positively nauseating to God.

Second, the living God is the God of the nations as well as of his covenant people. We Christians sometimes make the mistake which Israel made in the Old Testament when they concentrated exclusively on the God of the Covenant, who had chosen them out of all the nations to be the holy nation, and who had pledged himself to them, saying, "I will be your God and you shall be my people." To be sure, this was a glorious truth. The notion of "covenant" is a major biblical theme; the biblical revelation is unintelligible without it. But it is a dangerous half-truth. When Israel overemphasized it, they diminished the living God. They reduced him to the status of a tribal deity, a petty godling. He became Yahweh the god of the Israelites, more or less on a par with Chemosh the god of the Moabites and Milcom the god of the Ammonites. They also forgot the other nations, or simply despised and rejected them.

But the Bible begins with the nations, not Israel; with Adam not Abraham; with the creation not the Covenant. And when God chose Israel, he did not lose interest in the nations. Amos bravely gave voice to the word of the Lord: "Are not you Israelites the same to me as the Cushites [or Ethiopians]? . . . Did I not bring Israel up from Egypt, the Philistines from Caphtor [Crete] and the Arameans from Kir?" (Amos 9:7). Similarly, the arrogant emperor Nebuchadnezzar had to learn that "the Most High is sovereign over the kingdoms of men and gives them to anyone he wishes" (Daniel 4:32). He rules over the nations. Their destiny is under his control. Although Satan is called "the ruler of this world" and is de facto its usurper, God remains the ultimate governor of everything he has made. "From heaven the LORD looks down and sees all mankind; from his dwelling place he watches all who live on earth—he who forms the hearts of all, who considers everything they do" (Psalm 33:13–15). More than that, he has promised that in blessing Abraham and his posterity he will bless all the families of the earth, and that one day he will restore what the Fall has marred, and bring to perfection all that he has made.

Third, the living God is the God of justice as well as of justification.[43] Of course he is the God of justification, the Savior of sinners, "the compassionate and gracious God, slow to anger, abounding in love and faithfulness" (Exodus 34:6). But he is also concerned that our community life be characterized by justice.

> He upholds the cause of the oppressed
> and gives food to the hungry.
> The LORD sets prisoners free,
> the LORD gives sight to the blind,
> The LORD lifts up those who are bowed down,
> the LORD loves the righteous.
> The LORD watches over the alien
> and sustains the fatherless and the widow,
> but he frustrates the ways of the wicked.

(Psalm 146:7–9)

This does not mean that he does all these things invariably, but rather that this is the kind of God he is.

Moreover, God's concern for justice, though he expects it particularly among his own people, extends beyond them to all people. Social compassion and justice mattered to him in the nations as well as in Israel. There is no clearer evidence of this than in the first two chapters of the prophecy of Amos. Before Amos rebuked Judah for rejecting God's law and turning to idolatry, and Israel for crushing the poor and denying justice to the oppressed (2:4–8), he pronounced God's judgment on all the surrounding nations (1:3–2:3)—on Syria for savage cruelty, on Philistia for capturing whole communities and selling them into slavery, on Tyre for breaking a treaty of brotherhood, on Edom for pitiless hostility to Israel, on Ammon for atrocities in warfare, and on Moab for desecrating the bones of a neighboring king.

Several of the prophetic books similarly contain a section of oracles about or against the nations. That God is the God of justice and desires justice in every nation and community is particularly evident from the Book of Nahum, which is a prophecy against Nineveh, the capital and symbol of Assyria. Yahweh's denunciation of Assyria is not just because she was Israel's long-standing enemy (e.g., 1:9ff.; 2:2ff.), but because of her idolatry (1:14) and because she is a "city of blood, full of lies, full of plunder, never without victims" (3:1). Twice Yahweh says the terrible words, "I am against you" (2:13; 3:5), and the oracle ends with the rhetorical question (3:19): "Who has not felt your endless cruelty?"

It is clear from these Old Testament passages that God hates injustice and oppression everywhere, and that he loves and promotes justice everywhere. Indeed, wherever righteousness is to be found in our fallen world, it is due to the working of his grace. All human beings know this too. For we have an inbuilt sense of justice, to which the child's expostulation, "It isn't fair!" bears eloquent witness. It is solid evidence of Paul's teaching that God's moral law is written on the human heart (Romans 2:14, 15). Both God's law and God's gospel are for our good.

Here then is the living God of the Bible. His concerns are all-embracing— not only the "sacred" but the "secular," not only religion but nature, not only his covenant people but all people, not only justification but social justice in every community, not only his gospel but his law. So we must not attempt to narrow his interests. Moreover, ours should be as broad as his.

John Gladwin sums up this argument in his *God's People in God's World:* "It is because this is God's world, and he cared for it to the point of incarnation and crucifixion, that we are inevitably committed to work for God's justice in the face of oppression, for God's truth in the face of lies and deceits, for service in the face of the abuse of power, for love in the face of selfishness, for cooperation in the face of destructive antagonism, and for reconciliation in the face of division and hostility."[44]

(2) A Fuller Doctrine of Human Beings

All our philanthropic work (that is, work inspired by love for human beings) depends on our evaluation of them. The higher our view of their worth, the more we shall want to serve them.

Secular humanists, who are sincere in describing themselves as dedicated to "the human case and the human cause,"[45] sometimes appear more humane than Christians. But if we ask them why they are so committed to humankind, they are likely to reply with Julian Huxley that it is because of the human potential in the future aeons of evolution. "Thus the development of man's vast potential of realizable possibility," he wrote, "provides the prime motive for collective action."[46] The inadequacy of this as a basis for service is obvious. If the unimpeded progress of evolution were our chief concern, why should we care for the senile, the imbecile, the hardened criminal, the psychopath, the chronically sick, or the starving? Would it not be more prudent to put them to sleep like a well-loved dog, lest they hinder the evolutionary process? Compulsory euthanasia, not compassionate service, would be the logical deduction from the humanists' premise. The fact that they draw back from this abyss indicates that their heart is better than their head, and their philanthropy than their philosophy.

Christian people have a sounder basis for serving their fellow human beings. It is not because of what they may become in the speculative future development of the race, but because of what they already are by divine creation. Human beings are godlike beings made in God's likeness, and

34

possessing unique capacities which distinguish them from the animal creation. True, human beings are fallen, and the divine image is defaced, but despite all contrary appearances it has not been destroyed (Genesis 9:6; James 3:9). It is this which accounts for their unique worth and which has always inspired Christian philanthropy.

For these human but godlike creatures are not just souls (that we should be concerned exclusively for their eternal salvation), not just bodies (that we should care only for their food, clothing, shelter, and health), nor just social beings (that we should become entirely preoccupied with their community problems). They are all three. A human being might be defined from a biblical perspective as "a body-soul-in-a-community." For that is how God has made us. Therefore, if we truly love our neighbors, and because of their worth desire to serve them, we shall be concerned for their total welfare, the well-being of their soul, their body, and their community. And our concern will lead to practical programs of evangelism, relief, and development. We shall not just prattle and plan and pray, like that country vicar to whom a homeless woman turned for help, and who (doubtless sincerely, and because he was busy and felt helpless) promised to pray for her. She later wrote this poem and handed it a regional officer of Shelter.

I was hungry,
    and you formed a humanities group to discuss my hunger.
I was imprisoned,
    and you crept off quietly to your chapel and prayed for my
    release.
I was naked,
    and in your mind you debated the morality of my appearance.
I was sick,
    and you knelt and thanked God for your health.
I was homeless,
    and you preached to me of the spiritual shelter of the love of God.
I was lonely,
    and you left me alone to pray for me.
You seem so holy, so close to God
    but I am still very hungry—and lonely—and cold.

Motivated by love for human beings in need, the early Christians went everywhere preaching the Word of God, because nothing has such a humanizing influence as the gospel. Later they founded schools, hospitals, and refuges for the outcast. Later still they abolished the slave trade and freed the slaves, and they improved the conditions of workers in mills and mines, and of prisoners in jails. They protected children from commercial exploitation in the factories of the West and from ritual prostitution in the temples of the East. Today they bring leprosy sufferers both the compassion of Jesus and modern methods of reconstructive surgery and rehabilitation. They care for the blind and the deaf, the orphaned and the widowed, the sick and the dying. They get alongside junkies, and stay alongside them during the traumatic period of withdrawal. They set themselves against racism and political oppression. They get involved in the inner city, the slums, and the ghettos, and raise their protest against the inhumane conditions in which so many are doomed to live. They seek in whatever way they can to express their solidarity with the poor and the hungry, the deprived and the disadvantaged. I am not claiming that all Christians at all times have given their lives in such service. But a sufficiently large number have done so to make their record noteworthy. Why have they done it? Because of the Christian doctrine of man, male and female, all made in the image of God, though all also fallen. Because people matter. Because every man, woman, and child has an intrinsic, inalienable value as a human being. Once we see this, we shall both set ourselves to liberate people from everything dehumanizing and count it a privilege to serve them, to do everything in our power to make human life more human.

The film *The Elephant Man* made widely known the extraordinary story with which every English person was familiar at the end of the nineteenth century. It was in 1884 that Frederick Treves, a young surgeon and lecturer in anatomy at the London Hospital, found the Elephant Man in a rented shop opposite the hospital entrance. When Treves first saw his hunched-up form, he thought him "the embodiment of loneliness." He later described him as "the most disgusting specimen of humanity" he had ever seen. He had an "enormous misshapen head," with a huge bony mass projecting from his brow, and another from his upper jaw which gave him an elephantine appearance. Spongy, evil-smelling skin, like fungus or brown cauliflower, hung in bags from his back, his chest, the back of his head, and his right arm. His legs were deformed, his feet bulbous, and he had hip disease. His face was expressionless, and his speech spluttering, almost unintelligible. His left arm and hand, however, were as shapely and delicate as a young woman's.

To add to his suffering, he was treated like an animal, hawked from fair to fair, and exhibited to the curious for twopence a look. Treves wrote: "He was shunned like a leper, housed like a wild beast, and got his only view of the world from a peephole in a showman's cart." He received less kindness than a dog, and, terrified of staring eyes, he would creep into a dark corner to hide.

When he was abandoned by the circus showman, Treves had him accommodated and cared for in a room at the back of the London Hospital where three and half years later he died in his sleep, a few days after he had received his Easter Day Communion.

Treves had imagined that he was an imbecile, probably from birth. But in the hospital he discovered that he was a human being, Joseph Merrick by name, in his early twenties, highly intelligent, a voracious reader, with a passion for conversation, an acute sensibility, and a romantic imagination. He was also a "gentle, affectionate and lovable creature."

When the first woman visited Joseph Merrick, gave him a smile and a greeting, and actually shook him by the hand, he broke down into uncontrollable sobbing. But from that day his transformation began. He became a celebrity, and many notable people visited him. Gradually he changed "from a hunted thing into a man," wrote Treves. But actually he had always been a man. Treves may never have articulated the Christian doctrine of human beings made in the image of God. Nevertheless, it was his remarkable respect for Joseph Merrick which enabled him to lift up his poor misshapen head, and gain some measure of self-respect before he died.[47]

(3) A Fuller Doctrine of Christ

There have been many different reinterpretations and reconstructions of Jesus. Indeed, it is right that every generation of Christians should seek to understand and to present him in terms appropriate to their own age and culture. So we have had Jesus the ascetic, the sufferer, the monarch, the gentleman, the clown, the superstar, the capitalist, the socialist, the revolutionary, the guerrilla, the wonder drug. Several of these portraits are mutually contradictory, of course, and others have little or no historical warrant.

We need then to recover an authentic picture of him whom the Lausanne Covenant calls "the historical, biblical Christ" (para. 4). We need to see him in his paradoxical fullness—his sufferings and glory, his servanthood and lordship, his lowly Incarnation and cosmic reign. It is perhaps the Incarnation which we evangelicals have tended to neglect most, in both its theological significance and its practical implications.

The Son of God did not stay in the safe immunity of his heaven. He emptied himself of his glory and humbled himself to serve. He became little, weak, and vulnerable. He entered into our pain, alienation, and temptations. He not only proclaimed the good news of the Kingdom of God, but demonstrated its arrival by healing the sick, feeding the hungry, forgiving the sinful, befriending the dropout, and raising the dead. He had not come to be served, he said, but to serve and to give his life as a ransom price for the release of others. So he allowed himself to become a victim of gross injustice in the courts, and as they crucified him he prayed for his enemies. Then in the awful God-forsaken darkness he bore our sins in his own innocent person.

Should not this vision of Christ affect our understanding of his commission, "As the Father has sent me, I am sending you" (John 20:21)? For if the Christian mission is to be modeled on Christ's mission, it will surely involve for us, as it did for him, an entering into other people's worlds. In evangelism it will mean entering their thought world, and the world of their tragedy and lostness, in order to share Christ with them where they are. In social activity it will mean a willingness to renounce the comfort and security of our own cultural background in order to give ourselves in service to people of another culture, whose needs we may never before have known or experienced. Incarnational mission, whether evangelistic or social or both, necessitates a costly identification with people in their actual situations. Jesus of Nazareth was moved with compassion by the sight of needy human beings, whether sick or bereaved, hungry, harassed, or helpless; should not his people's compassion be aroused by the same sights?

Leonidas Proaño was formerly Roman Catholic bishop of Riobamba, about a hundred miles south of Quito, Ecuador. Basing his thinking on the Bible, he was strongly committed to social justice in his country, not least for the Indians whose culture he wanted to see preserved against those who were threatening to erode and even destroy it. Although he refused to identify himself with Marxism, and was in fact not a Marxist, he was critical—indeed defiant—of the political and ecclesiastical systems in his country. He opposed feudalism and the oppressive power of the wealthy landowners. It is perhaps not surprising that he was threatened with assassination. At all events, after the overthrow and death in 1973 of President Salvador Allende of Chile, Bishop Proaño preached at a mass for Marxist students in Quito. He portrayed Jesus as the radical he was, the critic of the establishment, the champion of the downtrodden, the lover of the poor, who not only preached the gospel but also gave compassionate service to the needy. After the Mass there was a question-time, during which some students said: "If we had known this Jesus, we would never have become Marxists."

Which Jesus do we believe in? And which Jesus do we preach? Is it possible that in some parts of the Church such a false Jesus ("another Jesus"—2 Corinthians 11:4) is being presented to the young people, that we are repelling them from him and driving them into the arms of Karl Marx instead?

(4) A Fuller Doctrine of Salvation

There is a constant tendency in the Church to trivialize the nature of salvation, as if it meant no more than a self-reformation, or the forgiveness of our sins, or a personal passport to paradise, or a private mystical experience without social or moral consequences. It is urgent that we rescue salvation from these caricatures and recover the doctrine in its biblical fullness. For salvation is a radical transformation in three phases, beginning at our conversion, continuing throughout our earthly life, and brought to perfection when Christ comes. In particular, we must overcome the temptation to separate truths which belong together.

First, we must not separate salvation from the Kingdom of God. For in the Bible these two expressions are virtual synonyms, alternative models to describe the same work of God. According to Isaiah 52:7 those who preach good news of peace are also those "who proclaim salvation, who say to Zion, 'Your God reigns!'" That is, where God reigns, he saves. Salvation is the blessing of his rule. Again, when Jesus said to his disciples, "How hard it is to enter the kingdom of God," it seems to have been natural for them to respond with the question, "Who then can be saved?" (Mark 10:24–6). They evidently equated entering the Kingdom with being saved.

Once this identification has been made, salvation takes on a broader aspect. For the Kingdom of God is God's dynamic rule, breaking into human history through Jesus, confronting, combating, and overcoming evil, spreading the wholeness of personal and communal well-being, taking possession of his people in total blessing and total demand. The church is meant to be the Kingdom community, a model of what human community looks like when it comes under the rule of God, and a challenging alternative to secular society. Entering God's Kingdom is entering the new age, long promised in the Old Testament, which is also the beginning of God's new creation. Now we look forward to the consummation of the Kingdom when our bodies, our society, and our universe will all be renewed, and sin, pain, futility, disease, and death will all be eradicated. Salvation is a big concept; we have no liberty to reduce it.

Second, we must not separate Jesus the Savior from Jesus the Lord. It is little short of incredible that some evangelists teach the possibility of accepting Jesus the Savior, while postponing a surrender to him as Lord. But God has exalted Jesus to his right hand and made him Lord. From that position of supreme power and executive authority he is able to bestow salvation and the gift of the Spirit. It is precisely because he is Lord that he can save. The affirmations "Jesus is Lord" and "Jesus is Savior" are almost interchangeable. And his lordship extends far beyond the religious bit of our lives. It embraces the whole of our experience, public and private, home and work, church membership and civic duty, evangelistic and social responsibilities.

Third, we must not separate faith from love. Evangelical Christians have always emphasized faith. *Sola fide,* "by faith alone," was one of the great watchwords of the Reformation, and rightly so. "Justification," or acceptance with God, is not by good works which we have done or could do; it is only by God's sheer unmerited favor ("grace"), on the sole ground of the atoning death of Jesus Christ, by simple trust in him alone. This central truth of the gospel cannot be compromised for anything. But, though justification is by faith alone, this faith cannot remain alone. If it is living and authentic, it will inevitably issue in good works, and if it does not, it is spurious. Jesus himself taught this in his "sheep and goats" description of Judgment Day. Our attitude to him, he said, will be revealed in, and so be judged by, our good works of love to the least of his brothers and sisters. The apostles all lay the same emphasis on the necessity of good works of love. James teaches it: "Faith by itself, if it is not accompanied by action, is dead. . . . I will show you my faith by what I do" (2:17, 18). So does John: "If anyone has material possessions and sees his brother in need but has not pity on him, how can the love of God be in him?" (1 John 3:17). And so does Paul. Christ died to create a new people who would be "eager to do what is good" (Titus 2:14). We have been re-created in Christ "to do good works, which God prepared in advance for us to do" (Ephesians 2:10). Again, "the only thing that counts is faith expressing itself through love. . . . Serve one another in love" (Galatians 5:6, 13). This, then, is the striking sequence—faith, love, service. True faith issues in love, and true love issues in service.

It is specially those of us who are called "evangelical" Christians who need to take this New Testament emphasis to heart. We have to beware of magnifying faith and knowledge at the expense of love. Paul did not. If he were able to "fathom all mysteries and all knowledge," he wrote, and if he had "a faith that can move mountains," yet had no love, he would be nothing (1 Corinthians 13:2). For saving faith and saving love belong together. Whenever one is absent, so is the other. Neither can exist in isolation.

(5) A Fuller Doctrine of the Church

Many people think of the Church as a kind of club, rather like the local golf club, except that the common interest of its members happens to be God rather than golf. They are religious people who do religious things together. They pay their subscription and are entitled to the privileges of club membership. In that frame of mind they forget William Temple's perceptive phrase that "The church is the only cooperative society that exists for the benefit of nonmembers."[48]

In place of the "club" model of the Church, we need to recover the truth of the Church's "double identity." On the one hand, the Church is a "holy" people, called out of the world to belong to God. But on the other, it is a "worldly" people, in the sense of renouncing "otherworldliness" and being sent back into the world to witness and to serve. This is what Dr. Alec Vidler, following a lead of Bonhoeffer, has called the Church's "holy worldliness."[49] Seldom in its long and chequered history has the Church remembered or preserved its double identity. Sometimes, in a right emphasis on its "holiness," the Church has wrongly withdrawn from the world and become insulated from it. At other times, in a right emphasis on its "worldliness" (i.e., its immersion in the life of the world), the Church has wrongly become assimilated to the world's standards and values, and so become contaminated by them. Yet without the preservation of both parts of its identity, the Church cannot engage in mission. Mission arises out of the biblical doctrine of the Church in society. An unbalanced ecclesiology makes mission unbalanced too.

Jesus taught these truths himself, not only in his famous expression, "in the world but not of it" (see John 17:11–19), but in his vivid metaphors of the salt and the light. "You are the salt of the earth," he said, and "you are the light of the world" (Matthew 5:13–16). He implied (as we shall see more fully in Chapter 4) that the two communities, the new and the old, the Church and the world, are as radically different from one another as light from darkness and salt from decay. He also implied that, if they were to do any good, the salt must soak into the meat, and the light must shine into the darkness. Just so, Christians must penetrate non-Christian society. Thus, the double identity and responsibility of the Church are plain.

In a similar way the apostle Peter describes the members of God's new people on the one hand as "aliens and strangers in the world" and on the other as needing to be conscientious citizens in it (1 Peter 2:11–17). We cannot be totally "world-affirming" (as if nothing in it were evil), nor totally "world-denying" (as if nothing in it were good); we need to be a bit of both, and we particularly need to be "world-challenging," recognizing its potentiality as God's world and seeking to conform its life increasingly to his lordship.

This vision of the Church's influence on society is best described in terms of "reform" rather than of "redemption." As A. N. Triton has expressed it, "Redemption is not an infection of social structures. . . . It results in individuals restored to a right relationship to God. But that sets up horizontal shock waves in society from which all of us benefit. These benefits are in terms of reforming society according to God's law, and not redeeming it by the death of Christ."[50]

The effectiveness of the Church depends on its combination of "holiness" and "worldliness." We shall return to these images later.

Practical Action

I have assembled five doctrines and pleaded that we hold them in their biblical fullness—the doctrines of God (Creator, Lawgiver, Lord, and Judge), of human beings (their unique worth because made in God's image), of Christ (who identified with us and calls us to identify with others), of salvation (a radical transformation), and of the Church (distinct from the world as its salt and light, yet penetrating it for Christ). These five doctrines constitute the biblical basis for mission, for both evangelistic and social responsibility. They lay upon us an obligation to be involved in the life of the world. But how?

Take the individual Christian first. In general terms, every Christian is called to be both a witness and a servant. For each of us is a follower of the Lord Jesus who both witnessed a good confession and said, "I am among you as a serving man." Thus *diakonia* (service) and *marturia* (witness) are inseparable twins. Yet different Christians are called to different specialist ministries, just as the Twelve were called to the ministry of the Word and prayer, while the Seven were called to take charge of the daily distribution to the widows (see Acts 6). The metaphor of the Church as the Body of Christ enforces the same lesson. Just as each member of the human body has a different function, so each member of the Body of Christ has a different gift and so a different ministry. At the same time, whatever our specialist calling may be, emergencies will override it. The priest and the Levite in the Parable of the Good Samaritan could not excuse their shameful neglect of the man who had been assaulted and robbed by saying that their calling was to work in the Temple. If we are called to a predominantly social ministry, we still have an obligation to witness. If we are called to a predominantly evangelistic ministry, we still cannot say that we have no social responsibilities.

As for the local church, the versatility of its outreach can be greatly increased if full use is made of all its members with their different gifts and callings. It is a very healthy thing for the local church's oversight or leadership to encourage people with similar concerns to coalesce into "special interest" groups or "study and action" groups. Some will have an evangelistic objective—house-to-house visitation, a music group, a world mission group. Other groups will have a social concern—sick and welfare visiting, a housing association, community or race relations, the care of the natural environment, pro-life, anti-abortion campaigning, the needs of an ethnic minority. Such specialist groups supplement one another. If an occasional opportunity is given to them to report back to the church membership as a whole, the representative nature of their work will be affirmed, and they can receive valuable support from their parent body in terms of advice, encouragement, prayer, and financial backing.

No one Christian could, or should try to, get involved in every kind of ministry. But each local church (at least of any size) can and should get involved in as many as possible, through its groups. The groups make it realistic for the church greatly to diversify its concern and action.[51]

I end this chapter with what may be a rather surprising reference to the Roman Catholic Mass. The word "Mass" is said to be derived from the final sentence of the old Latin rite, *ite missa est*. In polite English it might be rendered, "Now you are dismissed." In more blunt language it could be just, "Get out!"—out into the world which God made and God-like beings inhabit, the world into which Christ came and into which he now sends us. For that is where we belong. The world is the arena in which we are to live and love, witness and serve, suffer and die for Christ.

2

Complexity:
Can We Think Straight?

Let us suppose we are agreed that our doctrines of God, human beings, Christ, salvation, and the Church commit us inescapably to becoming socially involved—not only in social service, caring in Christ's name for the victims of oppression, but also in social action, concerned for justice and social change. To be thus strongly motivated is essential, but it is not enough. Any contribution we may hope to make will depend on our comprehension of the issues. We will be wise not to blunder unprepared into the minefield of social ethics. As I once heard the late John Mackay say when he was president of Princeton Theological Seminary, "Commitment without reflection is fanaticism in action, though reflection without commitment is the paralysis of all action."

We should certainly not underestimate the complexity of the issues which confront humankind today. True, every generation has felt baffled by its contemporary problems; so it is not surprising that we should feel the same way. Yet the number, scale, and gravity of the questions facing us at the turn of the millennium do seem to be unprecedented, owing particularly to the scientific revolution. For example, the problem of war and peace has always troubled the Christian conscience, but the international stockpiling of nuclear weapons has greatly aggravated it. Similarly, the birth of the internet and of sophisticated information technologies have brought basic questions of identity and privacy to the forefront of discussion. And the cloning of a sheep in Scotland and of monkeys in the United States has jolted the world into a recognition of the need for serious thinking in the still young field of bioethics.

Clearly, individual Christians cannot make themselves authorities in all these areas, and it is also doubtful whether the Church as such should be recommending particular and detailed policies. William Temple, who has certainly been the most socially concerned Archbishop of Canterbury in the twentieth century, made much of the need to distinguish between principles and policies. Writing in 1941 of continuing poverty and malnutrition in Britain, and of "the industrial life of the country . . . disgraced by chronic unemployment," he went on: "The Church is both entitled and obliged to condemn the society characterized by these evils; but it is not entitled in its corporate capacity to advocate specific remedies."[1] Instead, the Church should inspire its influential members (whether politicians, civil servants, businesspeople, trade unionists, or leaders in other areas of public life) to seek and apply appropriate remedies. "In other words, the Church lays down principles; the Christian citizen applies them; and to do this he utilizes the machinery of the State."[2] Again, "The Church cannot say how it is to be done; but it is called to say that it must be done."[3]

The following year, in his better known book *Christianity and the Social Order*, Temple was still emphasizing the same distinction. "The Church is committed to the everlasting Gospel . . . it must never commit itself to an ephemeral programme of detailed action."[4] Readers of Temple will know that he was very far from saying that religion and politics do not mix. His point was different, namely, that "the Church is concerned with principles and not policy."[5] The reasons why he believed the Church as a whole should refrain from "direct political action" by developing and advocating specific programs could be summed up as "integrity" (the Church lacks the necessary expertise, though some of her members may have it), "prudence" (she may prove to be mistaken and so be discredited), and "justice" (different Christians hold different opinions, and the Church should not side with even a majority of its members against an equally loyal minority).

Even if we agree with this clarification of roles, and concede that not all Christians are responsible for working out policies, we still have to grapple with the principles, and these are by no means always easy to formulate.

Some Christians in this situation give up in despair. "The age-long problems such as war, economics, and divorce," they say, "have always divided Christians. There have always been pacifists and nonpacifists, capitalists and socialists, lax and rigid attitudes to divorce. And our modern problems, being more complex, are also more divisive. Besides," they continue, "there's no such thing as 'the Christian view' on any of these problems; there is a whole spectrum of Christian views. Even the Bible does not always help us; it was written in such ancient cultures that it does not speak to our modern problems. So let us leave it to the experts and give up hope of finding a Christian answer ourselves." Such despair denigrates God, because it denies the usefulness of his revelation as "a lamp to our feet and a light for our path" (Psalm 119:105). To abandon hope of having anything Christian to say may even be mental laziness in the guise of a false humility.

True humility will lead us to sit patiently under the revelation of God and to affirm by faith that he can bring us to a substantially common mind. How can we believe in the Word and Spirit of God, and deny this? What is needed is more conscientious group study in which (1) we learn to pray together, (2) we listen attentively to each other's positions, and to the deep concerns that lie behind them, and (3) we help each other to discern the cultural prejudices which make us reluctant and even unable to open our minds to alternative viewpoints. This kind of discipline can be painful, but Christian integrity demands it. As a result, we shall refuse to acquiesce in superficial polarizations, for the truth is always more subtle and sophisticated than that. Instead, we shall undertake some careful mapwork, plotting (and emphasizing) areas of common ground, and clarifying residual disagreements with which we will continue perseveringly to wrestle.

If despair is one reaction to the complexity of modern ethical problems, its opposite is a naive oversimplification. Some Christians (particularly evangelical Christians, I fear) have tended to jump in head first. Either unwilling or unable to grasp the issues, we have sometimes denied that there are any. Or we have reasserted our evangelical watchword about the "perspicuity" of Scripture (namely, that its message is plain or transparent), as if this meant that there are no problems. We have then given glib answers to complex questions and have treated the Bible as if it resembled either a slot-machine (in goes your penny, out comes your answer) or that extraordinary Victorian almanac entitled *Enquire Within*, which offered information on everything.

Certainly, the way of salvation is plain or "perspicuous," which is what the Reformers meant by the term. But how can we assert that Scripture contains no problems when the apostle Peter himself declared that in his brother apostle Paul's letters there were "some things that are hard to understand" (2 Peter 3:16)? Applying God's ancient Word to the modern world is also hard. To deny this is another way of denigrating God, this time by misunderstanding the nature of his self-revelation.

Thus, we dishonor God both if we assert that there are no solutions, and if we offer slick solutions. For on the one hand, he has revealed his will to us, and on the other he has not revealed it in a set of neat propositions.

A Christian Mind

There is a third, better, and more Christian way to approach today's complicated questions, which is to develop a Christian mind, namely, a mind that has firmly grasped the basic presuppositions of Scripture and is thoroughly informed by biblical truth. It is only such a mind which can think with Christian integrity about the problems of the contemporary world.

This proposal immediately provokes opposition, however, from those Christians who have assimilated the anti-intellectual mood of today's world. They do not want to be told to use their minds, they say. Some even declare that it is "unspiritual" to do so. In response, we draw attention to Paul's injunction to the Corinthians: "Stop thinking like children. In . . . your thinking be adults" (1 Corinthians 14:20). The fact is that a proper use of our minds is wonderfully beneficial. (1) It glorifies God, because he has made us rational beings in his own image and has given us in Scripture a rational revelation which he intends for us to study. (2) It enriches us, because every aspect of our Christian discipleship (e.g., our worship, faith, and obedience) depends for its maturing on our reflection, respectively, upon God's glory, faithfulness, and will. (3) It strengthens our witness in the world, because we are called like the apostles not only to "preach" the gospel, but also to "defend" and "argue" it and so "persuade" people of its truth (e.g., Acts 17:2f.; 19:8, 2 Corinthians 5:11; Philippians 1:7).

Toward the beginning of Romans 12 Paul uses the expression "the renewing of your mind." He has just issued his famous appeal to his Roman readers that, in gratitude for God's mercies, they should present their bodies to him as a "living sacrifice" and as their "spiritual worship." Now he goes on to explain how it is possible for God's people to serve him in the world. He sets before us an alternative. One way is to "be conformed" to this world or "age," to its standards (or lack of them), its values (largely materialistic), and its goals (self-centered and godless). These are the characteristics of Western culture. Moreover, the prevailing culture (like the prevailing wind) is not easy to stand up against. It is easier to take the line of least resistance and bow down before it, like "reeds swayed by the wind." Contemporary secularism is strong and subtle; the pressures to conform are great.

Paul exhorts us, however, not to be conformed to the world, but instead to "be transformed" by the renewing of our minds with a view to discerning God's pleasing and perfect will. Here, then, is the apostle's assumption both that Christians have or should have renewed minds, and that our renewed minds will have a radical effect on our lives, since it will enable us to discern and approve God's will, and so transform our behavior. The sequence is compelling. If we want to live straight, we have to think straight. If we want to think straight, we have to have renewed minds. For once our minds are renewed, we shall become preoccupied not with the way of the world, but with the will of God, which will change us.

For Christian conversion means total renewal. The Fall led to total depravity—a doctrine rejected, I suspect, only by those who misunderstand it. It has never meant that every human being is as depraved as he could possibly be, but rather that every part of our humanness, including our mind, has become distorted by the Fall. So redemption involves total renewal (meaning not that we are now as good as we could be, but that every part of us, including our mind, has been renewed). The contrast is clear. Our old outlook led to conformity to the crowd; our new outlook has led us into moral nonconformity, out of concern for the will of God. Our fallen mind followed the way of the world; our renewed mind is engrossed with the will of God, as revealed in the Word of God. Between the two lies repentance, *metanoia,* a complete change of mind or outlook.

Paul writes not only of a "renewed mind" but also of "the mind of Christ." He exhorts the Philippians: "Let this mind be in you which was also in Christ Jesus" (2:5). That is, as we study the teaching and example of Jesus, and consciously put our minds under the yoke of his authority (Matthew 11:29), we begin to think as he thought. His mind is gradually formed within us by the Holy Spirit, who is the Spirit of Christ. We see things his way, from his perspective. Our outlook becomes aligned to his. We almost dare to say what the apostle could say: "we have the mind of Christ" (1 Corinthians 2:16).

"The renewed mind." "The mind of Christ." "A Christian perspective." "The Christian mind." It was Harry Blamires who popularized this fourth expression in his book of that title, which since its publication in 1963 has had widespread influence. By a "Christian mind" he was referring not to a mind occupied with specifically "religious" topics, but to a mind which could think about even the most "secular" topics "Christianly," that is, from a Christian perspective. It is not the mind of a schizoid Christian who "hops in and out of his Christian mentality as the topic of conversation changes from the Bible to the day's newspaper."[6] No, the Christian mind, he writes, is "a mind trained, informed, equipped to handle data of secular controversy within a framework of reference which is constructed of Christian presuppositions."[7] Blamires laments the contemporary loss of Christian thinking even among church leaders: "The Christian mind has succumbed to the secular drift with a degree of weakness and nerveless-ness unmatched in Christian history."[8] Having deplored its loss, Harry Blamires sets about canvassing its recovery. He wants to witness the rise of the kind of Christian thinker who "challenges current prejudices . . . disturbs the complacent . . . obstructs the busy pragmatists . . . questions the very foundations of all about him, and . . . is a nuisance."[9]

Mr. Blamires then goes on to list what he sees as the six essential "marks" of a Christian mind: (1) "its supernatural orientation" (it looks beyond time to eternity, beyond earth to heaven and hell, and meanwhile inhabits a world fashioned, sustained, and "worried over" by God); (2) "its awareness of evil" (original sin perverting even the noblest things into instruments of "hungry vanity"); (3) "its conception of truth" (the givenness of

49

divine revelation which cannot be compromised); (4) "its acceptance of authority" (what God has revealed requires from us "not an egalitarian attachment, but a bending submission"); (5) "its concern for the person" (a recognition of the value of human personality over against servitude to the machine); and (6) "its sacramental cast" (for example, recognizing sexual love as "one of God's most efficient instruments" for the opening of man's heart to Reality).

Dr. David Gill, formerly of New College, Berkeley, in his *The Opening of the Christian Mind*, proposes an alternative cluster of six characteristics which mark the Christian mind—namely, it is (1) "theological" (focused on God and his incarnate Word), (2) "historical" ("informed by the past, responsibly alive in the present and thoughtful about the future"), (3) "humanist" (deeply concerned for persons), (4) "ethical" (submissive to God's moral standards), (5) "truthful" (committed to God's self-revelation in nature and Scripture), and (6) "aesthetic" (appreciative of beauty as well as truth and goodness). Thus the Christian mind's "basic contours" relate to "God, history, persons, ethics, truth and beauty."[10]

Both lists of six characteristics, Harry Blamires's and David Gill's, are true and valuable. But I have personally found it yet more helpful to adopt the framework provided by Scripture as a whole. For the truly Christian mind has repented of "proof-texting" (the notion that we can settle every doctrinal and ethical issue by quoting a single, isolated text, whereas God has given us a comprehensive revelation), and instead saturates itself in the fullness of Scripture. In particular, it has absorbed the fourfold scheme of biblical history. For the Bible divides human history into epochs, which are marked not by the rise and fall of empires, dynasties, or civilizations, but by four major events—the Creation, the Fall, the Redemption, and the Consummation.

First, the Creation. It is absolutely foundational to the Christian faith (and therefore to the Christian mind) that in the beginning, when time began, God made the universe out of nothing. He went on to make the planet earth, its land and seas and all their creatures. Finally, as the climax of his creative activity, he made man, male and female, in his own image. The Godlikeness of humankind emerges as the story unfolds: men and women are rational and moral beings (able to understand and respond to God's commands), responsible beings (exercising dominion over nature), social beings (with a capacity to love and be loved), and spiritual beings (finding their highest fulfillment in knowing and worshiping their Creator). Indeed, the Creator and his human creatures are depicted as walking and talking together in the garden. All this was the Godlikeness which gave Adam and Eve their unique worth and dignity.

Next, the Fall. They listened to Satan's lies, instead of to God's truth. In consequence of their disobedience they were driven out of the garden. No greater tragedy has befallen human beings than this: though made by God like God and for God, they now live without God. All our human alienation, disorientation, and sense of meaninglessness stem ultimately from this. In addition, our relationships with each other have become skewed. Sexual equality was upset: "your husband . . . will rule over you" (Genesis 3:16). Pain came to haunt the threshold of motherhood. Cain's jealous hatred of his brother erupted into murder. Even nature was put out of joint. The ground was cursed because of man, the cultivation of the soil became an uphill struggle, and creative work degenerated into drudgery. Over the centuries men and women have slipped from the responsible stewardship of the environment entrusted to them, and have cut down the forests, created deserts and dustbowls, polluted rivers and seas, and fouled the atmosphere with poisons. "Original sin" means that our inherited human nature is now twisted with a disastrous self-centeredness. Evil is an ingrained, pervasive reality. Although our Godlikeness has not been destroyed, it has been seriously distorted. We no longer love God with all our being, but are hostile to him and under his just condemnation.

Third, the Redemption. Instead of abandoning or destroying his rebellious creatures, as they deserved, God planned to redeem them. No sooner had they sinned than God promised that the woman's seed would crush the serpent's head (Genesis 3:15), which we recognize as the first prediction of the coming Savior. God's redemptive purpose began to take clearer shape when he called Abraham and entered into a solemn covenant with him, promising to bless both him and through his posterity all the families of the earth—another promise which we know has been fulfilled in Christ and his worldwide community. God renewed his covenant, this time with Israel, at Mount Sinai, and kept promising through the prophets that there was more, much more, to come in the days of the messianic Kingdom. Then in the fullness of time the Messiah came. With him the new age dawned, the Kingdom of God broke in, the end began. Now today, through the death, resurrection, and Spirit-gift of Jesus, God is fulfilling his promise of redemption and is remaking marred humankind, saving individuals and incorporating them into his new, reconciled community.

Fourth will come the Consummation. For one day, when the good news of the Kingdom has been proclaimed throughout the whole world (Matthew 24:14), Jesus Christ will appear in great magnificence. He will raise the dead, judge the world, regenerate the universe, and bring God's Kingdom to its perfection. From it all pain, decay, sin, sorrow, and death will be banished, and in it God will be glorified for ever. Meanwhile, we are living in between times, between Kingdom come and Kingdom coming, between the "now" and the "then" of redemption, between the "already" and the "not yet."

Here, then, are four events, which correspond to four realities—the Creation ("the good"), the Fall ("the evil"), the Redemption ("the new"), and

51

the Consummation ("the perfect"). This fourfold biblical reality enables Christians to survey the historical landscape within its proper horizons. It supplies the true perspective from which to view the unfolding process between two eternities, the vision of God working out his purpose. It gives us a framework into which to fit everything, a way of integrating our understanding, the possibility of thinking straight, even about the most complex issues.

For the four events or epochs we have been thinking about, especially when grasped in relation to one another, teach major truths about God, human beings, and society, which give direction to our Christian thinking.

The Reality of God

First, the reality of God. The fourfold biblical scheme is essentially God-centered; its four stages are disclosed from his point of view. Even the Fall, though an act of human disobedience, is presented in the context of divine commandments, sanctions, and judgment. Thus, it is God who creates, judges, redeems, and perfects. The initiative is his from beginning to end. In consequence, there is a cluster of popular attitudes that are fundamentally incompatible with Christian faith: the concept of blind evolutionary development; the assertion of human autonomy in art, science, and education; and the declarations that history is random, life is absurd, and everything is meaningless. The Christian mind comes into direct collision with these notions precisely because they are "secular"—they leave no room for God. It insists that human beings can be defined only in relation to God, that without God they have ceased to be truly human. For we are creatures who depend on our Creator, sinners who are accountable to him and under his judgment, waifs and strays who are lost apart from his redemption.

This God-centeredness is basic to the Christian mind. The Christian mind is a godly mind. More than that, it understands "goodness" above all in terms of "godliness." It cannot describe as "good" a person who is "ungodly." This is the clear testimony of the Bible's Wisdom Literature. The five books of Wisdom (Job, Psalms, Proverbs, Ecclesiastes, and the Song of Songs) all focus, in different ways and with different emphases, on what it means to be human, and on how suffering, evil, oppression, and love fit into our humanness. The Book of Ecclesiastes is best known for its pessimistic refrain, "vanity of vanities, all is vanity," well translated by the NIV as "meaningless, meaningless, utterly meaningless." It demonstrates the folly and futility of a human life circumscribed by time and space. If life is restricted to the average brief lifespan, is overshadowed by pain and injustice, and culminates for everybody in the same fate, death; if it is also restricted by the dimensions of space to human experiences "under the sun," with no ultimate reference point beyond the sun—then indeed life is as profitless as "a chasing after wind." Only God, Creator and Judge, Beginning and End, by adding to human life the missing dimensions of transcendence and eternity, can give it meaning, and so turn folly into wisdom.

Over against the pessimism of Ecclesiastes we read the oft-repeated maxim of the Wisdom Literature, namely, "The fear of the LORD—that is wisdom [or its "beginning" or "principle"], and to shun evil is understanding" (Job 28:28; cf. Psalm 111:10; Proverbs 1:7, 9:10; Ecclesiastes 12:13). Here are the two major realities of human experience, God and evil. They are not equal realities, for Christians are not dualists. But they dominate life on earth. The one (God) brings human fulfillment, even ecstasy; the other (evil) human alienation, even despair. And wisdom consists in adopting a right attitude to both: loving God and hating evil, "fearing" God with the worship which acknowledges his infinite worth, and "shunning" evil in the holiness which despises it for its worthlessness. It is because God has made us spiritual and moral beings that religion and ethics, godliness and goodness, are fundamental to authentic humanness. Hence the tragedy of "secularism," the closed worldview which denies God and even glories in the spiritual vacuum it creates. T. S. Eliot was right to call it a "waste land," and Theodore Roszak in *Where the Wasteland Ends* to characterize it as a desert of the spirit. "For what science can measure is only a portion of what man can know. Our knowing reaches out to embrace the sacred." Without transcendence "the person shrinks."[11] Secularism not only dethrones God; it destroys human beings.

If, because of the reality of God, the Christian mind is a godly mind, it is also a humble mind. This is another consistent theme of Scripture. When Nebuchadnezzar strutted like a peacock around the flat rooftop of his Babylonian palace claiming for himself instead of God the kingdom, the power and the glory, he went mad. Only when he acknowledged the rule of God and worshiped him, were his reason and his kingdom simultaneously restored to him. Daniel pointed out the moral: "Those who walk in pride he is able to humble" (Daniel 4:28–37). It is a sobering story. If pride and madness go together, so do humility and sanity.

Jesus' contemporaries must have been dumbfounded when he told adults that they had to become like children if they wanted to enter God's Kingdom, and (even worse) that greatness in the Kingdom would be measured by childlike humility. We are too familiar with this teaching; it has lost its power to shock or stun. Yet Jesus not only taught it; he exhibited it. He emptied himself and humbled himself. So now, Paul adds, "let this mind be in you which was in him." The medieval moralists were right to see pride as the worst of the "seven deadly sins" and as the root of the others. There is nothing so obscene as pride, nothing so attractive as humility.

Probably at no point does the Christian mind clash more violently with the secular mind than in its insistence on humility and its implacable hostility to pride. The wisdom of the world despises humility. Western culture has imbibed more than it knows of the power philosophy of Nietzsche. The world's model, like Nietzsche's, is the "superman"; the model of Jesus remains the little child.

Thus the reality of God (as Creator, Lord, Redeemer, Father, Judge) gives to the Christian mind its first and most fundamental characteristic. Christians refuse to honor anything which dishonors God. We learn to evaluate everything in terms of the glory it gives to, or withholds from, God. That is why, to the Christian mind, wisdom is the fear of God and the preeminent virtue is humility.

The Paradox of Our Humanness

I turn now from God to man, from the unalloyed splendor which characterizes whatever is "divine" to the painful ambiguity which attaches to everything "human." We have already seen that the biblical understanding of humankind takes equal account of the Creation and the Fall. It is this that constitutes "the paradox of our humanness." We human beings have both a unique dignity as creatures made in God's image and a unique depravity as sinners under his judgment. The former gives us hope; the latter places a limit on our expectations. Our Christian critique of the secular mind is that it tends to be either too naively optimistic or too negatively pessimistic in its estimates of the human condition, whereas the Christian mind, firmly rooted in biblical realism, both celebrates the glory and deplores the shame of our human being. We can behave like God in whose image we were made, only to descend to the level of the beasts. We are able to think, choose, create, love, and worship, but also to refuse to think, to choose evil, to destroy, to hate, and to worship ourselves. We build churches and drop bombs. We develop intensive care units for the critically ill and use the same technology to torture political enemies who presume to disagree with us. This is "man," a strange, bewildering paradox, dust of earth and breath of God, shame and glory. So, as the Christian mind applies itself to human life on earth, to our personal, social, and political affairs, it seeks to remember what paradoxical creatures we are—noble and ignoble, rational and irrational, loving and selfish, Godlike and bestial.

Perhaps I can best illustrate this dialectic by taking two examples, first our sexuality and second the political process.

It is pertinent to begin with our sexuality, partly because we are all sexual beings, and partly because, of all the social revolutions which have taken place this century, the sexual revolution may well be the most profound. Sexual roles (masculinity and femininity), the context for sexual intercourse (in or out of marriage), whether the traditional understandings of marriage and the family can (or even should) survive the option of homosexual partnerships, contraception, in vitro fertilization, artificial insemination by donor, abortion, and divorce—these are some aspects of human sexuality about which radical questions are being asked today. Although the Bible gives clear instructions on some of them, we will be far better placed to grapple with individual issues if we first gain a bird's-eye view of sexuality in general by seeing it in the light of Scripture's fourfold scheme.

According to Genesis 1 and 2 God created humankind male and female in his own image from the beginning, and told them to be fruitful. Although he pronounced Creation "good," he needed to add that "It is not good for the man to be alone." And he went on to ordain that the sexual complementarity of men and women was to be consummated in the mysteries of the "one flesh" experience. Thus human sexuality, marriage, sexual intercourse, and the family are all part of the creative purpose of God. Marriage (a publicly pledged, permanent, exclusive, heterosexual union) is not a human but a divine institution, which therefore in itself is not affected by changing culture. Sexual intimacy within marriage is a good gift of a good Creator.

But after the Creation came the Fall. Sin has distorted our sexuality, as it has every other human instinct, faculty, and appetite. Sex has surely become a far more imperious drive than God originally intended. Unnatural sexual deviations have arisen. Although sexual love can still be enjoyed, and even wonderingly celebrated as in the Song of Songs, nevertheless it is also often spoiled by selfish demands, fears, exploitation, and cruelty.

The redeeming work of Christ through his Spirit has made possible a whole new attitude toward sex. This includes (in addition to a recognition of the Creator's purpose and gift) the control and sanctification of our sexual drive, a vision of self-giving love in marriage as a reflection of the relation between Christ and his Church, and a partnership between the sexes which, while not denying the responsible and caring headship which God has given to man (rooted in Creation, not culture), also rejoices that in the married couple's relationship to God "there is neither male nor female," since they are now equally justified in Christ and equally adopted into God's family (Galatians 3:26–29). At the same time, Jesus taught that for a variety of reasons some will remain single (Matthew 19:10f.; cf. 1 Corinthians 7:1ff.).

What about the consummation? In the next world after the resurrection, Jesus said, "they will neither marry nor be given in marriage; they will be like the angels in heaven" (Mark 12:25). So although love is eternal, marriage is not. Procreation will no longer be necessary. Relationships of love will transcend the physical, and will probably be less exclusive (though surely not less rich) than in marriage. The importance of adding this fourth stage should be clear. It contains a message both for the married (lest the union become selfish to the point even of idolatry) and for the single (that marriage is not indispensable to the attainment of full humanness).

As we try to respond Christianly to the radical sexual challenges of today, we will find it easier to struggle with particular issues within this general biblical framework.

My second example related to "the paradox of our humanness" concerns the political process. The nature of man (i.e., what it means to be human) has arguably been the basic political issue of the twentieth century. It has certainly been one of the chief points of conflict between Marx and Jesus, and therefore between the East and the West, namely, whether human beings have any absolute value because of which they must be respected, or whether their value is only relative to the community, for the sake of which they may be exploited. More simply, are the people the servants of the institution, or is the institution the servant of the people? As John S. Whale has written, "ideologies . . . are really anthropologies";[12] they reflect different doctrines of our humanity.

Christians should be careful not to "baptize" any political ideology (whether of the right, the left, or the center), as if it contained a monopoly of truth and goodness. At best a political ideology and its program are only an approximation to the will and purpose of God. The fact is that Christians are to be found in most political parties and are able to defend their membership on conscientious Christian grounds. Thus, to indulge in a blunt oversimplification, both the main political ideologies in Western societies appeal to Christians for different reasons. Capitalism appeals because it encourages individual human initiative and enterprise, but also repels because it seems not to care that the weak succumb to the fierce competition it engenders. Socialism appeals, on the other hand, because it has great compassion for the poor and the weak, but also repels because it seems not to care that individual initiative and enterprise are smothered by the big government which it engenders. Each attracts because it emphasizes a truth about human beings, either the need to give free play to their creative abilities or the need to protect them from injustice. Each repels because it fails to take with equal seriousness the complementary truth. Both can be liberating. But both can also be oppressive. A wit has put this well: "The difference between Capitalism and Socialism is that in Capitalism man exploits man, while in Socialism it's the other way round!" It is understandable that many Christians dream of a third option which overcomes the present confrontation and incorporates the best features of both.

Whatever our political color may be, all Christians tend to advocate democracy, which was popularly defined by Abraham Lincoln as "government of the people, by the people, for the people." Not that it is "perfect or all-wise," as Winston Churchill conceded in the House of Commons on 11 November 1947. "Indeed," he continued, "it has been said that democracy is the worst form of government—except for all those other forms that have been tried from time to time." The fact is that it is the wisest and safest form of government yet devised. This is because it reflects the paradox of our humanness. On the one hand, it takes the Creation seriously (that is, human dignity), because it refuses to govern human beings without their consent, and insists instead on giving them a responsible share in the decision-making process. On the other hand, it takes the Fall seriously (that is, human depravity), because it refuses to concentrate power in the hands of one person or of a few people, and insists instead on dispersing it, thus protecting human beings from their own pride and folly. Reinhold Niebuhr put it succinctly: "Man's capacity for justice makes democracy possible; but man's inclination to injustice makes democracy necessary."[13]

The Future of Society

A third sphere to which it may be helpful to apply the Bible's fourfold scheme is that of the possibility of social change. What expectation should we cherish that society can be improved? On this issue Christians of different traditions are to be found along a broad spectrum.

"Liberal" Christians have tended to be social activists. Because of their almost boundless confidence in human achievement, they dream dreams of building Utopia (sometimes mistakenly identified as "the Kingdom of God") on earth.

"Evangelical" Christians, on the other hand, have tended—at least earlier in the twentieth century—to be social quietists. Because of their gloomy view of human depravity, they lack confidence in human beings (at least until they have been born again). They therefore consider social action a waste of time and social transformation all but impossible.

I have deliberately expressed both positions in their more extreme forms. Stated thus, the polarization fails to hold together the two parts of the human paradox.

Because human beings are made in the image of God, and the divine image (though marred) has not been wholly lost, they retain some perception of the just and compassionate society which would please him, and some desire to bring it about. On the whole, all humankind still prefers peace to war, justice to oppression, harmony to discord, order to chaos. So social change is possible, and indeed has happened. In many parts of the world we can see rising standards of hygiene and health care, a greater respect for women and children, the increasing availability of education, a clearer recognition of human rights, a growing concern to conserve the natural environment, and better conditions in mine, factory, and prison. Much of this has been due (directly or indirectly) to Christian influence, although by no means all social reformers have been committed Christians. But whenever God's people have been effective as salt and light in the community, there has been less social decay and more social uplift. In the United States, for example, after the early-nineteenth-century awakening associated with Charles G. Finney, "born-again Christians were in the forefront of every major social reform in America. . . . They spear-headed the abolitionist movement, the temperance movement, the peace movement, and the early feminist movement."[14]

Because human beings are fallen, however, and inherit a twist of self-centeredness, we shall never succeed in building a perfect society. Improvement—yes; perfect justice—no. Utopian dreams are unrealistic; they belong to the world of fantasy. All human plans, though launched with great hopes, have to some degree disappointed the planners, for they have foundered on the rock of human selfishness. Christians have usually remembered this. As William Temple put it, "Its assertion of Original Sin should make the Church intensely realistic and conspicuously free from Utopianism."[15] Certainly, the evangelical Christians who gathered in Lausanne at the great International Congress on World Evangelization (1974) declared forthrightly in their Covenant: "We . . . reject as a proud, self-confident dream the notion that man can ever build a utopia on earth."[16] It is Socialists who have tended to be too optimistic about human achievement. Professor C. E. M. Joad is a good example. Having been brought up on the confessions and collects of the Church of England's 1662 *Book of Common Prayer*, he began by believing in the inherent sinfulness of human beings. But later he discarded this notion in favor of their "infinite perfectibility," until World War II shattered this illusion and convinced him again that "evil is endemic in man." He wrote candidly in his book *Recovery of Belief* (1952): "It is because we rejected the doctrine of original sin that we on the Left were always being disappointed; disappointed by the refusal of people to be reasonable, by the subservience of intellect to emotion, by the failure of true Socialism to arrive . . . above all, by the recurrent fact of war."[17]

It is difficult to avoid extremes of pessimism and optimism about the possibility of social change. Robert McNamara nearly did, in what has been described as perhaps his "most eloquent speech" while in office as U.S. Defense Secretary: "All the evidence of history suggests that man is indeed a rational animal, but with a nearly infinite capacity for folly. His history seems largely a halting but persistent effort to raise his reason above his animality. He draws blueprints for Utopia, but never quite gets it built."[18] But even this sounds a trifle cynical.

How, then, can we sum up an attitude to the possibility of social change which reflects "neither the easy optimism of the humanist, nor the dark pessimism of the cynic, but the radical realism of the Bible"?[19] How can we do equal justice to the truths of the Creation, the Fall, the Redemption, and the Consummation? I suggest that the biblical balance is well expressed by Paul in 1 Thessalonians 1:9–10, where he describes the results of conversion from idols to God as being "to serve the living and true God, and to wait for his Son from heaven." The combination of "serving" and "waiting" is striking, since the former is actively getting busy for Christ on earth, while the latter is passively looking for him to come from heaven. We must serve, but there are limits to what we can achieve. We must wait, but have no liberty to do so in idleness. Thus "working" and "waiting" go together. The need to wait for Christ from heaven will rescue us from the presumption which thinks we can do everything; the need to work for Christ on earth will rescue us from the pessimism which thinks we can do nothing. Only a Christian mind which has developed a biblical perspective can enable us to preserve the balance.

I began this chapter by admitting the complexity of the problems of personal and social ethics which confront us today. Neat, cut-and-dried solutions are usually impossible. Simplistic shortcuts, which ignore the real issues, are unhelpful. At the same time, it is not Christian to give up in despair.

We need to remember for our encouragement that God has given us four gifts.

His first gift is a mind with which to think. He has made us rational, intelligent creatures. He still forbids us to behave like horses and mules which lack understanding, and tells us in our thinking to be not babies but adults (Psalm 32:9; 1 Corinthians 14:20).

Second, he has given us the Bible and its witness to Christ, in order to direct and control our thinking. As we absorb its teaching, our thoughts will increasingly conform to his. This is not because we memorize a lot of proof texts, which we trot out at appropriate moments, each text labeled to answer its own question. It is rather that we have grasped the great themes and principles of Scripture and the fourfold framework which we have been considering in this chapter.

God's third gift is the Holy Spirit, the Spirit of truth, who opens up the Scriptures to us and illumines our minds so that we can understand and apply them.

Fourth, God has given us the Christian community as the context in which to do our thinking. Its heterogeneity is the best safeguard against blinkered vision. For the Church has members of both sexes, and of all ages, temperaments, experiences, and cultures. And each local church should reflect this colorful diversity. With rich insights contributed to the interpretation of Scripture from different backgrounds, it will be hard to maintain our prejudices.

With these four gifts, used in concert—a mind, a textbook, a Teacher, and a school—it should be possible for us to develop an increasingly Christian mind and to learn to think straight.

An Appendix on Postmodernity

The very possibility of being able to think straight about contemporary issues, and find solutions to contemporary problems, is being challenged today by postmodernity and its almost total skepticism about truth. A fundamental paradigm shift is taking place around us, as the "modern" Enlightenment culture, which replaced the "premodern," is itself being replaced by the "postmodern." These are slippery words, however, which elude the firm grasp of precise definition. Different scholars use them in different ways. Perhaps they are most easily understood in relation and reaction to each other.

The premodern mind-set was essentially medieval and prescientific. It was characterized by an unquestioning submission to feudal authority in church and state, and by an uncritical acceptance of the supernatural, to the point of gross superstition.

The modern mind-set, which budded in the Renaissance, blossomed in the eighteenth-century European Enlightenment. Its foundation was confidence in man rather than God. It celebrated the emergence of human beings from the bondage of tradition, and so from social and intellectual childhood. It sought to replace divine revelation by human reason; supernatural religion by natural science (the world being a closed, mechanistic system of cause and effect, with no room for miracles or indeed for an interfering God); laissez-faire economics by planning; feudalism by human rights; original sin by the fundamental goodness of human beings and the inevitability of material and moral progress; and morality by utilitarianism (behavior is right if it is beneficial).

The postmodern mind-set is best seen as a reaction against the "modernity" of both Renaissance and Enlightenment. Anticipated by the romanticism of the early nineteenth century, by the existentialism of the middle of the twentieth century, and by the counterculture of the 1960s, postmodernism rejects Enlightenment self-confidence and optimism. Far from fulfilling its promises, science has given birth to a dehumanizing technology. The dream of continuous progress has been shattered by two World Wars and the Holocaust, by the nightmare fears of nuclear and environmental destruction, and by the specters of nationalism and tribalism. In place of the old triumphalism, disillusion now reigns, along with her twin sisters skepticism and cynicism. In consequence, the postmodern mood distrusts all authorities, and rejects all so-called metanarratives, which propose grandiose, universal solutions. Where today are the economic liberation promised by Marx, the evolutionary progress implied by Darwin, and the psychoanalytical therapy propounded by Freud? Their pretentious theories offered much, but delivered little.

Truth to the postmodernist is purely subjective; it is merely what happens to make sense to me. Something quite different may make sense to you; it then becomes your truth. Moreover, there are no documents of law, history, tradition, or religion which can guide or unite us. For what is decisive in the interpretation of a text is not the identity and intention of its author (which in any case may not be discoverable), but rather the impact which it makes on each reader. Thus, it is left to each of us to construct our own reality, believe our own truth, tell our own story, and create our own identity.

The Christian critique of postmodernism is not wholly negative, however, for we share some of its quarrel with modernism. We, too, reject rationalism, that is, the proclamation of the autonomy and omni-competence of the human mind; yet we affirm the essential rationality of human beings, since God has made us rational in his own image. We also reject modernity's naive confidence in the inevitability of human progress and its dreams of Utopia; yet we refuse to lapse into postmodern cynicism, since through the power of the gospel and through the influence of the Church as salt and light, God can improve society and has in fact done so.

Again, we cannot help acknowledging that the very concept of truth has many limitations. First, ultimate reality has mysteries which science and religion cannot fathom and which language cannot describe. Second, the truth we do know is inevitably colored by our cultural presuppositions and perspectives. Third, the pursuit of truth has sometimes degenerated into a concealed hunger for power to oppress people. Nevertheless, even when these humbling confessions have been made, Christians still affirm that God has revealed himself in Christ and in the biblical witness to Christ, and that the truth of his self-revelation is objective in its character, absolute in its quality, and universal in its application. The gospel is, in fact, the authentic metanarrative.

3

Pluralism:
Should We Impose Our Views?

We accept that we should get involved, and we struggle to think Christianly about the issues. In consequence, we develop some quite strong convictions. But others do not share them. Indeed, Western Christians find themselves increasingly out of step with a post-Christian society. So how can we hope to influence our country to return to Christian values, in its laws, its institutions, and its culture? Should Christians attempt to impose their views on a largely non-Christian nation?

In Europe and America, and in those Commonwealth countries that inherited the "Christian civilization" of the West, we certainly have to come to terms with the new "pluralism," meaning a society composed of different ethnic and religious groups. Pluralism is due largely to two factors. The first is the process of secularization, seen as the diminishing influence of the Church on both people and institutions. Accurate statistics are notoriously hard to obtain and to interpret. It seems to be clear, however, that adult membership of the Protestant churches of the United Kingdom dropped from 12 percent of the adult population in 1975 to 9 percent in 1994. This shows a 19 percent loss in church membership over the twenty-year period in spite of roughly an 8 percent growth in population.[1] It is significant to note that these declining numbers are part of a larger pattern of decline that has been in place since World War II.

Again, between 1968 and 1990 around 1,200 Church of England churches were declared redundant, and were either demolished or appropriated to other uses (cultural, residential, etc.). While overall church membership has continued to decline in recent years, the statistics are not as depressing as they may seem at first glance. Although just over six churches close down every week, six churches are being opened every week too, with an average of two hundred members joining churches every day.[2] Nevertheless, in contrast to half a century ago, let alone the nineteenth century, there can be no doubt that the Church has lost a great deal of ground.

Alongside the Christian decline has gone an increase in non-Christian alternatives. For the second cause of pluralism is the liberal immigration policy of the immediate postwar years. As a result, most Western countries now include in their population sizable ethnic groups from Africa, Asia, the Middle East, and the Caribbean. This makes possible for all of us a rich experience of cultural diversity. But it also leads to religious competition and to consequent demands for recognition of other religions in those countries' educational systems, laws, and institutions. In 1994 the adult membership of non-Christian religious groups in the United Kingdom was as follows:[3]

- Muslims—575,000 active members (estimates for the whole community range from 1.15 million to 3 million)
- Sikhs—325,000 (although the Sikh Cultural Society estimates 500,000)
- Jews—97,300 (heads of household who represent about one-third of the whole Jewish community)
- Hindus—144,000 (this is the estimated active membership representing approximately one-third of the Hindu community)
- Mormons—168,302
- Jehovah's Witnesses—129,852

If we add together the adult membership of all non-Christian religious minorities in the United Kingdom (including Spiritualists, Christian Scientists, Christadelphians, etc.), it comes to over 1.2 million, with the total community (including children, cultural adherents, etc.) nearing 4 million.[4] This is a significant minority, exercising noticeable influence. As for unbelievers, since the most generous estimate of the combined numbers of all religious communities in Britain (including children and nonpracticing adherents) is 72 percent of the total population, there must be 28 percent who make no religious profession at all.[5]

Elsewhere in the world, even if Christians represent a substantial minority, the predominant culture is either Hindu or Buddhist, Jewish or Islamic, Marxist or secular. So here, too, usually in a more acute form, Christians are faced with the same dilemma. On many issues they believe they know the will of God. They also believe it is their Christian duty to pray and work for God's will to be done. Should they hope to impose their Christian convictions on non-Christians? If it is possible, is it desirable? Even if they could, should they try?

The two most common responses to these questions represent opposite extremes. One is "imposition," the crusading attempt to coerce people by legislation to accept the Christian way. The other is "laissez-faire," the defeatist decision to leave people alone in their non-Christian ways, and not interfere or try to influence them in any way. We need to look carefully at these alternatives, with some historical examples, before we shall be ready for a third and better option.

Imposition

Here are Christians with a commendable zeal for God. They believe in revelation, and they care deeply about God's revealed truth and will. They long to see society reflecting it. So the desire to achieve this end by force is an understandable temptation.

My first historical illustration is the Inquisition in Europe, which was a special tribunal set up by the Roman Catholic Church in the thirteenth century to combat heresy. Suspected heretics were first hunted out, then invited to confess, and then, if they refused, brought to trial. By Pope Innocent IV's bull *Ad extirpanda* of 1252, torture was permitted in addition to trial. Impenitent heretics were punished by excommunication or imprisonment or confiscation of goods, or were handed over to the state to be burned alive. The Inquisition lasted about three hundred years. It was suppressed in 1542, although the Spanish Inquisition (which was the most cruel), instituted at the end of the fifteenth century by Ferdinand and Isabella for purposes of national security and used especially against Jews, Moors, and Protestants, was abolished only in the year 1834.[6] Today, I imagine, Christians of all traditions are deeply ashamed that such methods could ever have been used in the name of Jesus Christ. The Inquisition remains a horrible blot on the pages of Church history, never to be reinstated. Yet dictatorships of the extreme left and right are still guilty of trying by force to abolish opposition and compel assent. All Christians affirm, however, that totalitarianism and torture are both wholly incompatible with the mind and spirit of Jesus.

My second and more recent historical example is that of Prohibition in the United States, namely, the legal ban on the manufacture and sale of alcoholic liquor. The National Prohibition Party was formed in 1869 by a group of white Protestants. Their motives were admirable. Dismayed by the increase in heavy drinking and drunkenness, especially among poor immigrants, and perceiving this as a threat to public order, they committed themselves to work for the total prohibition of alcoholic beverages. In 1895 the

"Anti-Saloon League of America" was founded by a group of church leaders, and after a campaign of about twenty-five years Congress passed in 1919 the Eighteenth Amendment to the Constitution, prohibiting the manufacture, sale, and transportation of liquor. It came into force a year later, and forty-six out of forty-eight states had ratified it within about two years.

The result, however, was that the law was widely broken. Bootleggers made, sold, and smuggled alcoholic drinks illegally, and speakeasies (stores in which liquor was sold clandestinely) flourished. So in 1933, thirteen years after the so-called Noble Experiment began, the Twenty-First Amendment, which voided the Eighteenth, was signed by President Roosevelt, and Prohibition ended. Far from abolishing alcohol abuse, it had provoked and increased it. And the law had been brought into disrepute.

So, was Prohibition foisted on the country, or did the people want it? Opinions differ. The "drys" claim that there was a national consensus; the "wets" that this was obtained by legislative action, not by direct popular vote, and only when the nation's mind was preoccupied with America's entry into World War I. John Kobler writes: "The accessible evidence confirms neither claim. It precludes any flat answer and leaves the question for ever unsettled." Nevertheless, this is how he concludes his historical inquiry: "In sum, it appeared that rural, agricultural America with its large Protestant, native-born population thrust prohibition upon urban, industrial America, with its heterogeneity of races, religions and foreign backgrounds."[7]

Looking back at these two examples, one European and the other American, the Inquisition was an attempt to impose belief, and Prohibition an attempt to impose behavior. Both were seen in the end to be unproductive, for you cannot force people to believe what they do not believe, or to practice what they do not want to practice. Similarly, to imagine today that we can force Christian convictions and standards on Europe is totally unrealistic. It is a foolish, nostalgic desire for a Christendom which has long since vanished.

Laissez-Faire

The opposite of imposition, I suggest, is laissez-faire.The term was originally used in the eighteenth century of Free Trade economists, and the concept dominated nineteenth-century society. It had no overtones of the lackadaisical about it. On the contrary, it was a principled belief in the necessity of noninterference by government. The use of the term has changed with the centuries, however, and in popular parlance today it describes a mood of apathy and indifference. It is applied to citizens as much as to governments. Far from imposing our views, we say, we will not even propagate or commend them. We shall leave other people alone to mind their own business, as we devoutly hope they will leave us alone to mind ours. Laissez-faire has even sometimes been an attitude adopted by Christian people in the name of tolerance.

Tolerant in spirit Christians should certainly be, showing respect toward those who think and behave differently. Socially tolerant too, in the sense that we should want to see political and religious minorities accepted in the community and protected by law, just as the Christian minority in a non-Christian country expects to be legally free to profess, practice, and propagate the gospel. But how can we Christians be intellectually tolerant of opinions we know to be false or actions we know to be evil? What kind of unprincipled indulgence is this? Societies smell sweet or acrid in the nostrils of God. He is not indifferent to questions of social justice, so how can his people be? To remain silent and inactive when error or evil is being canvassed has very serious consequences. For the Christian option has then gone by default. Is it not at least partly because Christians have failed to raise their voices for Jesus Christ, that our country has slipped its Christian moorings and drifted away from them?

The gravest modern example of Christian laissez-faire is the failure of German churches to speak out against the Nazis' treatment of the Jews. It is a long and dismal story, thoroughly documented by Richard Gutteridge in his book *Open Thy Mouth for the Dumb*.[8] He traces Christian complicity in German anti-Semitism back to the nineteenth century, when Christianity became identified with a mystical German patriotism, which increased after defeat in World War I. It was at this time that several misguided attempts were made to theologize the intrinsic value of the Aryan *Volk*. For example, Paul Althaus wrote in 1932: "It is God's will that we maintain our Race and our *Volkstum* in purity, that we remain German men, and do not become a bastard-*Volk* of Jewish Aryan blood."[9] At that time the Church seemed to be in alliance with the National Socialist Movement. Only a few brave voices (like those of Karl Barth and Paul Tillich) were raised in protest. But meanwhile the "Faith Movement of German Christians," under the patronage of the Nazi Party, affirmed the Aryan Race.

After Hitler came to power in 1933 a law was passed to purge the Civil Service of officials of non-Aryan descent, and, incredible as it may seem, the racially compromised "German Christians" wanted to apply this "Aryan Clause" to the Church. Several synods adopted it, against the opposition of men like Martin Niemöller, Walter Künneth, Hans Lilje, and Dietrich Bonhoeffer. Yet "the Evangelical Church never spoke out officially against the Aryan legislation in general." Bonhoeffer was deeply upset by the Church's silence and frequently quoted Proverbs 31:8: "Open thy mouth for the dumb."[10]

In the terrible pogrom of November 1938, 119 synagogues were set on fire (of which 76 were destroyed), 20,000 Jews were arrested, shops were looted, and prominent Jewish citizens were publicly humiliated. The general public was aghast, and some church leaders protested. But "there was no chance of the Evangelical Church as a whole voicing her horror and indignation, and the Catholic Church kept almost completely silent, and their hierarchy found no word to say."[11] Hitler's appalling "Final Solution," which he had already decided upon before World War II broke out, began to be implemented in 1941. Not until two years later, however, did a conference of Lutheran Church leaders resolve to attack the Reich government for its anti-Jewish atrocities. This is how Richard Gutteridge sums up his thesis: "The Church as Church did not find a decisive word from Scripture as a whole to embrace the issue as a whole. . . . Throughout the conflict nobody in a position of authority made a full and plain denunciation of anti-Semitism as such."[12] Barth called it "the sin against the Holy Ghost" and a "rejection of the grace of God."[13] Some other church officials were equally bold, and paid dearly for their courage. But when evangelical church leaders met soon after the end of the war and issued their "Stuttgart Declaration," they had to acknowledge: "It is our self-indictment that we have not made a more courageous confession."[14] Gutteridge concludes: "The ultimate failure of the Church lay not in the inability of bishops and synods to make plain and outspoken pronouncements in public," though it included that, but rather "what was missing was a spontaneous outburst at any point by ordinary decent Christian folk. . . . A really widespread, public, visible expression of righteous indignation would have had to have been taken very seriously indeed by the Nazi leaders, and would assuredly have had a profound effect in curbing the most iniquitous excesses and brutalities, if not in bringing about the downfall of so monstrous and unprincipled a tyranny."[15]

The story Richard Gutteridge tells speaks for itself. It needs no additional comment from me. The complicity of the "German Christians," who failed to develop a biblical critique of the Nazis' blatant racism, should be enough to outlaw laissez-faire forever. Could they not have prevented the Holocaust?

Persuasion

Better than the extremes of imposition and laissez-faire is the strategy of persuasion by argument. This is the way the Christian mind advocates, for it arises naturally from the biblical doctrines of God and human beings.

The living God of the biblical revelation, who created and sustains the universe, intended the human beings he made to live in loving community. Moreover, his righteousness is an essential expression of his love. He loves justice and hates oppression. He champions the cause of the poor, the alien, the widow, and the orphan. He feeds the hungry, clothes the naked, heals the sick, finds the lost. He wants all humankind to be saved and to come to know the truth in his Son Jesus Christ. Now this biblical vision of God profoundly affects our attitude to society, since God's concerns inevitably become his people's too. We also will respect men and women made in God's image, seek justice, hate injustice, care for the needy, guard the dignity of work, recognize the necessity of rest, maintain the sanctity of marriage, be zealous for the honor of Jesus Christ, and long that every knee will do homage to him and every tongue confess him. Why? Because all these are God's concerns. How can we acquiesce in things which passionately displease him, or be nonchalant about things he is strongly committed to? The policy of laissez-faire is inconceivable to Christians who hold a biblical doctrine of God.

But then the policy of imposition is impossible to those who hold a biblical doctrine of human beings. For God made male and female to be responsible beings. He told them to be fruitful (exercise their powers of procreation), to subdue the earth and rule its creatures, to work and to rest, and to obey him ("you may . . . you must not . . ."). These injunctions would be meaningless if God had not endowed humankind with two unique gifts—conscience (to discern between alternatives) and freedom (to choose between them). The rest of the Bible confirms this. It is assumed throughout that human beings are moral beings, who are accountable for their actions. They know the moral law, since it is "written on their hearts" (Romans 2:14–15), and are exhorted to obedience and warned of the penalties for disobedience. But they are never coerced. No compulsion is ever used. Only persuasion by argument: "Come now, let us reason together, says the LORD" (Isaiah 1:18).

A basic ground for this is that the human conscience must be treated with the greatest respect. Paul expresses his personal determination "to keep my conscience clear before God and man" (Acts 24:16). He also has much to say about other people's consciences. They may be "strong" (well-educated and free) or "weak" (overscrupulous and full of qualms). But whatever the condition of a person's conscience, even when it is mistaken, it is to be respected. Weak consciences need to be strengthened, and deceiving consciences enlightened, but there must be no bullying of consciences. Only in the most extreme circumstances should people be induced to act against their consciences. In general, consciences are to be educated, not violated. This principle, which arises out of the Christian doctrine of human beings, should affect our social behavior and institutions. It is the reason why Christians oppose autocracy and favor democracy. Autocracy crushes consciences; democracy (at least in theory) respects them, since democratic governments derive "their just powers from the consent of the governed" (The

American Declaration of Independence).[16] Once laws have been promulgated, however, all citizens (in a democracy as in an autocracy) are under constraint to obey them. They may not do as they please. Yet in matters of great moment (e.g., conscription in time of war) a civilized government will allow "conscientious objection." This provision is also the product of Christian thinking.

So both the biblical doctrine of God and that of human beings guide our behavior in a pluralist society, the former ruling out laissez-faire, and the latter ruling out imposition. Because God is who he is, we cannot be indifferent when his truth and law are flouted, but because human beings are who they are, we cannot try to impose them by force.

What, then, should Christians do? We should seek to educate the public conscience to know and desire the will of God. The Church should seek to be the conscience of the nation. If we cannot impose God's will by legislation, neither can we convince people of it merely by biblical quotation. For both these approaches are examples of "authority from above," which people resent and resist. More effective is "authority from below," the intrinsic truth and value of a thing which is self-evident and therefore self-authenticating. (Not that the two are incompatible; God's authority is essentially both.) This principle applies equally in evangelism and social action.

In evangelism we should neither try to force people to believe the gospel, nor remain silent as if we were indifferent to their response, nor rely exclusively on the dogmatic proclamation of biblical texts (vital as authoritative biblical exposition is), but rather, like the apostles, we should reason with people from both nature and Scripture, commending God's gospel to them by rational arguments.

In social action, similarly, we should neither try to impose Christian standards by force on an unwilling public, nor remain silent and inactive before the contemporary landslide, nor rely exclusively on the dogmatic assertion of biblical values, but rather reason with people about the benefits of Christian morality, commending God's law to them by rational arguments. We believe that God's laws are both good in themselves and universal in their application because, far from being arbitrary, they fit the human beings God has made. This was God's claim for his laws from the beginning. He gave them, he said, "for your own good" (Deuteronomy 10:13), and pleaded with the people to obey them "so that it might go well with them and their children for ever" (Deuteronomy 5:29 etc.). There was thus an essential correspondence between what was "good and right in the eyes of the LORD" and what was "well with them" (Deuteronomy 12:28). The "good" and the "well" coincided. We believe, moreover, that everybody has an inkling that this is so. But because they may be either unable or unwilling to acknowledge it, we have to deploy arguments to demonstrate that God's laws are for the well-being both of individuals and of society.

We therefore need a doctrinal apologetic in evangelism (arguing the truth of the gospel) and an ethical apologetic in social action (arguing the goodness of the moral law). Apologists of both kinds are needed urgently in today's Church and world.

Examples of Persuasion by Argument

Let me try to supply some examples. The Christian standards of chastity before marriage and fidelity within it are increasingly challenged and repudiated. Sexual promiscuity is spreading, even though the AIDS scare has provoked a greater degree of self-control in some, and in others even a new celibate lifestyle. At the same time, experimental living together before marriage is not only widely practiced, but widely recommended. Cohabitation without marriage, not just in the old sense of de facto "common law marriage" but in the sense of deliberately dispensing with marriage altogether as an obsolete custom, now provokes little if any social displeasure. Wife-swapping is regarded as an amusing suburban game. "Open marriages," in which the husband knows his wife has other sexual partners, and the wife knows the same about her husband, and both approve of the fact, and even encourage it, are not unusual. In some circumstances a series of successive marriages through easy divorce is regarded as "enriching" (the suffering of the children being conveniently ignored or rationalized), and a homosexual partnership is more and more considered a legitimate alternative to a heterosexual marriage.

In the face of this sexual revolution, Christians should of course both themselves obey, and make known to others, the unchanging standards of God's law. Nevertheless, it will not be enough to climb Mount Sinai and proclaim the Ten Commandments from that pinnacle of authority. Even when people are converted and regenerated (which remains our paramount concern and the surest route to moral uprightness), they still need reasons for obedience. So what arguments can we deploy? The first is anthropological. It was Raymond Johnston who in his 1978 London Lectures in Contemporary Christianity introduced me to J. D. Unwin's book *Sex and Culture* (1934). He described it as "one of the monumental works of comparative anthropology."[17] Unwin confessed that he began his investigation "with carefree open-mindedness" and "in all innocence." With no axe to grind, and no idea where his researches might lead him, he wanted to test the conjecture that civilization and sexual self-control were related to each other. He studied eighty primitive and sixteen civilized societies, and found that a society's cultural energy (art, science, technology, etc.) increases as its sexual energy is controlled.

His study of certain "vigorous societies" revealed that "in each case they reduced their sexual opportunity to a minimum by the adoption of absolute monogamy; in each case the ensuing compulsory continence produced great social energy. The group within the society which suffered the greatest continence displayed the greatest energy, and dominated the society." Conversely, whenever monogamy was modified, the society's cultural energy decreased. The conclusion of his book was that if a vigorous society "wishes to display its productive energy for a long time," it must regulate relations between the sexes by practicing monogamy. Then "its inherited tradition would be continually enriched; it would achieve a higher culture than has yet been attained; by the action of human entropy (the generation of fresh cultural energy) its tradition would be augmented and refined in a manner which surpasses our present understanding."[18] Freud had taught similarly that the flourishing of culture and the restraining of instincts belong together.

To this sociological evidence a psychological argument may be added. It is well known that male and female sexual experiences differ. The male sexual appetite is largely physical, is quickly aroused and quickly satisfied. With women, however, sexual intercourse is not in itself a wholly satisfying experience, for it arouses other desires which are not so easily met—desires for the security of husband, home, and children. For men to arouse such desires, when they have no intention of fulfilling them, can only be described as cruel.[19]

Some years ago I read a confirmation of this in an unlikely place, the November 1977 edition of the American magazine *Seventeen*. It carried an article entitled "The Case Against Living Together," which took the form of an interview with Dr. Nancy Moore Clatworthy, a sociologist at Ohio State University in Columbus, Ohio. For ten years she had been studying the phenomenon of unmarried couples living together. When she began, she was predisposed toward it. Young people had told her it was "wonderful," and she had believed them. It seemed to her a "sensible" arrangement, "a useful step in courtship," during which couples got to know each other. But her research (which involved the testing of hundreds of couples, married and unmarried) led her to change her mind. "The things people say living together is doing for them, it's not doing," she said. The problem was especially with the young women, whom she found uptight, fearful, and looking "past the rhetoric to the possible pain and agony."

She made two points in particular. First, regarding problems. "In the areas of adjustment, happiness and respect," couples who had lived together before marriage had more problems than those who had married first. They also argued more, for example, about money, friends, and sex. "In every area the couples who had lived together before marriage disagreed more often than the couples who had not." It was evident, she concluded, that living together first does not solve problems. Dr. Clatworthy's second point was about commitment. "Commitment is the expectation a person has about the outcome of a relationship. . . . Commitment is what makes marriage, living together or any human relationship work." But "knowing that something is temporary affects the degree of commitment to it." So unmarried couples are less than wholehearted in working to sustain and protect their relationship; and consequently 75 percent of them break up. It is especially the women who are badly hurt. Dr. Clatworthy concludes: "Statistically, you're much better off marrying than living together." "For people who are in love anything less than a full commitment is a cop-out."

When anthropology, sociology, and psychology all point in the same direction, the argument is powerful. We should not be afraid to use it. Nor should we be surprised about this convergence, because God has written his law in two places, on stone tablets and on the tablets of the human heart (Romans 2:14f.). The moral law is not alien to human beings, therefore. There is a fundamental correspondence between Scripture and human nature.

Sexual morality is only one example of the need to deploy arguments in our defense and commendation of Christian social ethics. We should seek to develop the same strategy in every sphere. The "just war theory," for instance, is a line of reasoning that is not expressly Christian. Although it has been developed by great Christian thinkers like Augustine and Thomas Aquinas, its origins go back to Plato, Aristotle, and Cicero in ancient Greece and Rome. So it is a tradition, although it has been refined and enriched by Scripture. Many non-Christians agree with its reasonableness, even though they may not accept the authority of Scripture.

Again, we can occupy common ground with non-Christians, and join hands with them in our desire both to protect human rights and to preserve the natural environment. Respect for human beings is a major concern of secular humanists, who are dedicated to the human cause, even if their reasons differ from those of Christians. As for conservation, it is possible to agree about the unity of spaceship earth, the delicate balance of nature, our common dependence on air, water, and earth, and the distinction between capital resources (like fossil fuels) and income—without ever quoting a text from Genesis 1 and 2 or from any other part of Scripture.

My last example concerns the use of Sunday. The duty to safeguard one day in seven for worship and rest is laid down in the fourth commandment, which is still in force. But we shall not secure Sunday observance merely by quoting God's law—or not until people are converted. Meanwhile, however, we believe that it is God's will to maintain this rhythm, that the nation is well served by legislative protection of Sunday as a different day, that family life is built up by it, that workers are thus protected against being compelled to work, and that at least "spectator sports" (which demand the transportation of large numbers of people and the provision of policing, catering, fire and ambulance services) should be prohibited. For why should some people get their rest and recreation at the expense of others who have to work to provide it? And when the biblical argument is unacceptable, the historical argument may convince. Several attempts have been made to change the one-day-in-seven rhythm, either by cancelling the day of rest altogether or by lengthening the working week. For example, the French revolutionaries, after abolishing the monarchy and setting up the Republic in 1792, introduced a new republican calendar with a ten-day week. But the experiment survived only a few years. People could not last nine days without a break. So in 1805 Napoleon restored the seven-day week. Something similar happened after the Russian revolution a century later. In sweeping away religious institutions, the revolutionary leaders turned Sunday into a working day. But again it did not last, and Stalin restored Sunday as a day of rest.

We should not be unduly concerned that the arguments mentioned in nearly all of my examples are based on self-interest. For when we are looking for reasoning that will appeal to the public at large, we have to be realistic. "The art of government, in fact," wrote William Temple, "is the art of so ordering life that self-interest prompts what justice demands."[20] People need to be convinced that the laws that govern their lives are for their good, and that it is to their advantage to be law-abiding. This is even more true of groups than it is of individuals. Indeed, the main thesis of Reinhold Niebuhr's book *Moral Man and Immoral Society* is that, whereas "individual men may be moral in the sense that they are able to consider interests other than their own in determining problems of conduct," we have to recognize "the brutal character of the behaviour of all human collectives, and the power of self-interest and collective egoism in all inter-group relations."[21]

Political Systems

Social action is not only a question of winning the public debate, but of securing legislation that makes public life more pleasing to God. Not that every sin should be made a crime, and all duty buttressed by legal sanctions. For there are areas of private life into which the law should not intrude. For example, in Muslim countries private sexual immorality is a punishable offense, whereas in Christian countries it is not, unless it harms other people in some way. The main function of the law is to safeguard the accepted values of society and to protect the rights of citizens. Laws must also be enforceable, which means that they must enjoy public approval. To frame and pass such laws requires political power, and in a democracy majority power in Parliament.

It is irrelevant to reply that Jesus and his apostles were not interested in politics, and that they neither required nor even commended political action, let alone engaged in it themselves. This is true. They did not. But we have to remember that they were a tiny, insignificant minority under the totalitarian regime of Rome. The legions were everywhere, and were under orders to suppress dissent, crush opposition, and preserve the status quo. The first-century Christians could not take political action; is this the reason why they did not? At least the fact that they did not because they could not is no reason why we should not—if we can. The question is: would they have been politically active if they had had both the opportunity to be and the likelihood of success? I believe they would. For without appropriate political action some social needs simply cannot be met. The apostles did not demand the abolition of slavery. But are we not glad and proud that nineteenth-century Christians did? Their campaign was based on biblical teaching regarding human dignity, and was a legitimate extrapolation from it. The apostles did not build hospitals either, or require them to be built, but Christian hospitals are a legitimate extrapolation from Jesus' compassionate concern for the sick. Just so, political action (which is love seeking justice for the oppressed) is a legitimate extrapolation from the teaching and ministry of Jesus.

What is necessary now is to take up the three possible attitudes to social change which we have been considering and give them a political twist, at the same time noting what view of human beings each presupposes.

Absolutism is the political expression of imposition. An absolutist government makes and enforces laws without the checks and balances of a Constitution or of consultation with the people. Absolutism arises from an entirely pessimistic view of human beings. Either they are thought to be too stupid to know what is good for themselves and for society, or, if they do know, it is thought that they cannot agree about it or that they do not want it. In consequence, the argument runs, "We have to tell 'em; we'll knock their heads together and make 'em conform." The public justification given is always that tight control is necessary for the sake of social order. And occasionally an autocracy has been genuinely benevolent. Nevertheless, it demeans citizens because it does not trust them to have any share in decision making.

Anarchy could be regarded as the political expression of laissez-faire. Not that it was in the nineteenth century, for its original advocates cherished the vision of an ordered society, with laissez-faire economics as the means to that end. But the modern laissez-faire attitude would naturally lead to the abolition of all government and law, and would arise from a naively optimistic view of human beings. It assumes that they are perfectly capable of governing themselves and that laws are unnecessary to create a just society. "Leave people alone," it is said, "and all will be well."

So, then, absolutism considers rigid control essential because it is pessimistic about human beings, denying their dignity due to their creation in God's image. Anarchy, on the other hand, considers unrestricted freedom safe because it is optimistic about human beings, denying their depravity due to the Fall. Both are politically mistaken because both are theologically mistaken, being based on false doctrines of humanity. They are also disastrous in practice. Absolutism leads to tyranny, not justice, and anarchy leads to chaos, not Utopia.

Democracy is the third option. It is the political expression of persuasion by argument. If absolutism, being pessimistic, imposes law arbitrarily, and anarchy, being optimistic, dispenses with law altogether, then democracy, being realistic about human beings as both created and fallen, involves citizens in the framing of their own laws. At least this is the theory. In practice, especially in countries with a large number of illiterates, the media can too easily manipulate them. And in every democracy there is the constant danger of trampling on minorities.

"The word 'democracy' and its derivatives apply to decision-procedures," writes John R. Lucas in his book *Democracy and Participation*. The word describes three aspects of the decision-making process. The first concerns who takes it. "A decision is democratically taken if the answer to the question 'who takes it?' is 'more or less everybody,' in contrast to decisions taken only by those best qualified to take them, as in a meritocracy, or those taken by only one man, as in an autocracy or monarchy." Second, democracy describes how a decision is reached. "A decision is taken democratically if it is reached by discussion, criticism and compromise." Third, democracy describes the spirit in which a decision is made, namely, "being concerned with the interests of all, instead of only a faction or a party."[22]

So modern democracy reflects the balanced biblical view of human beings, as we might expect in view of its roots in post-Reformation Christian Europe. It also gives Christians the opportunity to make a constructive contribution in a pluralistic society, by getting into the public debate (whether on disarmament or divorce, abortion or in vitro fertilization), and by seeking to influence public opinion until there is a public demand for legislation that would be more pleasing to God. For if democracy is government by consent, consent depends on consensus (or at least does so when electoral procedures are truly democratic), and consensus arises out of a discussion in which the issues become clarified.

Of course the democratic political process is also "the art of the possible." Because human beings are fallen there is bound to be a gap between the divine ideal and the human reality, between what God has revealed and what humans find possible. Jesus himself recognized this distinction within the law of Moses. For Moses' permission of divorce in a case of "indecency" or "immorality," he said, was given "because of the hardness of your hearts" (Mark 10:5). In other words, it was a concession to human weakness. But Jesus immediately added that "from the beginning it was not so," reminding them of the divine ideal.

There is a great need for more Christian thinkers in contemporary society who will throw themselves into the public debate, and for more Christian activists who will organize pressure groups to promote the work of persuasion. Their motivation will be thoroughly Christian—a vision of the God who cares about justice, compassion, honesty, and freedom in society, and a vision of humanity, made in God's image though fallen, moral, responsible, and with a conscience to be respected. It will be out of zeal for God and love for human beings that they will seek the renewal of society. They will make no attempt to conceal the origins of their concern. Yet in the parry and thrust of debate, and in the policies they develop, they will have to be content with the realities of a fallen world. And all the time, their target will be the shaping of public opinion.

Addressing the need for Christians to live in cheerful protest against the assumptions of the consumer society, John V. Taylor, former Bishop of Winchester, has written: "It is in the area of public opinion that this battle has to be fought. Nothing can achieve the change of policies which our very salvation demands but a profound reorientation of public opinion." He went on to quote Reg Prentice, who said in 1972, when Minister of Overseas Development, that the only way to increase Britain's concern for Third World nations was the "slow, hard grind of public education and political pressure within rich countries." Bishop Taylor concluded that Christ's "renewals and revolutions begin quietly, like faith itself. They start growing from one tiny seed, the staggering thought: things don't have to be like this. When that idea begins to trickle down into the structures and into the minds of ordinary people in our affluent society, the cry may at last go up: you're nothing but a pack of cards!"[23]

4

Alienation:
Have We Any Influence?

No single word captures more accurately, or expresses more eloquently, the modern sense of impotence than the word "alienation." To say "I'm alienated" means "I can't relate to society any longer and, what's worse, I can't do anything about it."

Marx popularized the term. But he was referring to an economic order in which the workers, because their products were sold by the factory owner, were thus alienated from the fruits of their labor. Contemporary Marxists give the word a broader application. Jimmy Reid, for example, when a Communist councillor of Glasgow, Scotland, and chief spokesman of the Upper Clyde Shipyard Workers, said in 1972: "Alienation is the cry of men who feel themselves to be the victims of blind economic forces beyond their control . . . the frustration of ordinary people excluded from the process of decision-making."[1]

So alienation is the feeling of economic and political powerlessness. The juggernauts of institutionalized power roll ruthlessly on their way, but the common man or woman cannot do anything to change their direction or speed, let alone stop them. We are nothing but spectators of a developing situation which we feel helpless to influence in any way. That is "alienation."

And in spite of my attempted theological defense of democratic theory, and my plea that Christians should take advantage of the democratic process and join in the public debate, I have to admit that democracy does not always cure alienation, for many are disillusioned with its realities. It is this gulf between theory and practice that lies at the heart of John R.

Lucas's book *Democracy and Participation*, from which I quoted in the previous chapter. People exercise their democratic right to vote, and, to be sure, "the vote constitutes a form of minimal participation" (p. 166). Thereafter, however, "democracy becomes an autocracy, in which all decisions save one are taken by the autocrat, and the only decision left to the people is the occasional choice of autocrat." So he renames democracy an "elective autocracy," because it "enables people to participate in government only to a derisory extent." It also "makes the government singularly insensitive to the wishes of the governed and the requirements of justice" (p. 184). Again, "although elective autocracy has its democratic aspect, it is deeply undemocratic as regards the way and the spirit in which decisions are taken. . . . It is non-participatory" (p. 198). Without doubt this disenchantment with the actual workings of democracy is widespread. Christians should share with others the concern to broaden the context of public debate, until parliamentary discussions "reverberate in every inn and workshop in the realm." Dr. Lucas ends his book with the delightful statement that "democracy can flourish only in a land of pubs" (p. 264).

To me it is sad that many Christians become contaminated by the mood of alienation. "To be sure," they agree, "the quest for social justice is our concern and we cannot escape this fact. But the obstacles are immense. Not only are the issues complex (we claim no expertise), but society is pluralistic (we claim no monopoly of power or privilege), and the forces of reaction dominate (we have no influence). The receding tide of Christian faith in the community has left us high and dry. In addition, human beings are selfish and society is rotten. It is entirely unrealistic to hope for social change."

The first antidote to this mixture of secular alienation and Christian pessimism is history. History is full of examples of social change as a result of Christian influence. Take England as an example. Social progress, especially as a result of biblical Christianity, cannot be denied. Think of some of the features that marred the country only two hundred years ago. Criminal law was so harsh that about two hundred offenses were punishable by death; it was justly named "the Bloody Code." Slavery and the slave trade were still being defended as legitimate, even respectable. Men were "press-ganged" into the army and navy. No education or health care was provided for the masses. Smallpox killed more than 10 percent of every generation. Travel by horse and coach was made perilous by highwaymen. Social feudalism imprisoned people in a rigid class system and condemned millions to abject poverty. Conditions in prisons, factories, and mines were unbelievably inhuman. Only Anglicans were eligible to enter university or Parliament, although a few dissenters got in through the practice of "occasional conformity." One is ashamed that only two centuries ago so much injustice tarnished England's national life.

But the social influence of Christianity has been worldwide. K. S. Latourette sums it up at the conclusion of his seven-volume *History of the Expansion of Christianity*. He refers in glowing terms to the effects of the life of Christ through his followers.

> No life ever lived on this planet has been so influential in the affairs of men. . . . From that brief life and its apparent frustration has flowed a more powerful force for the triumphal waging of man's long battle than any other ever known by the human race. . . . Through it hundreds of millions have been lifted from illiteracy and ignorance, and have been placed upon the road of growing intellectual freedom and of control over their physical environment. It has done more to allay the physical ills of disease and famine than any other impulse known to man. It has emancipated millions from chattel slavery and millions of others from thraldom to vice. It has protected tens of millions from exploitation by their fellows. It has been the most fruitful source of movements to lessen the horrors of war and to put the relations of men and nations on the basis of justice and peace.[2]

So Christian pessimism is historically unfounded. It is also theologically inept. We have seen that the Christian mind holds together the biblical events of the Creation, the Fall, the Redemption, and the Consummation. Christian pessimists concentrate on the Fall ("human beings are incorrigible") and the Consummation ("Christ is coming to put things right"), and imagine that these truths justify social despair. But they overlook the Creation and the Redemption. The divine image in human beings has not been obliterated. Though evil, they can still do good, as Jesus plainly taught (Matthew 7:11). And the evidence before our eyes confirms it. There are non-Christian people who have good marriages, non-Christian parents who love their children and bring them up well, non-Christian industrialists who run factories on a just basis, and non-Christian doctors who still take the Hippocratic standards as their guide and are conscientious in the care of their patients. This is partly because the truth of God's law is written on all human hearts, and partly because the values of the Kingdom of God, when embodied in the Christian community, are often recognized and to some extent imitated by people outside it. In this way the gospel has borne fruit in Western society over many generations.

In addition, Jesus Christ redeems people and makes them new. Are we saying that regenerated and renewed people can do nothing to restrain or reform society? Such an opinion is monstrous. This is the thrust of Charles Colson's book, *Kingdoms in Conflict*. The radical values of the Kingdom of God, which was inaugurated by Jesus Christ, confront, challenge, and change the kingdoms of men, especially through the agency of what Edmund Burke in the eighteenth century called "little platoons." Charles

Colson has in mind small voluntary associations of people who love God and their neighbor, exhibit transcendence in the midst of secularism, refuse to acquiesce in evil, oppose injustice, and spread mercy and reconciliation in the world.[3]

The combined witness of history and Scripture is that Christian people have had an enormous influence on society. We are not powerless. Things can be different. Nikolai Berdyaev summed the situation up admirably in these words: "The sinfulness of human nature does not mean that social reforms and improvements are impossible. It only means that there can be no perfect and absolute social order . . . before the transfiguration of the world."[4]

Salt and Light

From history and Scripture I turn to the expectation which Jesus had for his followers. He expressed it most vividly in the Sermon on the Mount by his use of the salt and light metaphors:

> You are the salt of the earth. But if the salt loses its saltiness, how can it be made salty again? It is no longer good for anything, except to be thrown out and trampled by men.
> You are the light of the world. A city on a hill cannot be hidden. Neither do people light a lamp and put it under a bowl. Instead they put it on its stand, and it gives light to everyone in the house. In the same way, let your light shine before men, that they may see your good deeds and praise your Father in heaven.

> (Matthew 5:13–16)

Everybody is familiar with salt and light. They are found in virtually every household in the world. Jesus, as a boy in his Nazareth home, must have often watched his mother Mary use salt as a preservative in the kitchen and light the lamps when the sun went down. He knew their practical usefulness.

So these were the images which Jesus later used to illustrate the influence he expected his disciples to exert in human society. At that time they were very few in number, the initial nucleus of his new society; yet they were to be salt and light to the whole earth. What did he mean? At least four truths cannot be missed.

First, Christians are fundamentally different from non-Christians, or ought to be. Both images set the two communities apart. The world is dark, Jesus implied, but you are to be its light. The world is decaying, but you are to be its salt and hinder its decay. In English idiom we might say they are as different as "chalk from cheese" or "oil from water"; Jesus said they are as different as light from darkness, and salt from decay. This is a major theme of the whole Bible. God is calling out from the world a people for himself, and the vocation of this people is to be "holy" or "different." "Be holy," he says to them again and again, "because I am holy."

Second, Christians must permeate non-Christian society. Although Christians are (or should be) morally and spiritually distinct from non-Christians, they are not to be socially segregated. On the contrary, their light is to shine into the darkness, and their salt is to soak into the decaying meat. The lamp does no good if it is put under a bed or a bowl, and the salt does no good if it stays in the salt cellar. Similarly, Christians are not to remain aloof from society, where they cannot affect it, but are to become immersed in its life. They are to let their light shine, so that their good deeds are seen.

Third, Christians can influence non-Christian society. Before the days of refrigeration, salt was the best known preservative. Either it was rubbed into fish and meat, or they were left to soak in it. In this way bacterial decay was retarded, though not of course entirely arrested. Light is even more obviously effective; when the light is switched on, the darkness is actually dispelled. Just so, Jesus must have meant, Christians can hinder social decay and dispel the darkness of evil. William Temple wrote of the "pervasive sweetening of life and of all human relationships by those who carry with them something of the mind of Christ."[5]

This prompts the question why Christians have not had a far greater influence for good on the non-Christian world. I hope my American friends will forgive me if I take the United States as my example; of course in principle the situation is the same in Europe. The published statistics of American Christianity are staggering.

According to Gallup polls conducted in 1994 and 1996, 96 percent of Americans said they believed in "God or a universal spirit," 28 percent attended church or synagogue at least once a week, 59 percent called themselves Protestant, and 41 percent said they would describe themselves as "born again" or "evangelical." Why then has this great army of Christian soldiers not been more successful in beating back the forces of evil? This is American futurologist Tom Sine's explanation: "We have been remarkably effective at diluting his [Christ's] extremist teaching and truncating his radical gospel. That explains why we . . . make such an embarrassingly little difference in the morality of our society."[6] More important than mere numbers of professing disciples are both the quality of their discipleship (maintaining Christ's standards without compromise) and their strategic deployment (capturing positions of influence for Christ).

Our Christian habit is to bewail the world's deteriorating standards with an air of rather self-righteous dismay. We criticize its violence, dishonesty, immorality, disregard for human life, and materialistic greed. "The world is going down the drain," we say with a shrug. But whose fault is it? Who is to blame? Let me put it like this. If the house is dark when nightfall comes, there is no sense in blaming the house; that is what happens when the sun goes down. The question to ask is "Where is the light?" Similarly, if the meat goes bad and becomes inedible, there is no sense in blaming the meat; that is what happens when bacteria are left alone to breed. The question to ask is "Where is the salt?" Just so, if society deteriorates and its standards decline, until it becomes like a dark night or stinking fish, there is no sense in blaming society; that is what happens when fallen men and women are left to themselves, and human selfishness is unchecked. The question to ask is "Where is the Church? Why are the salt and light of Jesus Christ not permeating and changing our society?" It is sheer hypocrisy on our part to raise our eyebrows, shrug our shoulders, or wring our hands. The Lord Jesus told us to be the world's salt and light. If therefore darkness and rottenness abound, it is largely our fault and we must accept the blame.

Fourth, Christians must retain their Christian distinctness. If salt does not retain its saltiness, it is good for nothing. If light does not retain its brightness, it becomes ineffective. So we who claim to be Christ's followers have to fulfill two conditions if we are to do any good for him. On the one hand, we have to permeate non-Christian society, and immerse ourselves in the life of the world. On the other, while doing so, we have to avoid becoming assimilated to the world. We must retain our Christian convictions, values, standards, and lifestyle. We are back with the "double identity" of the Church ("holiness" and "worldliness") which I mentioned in the first chapter.

If it be asked what the "saltiness" and "brightness" of Christian holiness are, the rest of the Sermon on the Mount gives us the answer. For in it Jesus tells us not to be like others around us: "Do not be like them" (Matthew 6:8). Instead, he calls us to a greater righteousness (of the heart), a wider love (even of enemies), a deeper devotion (of children coming to their Father), and a nobler ambition (seeking first God's rule and righteousness).[7] It is only as we choose and follow his way that our salt will retain its saltiness and our light will shine, that we shall be his effective witnesses and servants and exert a wholesome influence on society.

This purpose and expectation of Christ should be enough to overcome our sense of alienation. We may be ostracized by some at work or in our local community. Secular society may do its best to push us to the circumference of its concerns. But, refusing to be marginalized, we should seek to occupy a sphere of influence for Christ. Ambition is the desire to succeed. There is nothing wrong with it if it is genuinely subordinated to the will and glory of God. True, power can corrupt. True also, the power of Christ is best displayed in our weakness. And indeed we shall continue to feel our personal inadequacy. Yet we should determine by his grace to infiltrate some secular segment of society and raise his flag there, maintaining without compromise his standards of love, truth, and goodness.

But how can we exert some influence for Christ? What does it mean in practice to be the world's salt and light? What can we do for social change? I will try to develop six ways, in three pairs.

Prayer and Evangelism

First, there is the power of prayer. I beg you not to dismiss this as a pious platitude, a sop to Christian convention. For it really is not. We cannot read the Bible without being impressed by its constant emphasis on the efficacy of prayer. "The prayer of a righteous man is powerful and effective," wrote James (5:16). "I tell you," said Jesus, "that if two of you on earth agree about anything you ask for, it will be done for you by my Father in heaven" (Matthew 18:19). We do not claim to understand the rationale of intercession. But somehow it enables us to enter the field of spiritual conflict, and to align ourselves with the good purposes of God, so that his power is released and the principalities of evil are held back.

Prayer is an indispensable part of the individual Christian's life. It is also indispensable to the life of the local church. Paul gave it priority. "First of all, then, I urge that supplications, prayers, intercessions, and thanksgivings be made for all men, for kings and all who are in high positions, that we may lead a quiet and peaceable life, godly and respectful in every way. This is good, and it is acceptable in the sight of God our Saviour, who desires all men to be saved and to come to the knowledge of the truth" (1 Timothy 2:1–4 RSV). Here is prayer for national leaders, that they may fulfill their responsibility to maintain conditions of peace and order, in which the Church is free both to obey God and to preach the gospel.

In theory, we are convinced of this duty to pray. Yet some Christian social activists seldom stop to pray. And some churches hardly seem to take it seriously. If in the community (indeed, in the world), there is more violence than peace, more oppression than justice, more secularism than godliness, is it because Christians and churches are not praying as they should?

This is how the Church's obligation in this matter was expressed in the report of the International Consultation on the Relationship between Evangelism and Social Responsibility (1982):

> We resolve ourselves, and call upon our churches, to take much more seriously the period of intercession in public worship; to think in terms of ten or fifteen minutes rather than five; to invite lay people to share in leading, since they often have deep insight into the world's needs; and to focus our prayers both on the evangelization of the world (closed lands, resistant peoples, mis-

sionaries, national churches, etc.) and on the quest for peace and justice in the world (places of tension and conflict, deliverance from the nuclear horror, rulers and governments, the poor and needy, etc.). We long to see every Christian congregation bowing down in humble and expectant faith before our Sovereign Lord.[8]

We also rejoice over the growth of parachurch movements whose goal is to stimulate the prayers of the people of God (e.g., in the United Kingdom the Lydia Fellowship, Crosswinds, and Intercessors for Britain and in the United States Intercessors for America and the AD 2000 movement).

The successful ousting of President Marcos, the Filipino dictator, is usually referred to as either "the February Revolution" or "People Power." But a number of Christians have been saying, "It was not people power; it was prayer power." On 13 February 1986 the Roman Catholic bishops issued a bold statement declaring the 7 February elections fraudulent and the Marcos government illegitimate. Rejecting both extremes of apathy and violence, they went on to call for "the active resistance of evil by peaceful means," including prayer. At the huge rally in Luneta Park, Cory Aquino also called for prayer and nonviolent protest. When, a few days later, Defense Minister Juan Enrile and General Fidel Ramos declared Mrs. Aquino the rightful president, and made Camp Aguinaldo their headquarters, Cardinal Archbishop Sin over the radio told his nuns to get to their chapels in order to support and protect Enrile and Ramos. It is estimated that up to two million unarmed civilians, Protestants as well as Catholics, took to the streets and formed human barricades. And when the marines came in their tanks, they were stopped "not by anti-tank missiles but by the bodies of praying Filipinos."[9] The soldiers "could never shoot at people who were praying. They could have shot people who were throwing stones. . . . But this was the first time that they were confronted with prayers."[10] The marines withdrew and Marcos fled. "What is so remarkable about the story of the Philippines," concludes Charles Colson, "is that millions of people believed more in the power of prayer than in the power of politics."[11]

I turn now from the power of prayer to the power of the gospel, and so to evangelism. This book is about Christian social responsibility, not evangelism. Nevertheless, the two belong together. Although different Christians have received different gifts and callings, and although in some situations it is perfectly proper to concentrate on either evangelism or social action without combining them, nevertheless in general and in theory they cannot be separated. Our love for our neighbors will be fleshed out in a holistic concern for all their needs—for the needs of their bodies, souls, and community. That is why in the ministry of Jesus words and works were bracketed. As the Grand Rapids Report put it, evangelism and social activity are "like the two blades of a pair of scissors or the two wings of a bird."[12]

There are, however, two particular ways in which evangelism should be seen as a necessary prelude to and foundation of social action. First, the gospel changes people. Every Christian should be able to echo Paul's words with conviction: "I am not ashamed of the gospel, because it is the power of God for the salvation of everyone who believes" (Romans 1:16). We know it in our own lives, and we have seen it in the lives of others. If sin is at root self-centeredness, then the transformation from "self" to "unself" is an essential ingredient of salvation. Faith leads to love, and love to service. So social activity, which is the loving service of the needy, should be the inevitable result of saving faith, although we have to confess that this is not always so.

There are other situations in which positive social change is taking place apart from explicit Christian initiatives. So we must not bind evangelism and social change together so indissolubly as to say that the former always issues in the latter and the latter never happens without the former. Nevertheless, these are exceptions which prove the rule. We still insist that evangelism is the major instrument of social change. For the gospel changes people, and changed people can change society. We have seen that society needs salt and light; but only the gospel can create them. This is one way in which we may declare without embarrassment that evangelism takes primacy over social action. Logically speaking, "Christian social responsibility presupposes socially responsible Christians," and it is the gospel which produces them.[13]

When John V. Taylor, who later became the Bishop of Winchester, was still General Secretary of the Church Missionary Society, he described in his *CMS Newsletter* (May 1972) his reactions to Geoffrey Moorhouse's book, *Calcutta*, and indeed to the apparent hopelessness of that city's problems. "But invariably what tips the balance from despair to faith," he wrote, "is the person who rises above the situation." Such persons are neither "trapped" in the city, nor have they "escaped" from it. "They have transcended the situation. . . . Salvation is not the same as solution: it precedes it and makes it a possibility. . . . Personal salvation—salvation in first gear— is still the way in. It is the key to unlock the door of determinism and make possible the 'salvation' of corporate organizations and institutions—salvation in second gear—by providing those who can transcend the situation."

There is another way in which social uplift is facilitated by evangelism. When the gospel is faithfully and widely preached, it not only brings a radical renewal to individuals, but produces what Raymond Johnston once called "an antiseptic atmosphere," in which blasphemy, selfishness, greed, dishonesty, immorality, cruelty, and injustice find it harder to flourish. A country that has been permeated by the gospel is not a soil in which these poisonous weeds can easily take root, let alone luxuriate.

More than this. The gospel that changes people also changes cultures. One of the greatest hindrances to social change is the conservatism of culture. A country's laws, institutions, and customs have taken centuries to develop; they have a built-in resistance to reform. In some cases it is the moral ambiguity of culture which is the hindrance. Every political program, economic system, and development plan depends on values to motivate and sustain it. It cannot operate without honesty and some degree of altruism. So progress is effectively blocked if the national culture (and the religion or ideology that shapes it) connives at corruption and selfishness, and offers no incentive to self-control or self-sacrifice. Then culture stands in the way of development.

Professor Brian Griffiths (now Lord Griffiths) applied this principle with great insight to both capitalism and Marxism in his 1980 London Lectures in Contemporary Christianity, entitled *Morality and the Market Place*. To him capitalism had lost its legitimacy and Marxism was fatally flawed. "Capitalism suffers because of inadequate limits on the exercise of freedom," while communism "suffers from an inability to put adequate constraints on the urge to control." But this "inability to resolve the basic tension between freedom and control" is the crisis of secular humanism. Both capitalism and Marxism are, in fact, the product of the eighteenth-century Enlightenment: what they lack is Christian values.[14]

Brian Griffiths's last chapter is entitled "Third World Poverty and First World Responsibility." He takes issue with a key expression used by Herr Willy Brandt in his Introduction to the Brandt Commission Report: "We take it for granted that all cultures deserve equal respect, protection and promotion."[15] "But they do not" is Brian Griffiths's rejoinder. "Cultures express values which shape institutions and motivate people—some of which . . . promote wealth and justice and liberty, and others of which do not."[16]

It is entirely logical, therefore, that a book on economics, and in particularly on morality and the marketplace, should conclude with a passionate plea for world evangelism:

> Christianity starts with faith in Christ and it finishes with service in the world. . . . Because of this I believe that evangelism has an indispensable part to play in the establishment of a more just economic order. Obedience to Christ demands change, the world becomes his world, the poor, the weak and the suffering are men, women and children created in his image; injustice is an affront to his creation; despair, indifference and aimlessness are replaced by hope, responsibility and purpose; and above all selfishness is transformed by love.[17]

So the gospel changes both people and cultures. This is not to say that no development is possible without evangelism, but rather that development is hindered without, and greatly facilitated by, the cultural changes that the gospel brings. And the more the gospel spreads, the more hopeful the situation becomes. Even a few Christians in public life can initiate social change. But their influence is likely to be far greater if they have massive grassroots support, as the nineteenth-century British evangelical reformers had. So Christians in every country should pray for a widespread acceptance of the gospel. As the nineteenth-century American evangelicals clearly saw, revival and reform belong together.

Witness and Protest

We have seen that the gospel is God's power for salvation. But in fact all truth is powerful. God's truth is much more mighty than the devil's crooked lies. We should never be afraid of the truth. Nor do we ever need to be afraid for the truth, as if its survival hangs in the balance. For God watches over it and will never allow it to be completely suppressed. As Paul put it, "we cannot do anything against the truth, but only for the truth" (2 Corinthians 13:8). And as John put it, "The light shines in the darkness, and the darkness has not overcome it" (John 1:5, margin). One contemporary Christian thinker who is convinced about this is Solzhenitsyn. His Nobel Speech on Literature (1970) was entitled *One Word of Truth*. He confessed that writers lack all material weapons like rockets and tanks. So "what can literature do," he asked, "in the face of the merciless onslaught of open violence?" First, it can refuse "to take part in the lie." Second, writers and artists can "vanquish the lie." For "one word of truth outweighs the whole world. And on such a fantastic breach of the law of conservation of mass and energy are based my own activities and my appeal to the writers of the world."[18]

All Christians are called like their Master "to bear witness to the truth." This, Jesus added, was why he had been born and why he had come into the world (John 18:37). The supreme truth to which we testify is of course Jesus Christ himself, for he is the truth (John 14:6). But all truth—scientific, biblical, theological, moral—is his, and we are to be fearless in defending, maintaining, and arguing it. This is the place for developing an ethical apologetic, as I was urging in the previous chapter, and for entering into the public debate of contemporary issues. From the pulpit (still a much more influential "platform" than is commonly realized, especially in the shaping of public opinion), through letters to and articles in national and local newspapers, in discussions at home and work, through opportunities on radio and television, by poetry, drama, and popular songs, we are called as Christians to witness to God's law and God's gospel, without fear or apology. Moreover, as with Jesus so with his followers, the true witness (*martus*) must be prepared to suffer, and even if necessary to die, for his testimony.

Such costly testimony is the chief weapon of those who are denied the democratic process because they live under an oppressive regime.

In a much-publicized speech in 1974, Sir Keith Joseph spoke about the moral decline of Britain, the possibility of "remoralizing" the nation, and the power of ideas. "Are we to be destroyed from inside?" he asked, although the country had repelled successive attempts at invasion from outside by Philip of Spain, Napoleon, the Kaiser, and Hitler. "Are we to be destroyed by ideas, mischievous, wrongheaded, debilitating, yet seductive because they are fashionable and promise so much on the cheap?" Later in the speech he answered his own questions, and urged his listeners to go on to the offensive. "We must fight the battle of ideas," he cried, "in every school, university, publication, committee, TV studio, even if we have to struggle for our toe-hold there. We have the truth. If we fail to make it shine clear, we shall be to blame no less than the exploiters, the casuists and the commercializers."[19]

Here is an illustration of the power of the truth. The World Development Movement, to which many Christians and churches belong, exists to campaign for political changes in Britain's aid and trade policies toward the Third World. In October 1985 it organized the largest ever mass lobby of Parliament, when twenty-thousand people urged MPs to fight world poverty. Shortly afterward the government announced that Britain's aid program, instead of being reduced, would be increased by £47 million. In January 1987 WDM persuaded the government to double its contribution to UNICEF (the United Nations Children's Fund). The same month Christopher Patten, then Minister for Overseas Development, had the integrity to say: "WDM has taught me a great deal. As a result of the strength of their intellectual arguments, they have convinced me to change my mind on at least two specific matters of policy."

Alongside a positive witness to the truth must go its negative counterpart, protest against folly, deceit, and wickedness. Many seem to be disenchanted with the weapon of rational protest, but I think they should not be. Public agitation is an effective weapon. Let me give you some examples.

First, before the General Election in 1983, when William Whitelaw as Home Secretary published details of the Police and Criminal Evidence Bill which he intended to introduce into Parliament, there was an immediate outcry against its Clause 10, which would have given police the power to search for and remove confidential records held by clergymen, doctors, and social workers. Vigorous protests were made by lawyers and doctors, and fifty-five Church of England bishops signed a petition. Almost at once the Home Secretary announced that he would amend the clause.

My second example comes from West Germany. When details of the 1983 population census were published, and it became known that respondents would be required to divulge a great deal of private information about themselves, there was a groundswell of protest. A law student and two lawyers used the right of German citizens, when they believe that their civil liberties are being threatened, to appeal to the highest court of the land, the Federal Constitutional Court in Karlsruhe. The Court stopped the census, by what was virtually an interim injunction, in order to create time in which to study its legality in full.

Third, organized protest was very nearly successful in preventing a free-for-all in Sunday trading in England and Wales. The Shops Act of 1950 required Sunday closure, with a few exceptions. Everybody agreed that, as it stood, the law contained anomalies, was difficult to enforce, and needed reform. The Conservative government of the day, however, backed by powerful commercial interests, accepted the Auld Committee's recommendation that all legal restrictions on Sunday should be abolished.

Refusing to be intimidated by this deregulation lobby, a small Christian research group, the Jubilee Centre in Cambridge, launched the "Keep Sunday Special Campaign." This became a coalition of the churches of all major denominations, the shop workers' union, and several retail trade bodies, who were united in the pursuit of three goals: (1) to protect the special character of Sunday (for rest and recreation as well as worship); (2) to promote family life and social contact; and (3) to prevent hardship for shopworkers, shopkeepers, and residents near shopping areas.

The "Keep Sunday Special Campaign" was at first highly successful, not only because it was a grassroots campaign (more letters were written to MPs on this issue than on any other in 1986), but also because it looked beyond the defeat of deregulation to reform (not the repeal) of the Shops Act. As well as allowing all small shops to open, its positive "REST" proposals would have allowed for the registering and opening of large shops related to Recreation (e.g., sports and garden centers), Emergencies (e.g., chemists), Social gatherings (e.g., restaurants), and Travel (e.g., garages). All other large shops would have remained closed.

So what happened? The Thatcher government's "Sunday Trading Bill," providing for total deregulation, was introduced in 1985, but defeated during its second reading in 1986. Following this humiliation (the only parliamentary defeat suffered by Mrs. Thatcher's government), both sides of the debate rallied their forces, including the giant chainstores. For example, Tescos and Sainsburys tried to gain support for deregulation by openly flouting the laws from December 1991. The John Lewis Partnership, on the other hand, threw its weight behind the "REST" proposals. In a final twist to the saga, for reasons which remain unclear, the shopworkers' union changed sides shortly before the crucial vote and supported Sunday opening. As a result, the relatively restrictive KSSC proposals were lost in December 1993 by 304 votes to 286. The so-called compromise which won the day restricted large shops to opening for six hours on all Sundays except Easter Day (and Christmas when it falls on a Sunday). Although the "Keep Sunday Special Campaign" eventually salvaged only limited restraints on Sunday opening, it demonstrated that persuasive argument based on biblical values can rally the united support of both Christians and non-Christians. Let no one say that protest and campaigning are a waste of time and effort.

Example and Groups

Truth is powerful when it is argued; it becomes even more powerful when it is also exhibited. People need to understand the arguments, and see its benefits displayed. A Christian nurse in a hospital, teacher in a school, secretary in an office, assistant in a shop, or worker in a factory can have an influence out of all proportion to numbers and percentages. And who can calculate the influence for good on the whole neighborhood of a single Christian home, in which husband and wife are faithful to and find fulfillment in each other, their children grow up in the disciplined security of love, and the family is not turned in on themselves but outgoing to the community? Christians are marked people both at work and at home; the world is watching us.

More influential even than the example of Christian individuals and families is that of the local church. For the church is meant by God to be his new and redeemed community, which embodies the ideals of his Kingdom. We must not underestimate, writes Dr. John Howard Yoder, "the powerful . . . impact on society of the creation of an alternative social group." For "the primary social structure through which the gospel works to change other structures is that of the Christian community."[20]

But how does the new community change the old? The answer is well expressed in the Grand Rapids Report:

> First, the new community should constitute a challenge to the old. Its values and ideals, its moral standards and relationships, its sacrificial life-style, its love, joy and peace—these are the signs of the Kingdom . . . and present the world with a radically alternative society. . . .
>
> Secondly, as the world lives alongside the Kingdom community, some of the values of the Kingdom spill over into society as a whole, so that its industry, commerce, legislation and institutions become to some degree imbued with Kingdom values. So-called "Kingdomized" or "Christianized" society is not the Kingdom of God, but it owes a debt to the Kingdom which often is unrecognized.
>
> The "overspill" model has its limitations, however, because it pictures the two communities as independent of one another, like two vessels standing side by side, the contents of one spilling over into the other. The salt, light

and yeast metaphors which Jesus employed are more dynamic, since each implies the penetration of the old community by the new.[21]

Small groups of Christian people can be visible embodiments of the gospel. They can also make use of all the means of influencing society which I have mentioned so far. There is power in prayer and in the gospel; there is even more if we pray and evangelize together. There is power in witness and protest; there is even more if we testify and take action together. The group was our Lord's own chosen way. He began with the Twelve. And the long history of the Church abounds in examples of the strategic influence of small groups. In sixteenth-century Cambridge the early Reformers met in the White Horse Inn to study Erasmus's Greek New Testament; in eighteenth-century Oxford the Holy Club, to which the Wesleys and White-field belonged, although at first engaged in barren good works, was the background against which the evangelical revival began; and in nineteenth-century South London the Clapham Sect gave their support to Wilberforce in his antislavery campaign and to many other social and religious causes. Today one of the most promising features of modern church life is the hunger for the small group experience. Thousands of congregations have divided their membership into small fellowship or home groups. Many churches also encourage the formation of specialist groups—evangelistic visiting teams, missionary prayer groups, music groups, contemporary issue groups, reading groups, social study and action groups—the list is almost endless.

Then there are communities experimenting in new styles of living, shar-ing, and working together—for example, the Kairos Community in Buenos Aires (for theological reflection on discipleship in the secular world), the Sojourners Community in Washington, D.C. (involved in producing the *Sojourners'* magazine, in promoting its concern for peace and justice, and in serving local black families), and TRACI in New Delhi (The Research and Communication Institute of young Indian thinkers and writers). And in Britain there are groups like CARE Trust and CARE Campaigns (Christian Action, Research, and Education) which promote moral standards in soci-ety, and I might also mention The Institute for Contemporary Christianity in London, whose goals are to stimulate the integration of consistent Chris-tian thought and action in the world.

A widely respected Roman Catholic leader, long since retired, who believed strongly in the potential of small groups, is Dom Helder Camara, former Archbishop of Recife in northeast Brazil. Accused of being subver-sive, forbidden access to the media, under constant threat of assassination, this "violent peacemaker" (as he has been called) is committed to justice and peace. Having traveled half the world for several years, appealing to institutions, he came to put more faith in groups. He encourages the formation of "Abrahamic minorities" (so-called "because like Abraham we are hoping against hope")[22] in neighborhoods, universities, and unions, within the media, in management, among politicians, and in the armed forces. Sharing a common thirst for justice and freedom, they gather information; they try to diagnose the problems relating to housing, unemployment, sweated labor, and social structures; they pool experiences and carry out whatever form of "peaceful violence" they deem appropriate. Dom Helder believes that such minority groups have "the power for love and justice which could be likened to nuclear energy locked for millions of years in the smallest atoms and waiting to be released."[23] "All these minorities united could become an irresistible force," he adds.[24] Some ridicule him, but he perseveres. "My plan, I am well aware," he has written, "may call to mind the combat against Goliath. But the hand of God was with the young shepherd, and David conquered the Philistine with his faith, a sling and five small stones."[25] "Keep in mind," he urges elsewhere, "that throughout the centuries humanity has been led by daring minorities."[26]

This contrast between the giant and the boy, the sword and the slingstones, arrogant boasting and humble trust, is characteristic of God's activity in the world. Tom Sine has captured it well in his book *The Mustard Seed Conspiracy*, whose title alludes to the tiny seed out of which a large bush grows. Its subtitle is "You can make a difference in tomorrow's troubled world." He writes:

> Jesus let us in on an astonishing secret. God has chosen to change the world through the lowly, the unassuming and the imperceptible.... That has always been God's strategy—changing the world through the conspiracy of the insignificant. He chose a ragged bunch of Semite slaves to become the insurgents of his new order.... And who would have ever dreamed that God would choose to work through a baby in a cow stall to turn the world right side up! "God chose the foolish things ... the weak things ... the lowly things ... the things that are not." ... It is still God's policy to work through the embarrassingly insignificant to change his world and create his future.[27]

"The embarrassingly insignificant." I feel the need to underline this topsy-turvy policy which God has adopted. At the same time, I am anxious that we should grasp that it is realistic. What minorities lack in numbers, they can make up in conviction and commitment. In support of this contention I call on the witness of the well-known American sociologist Robert Bellah. Chief author of *Habits of the Heart*, "a study in American individualism,"[28] he is a specialist in "civil religion," and in the influence of religion and ethics on politics. He lectures in the Department of Sociology at the University of California, Berkeley, and also in its Center for Japanese and

Korean Studies. In an interview with Sam Keen in *Psychology Today* (January 1976), he said:

> I think we should not underestimate the significance of the small group of people who have a new vision of a just and gentle world. In Japan a very small minority of Protestant Christians introduced ethics into politics, and had an impact beyond all proportion to their numbers. They were central in beginning the women's movement, labour unions, socialist parties, and virtually every reform movement. The quality of a culture may be changed when two per cent of its people have a new vision.

Christians are less than one percent in Japan, but many more than 2 percent in a large number of countries. We could have an enormous influence on society, in terms of both evangelism and social action, for the glory of God. There is little justification for a sense of alienation.

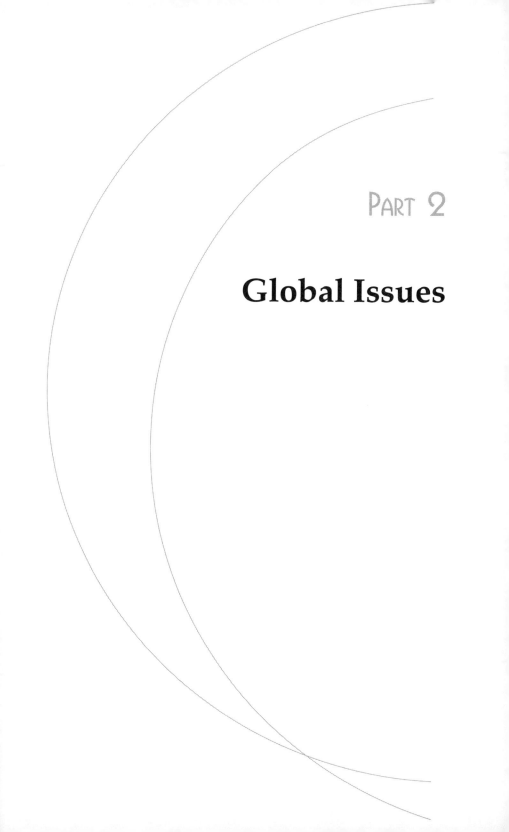

PART 2

Global Issues

5

Wars and Rumors of Wars

Of all the global problems that confront the human race today none is graver than the threat of a nuclear holocaust. War has always been horrible, whether fought by sticks and stones, bows and arrows, swords and spears, muskets and rifles, or bayonets and bombs. But in the case of these so-called conventional weapons, there has been the possibility of controls and limits, and war has involved an engagement between armies. The arrival of the nuclear age, however, has rendered most military traditions obsolete. "The unleashed power of the atom," said Albert Einstein, "has changed every-thing save our modes of thinking; and thus we are drifting towards unpar-alleled catastrophe. . . . A new type of thinking is essential if mankind is to survive."[1] He was not exaggerating. Now that we have the power to destroy the total legacy of past civilizations, the present delicate ecological balance of the biosphere, and through radiation the genetic potential of the future, it is the very survival of the human race and of our planet which is at stake.

Contemporary Realities

The Christian mind cannot operate in a vacuum. However strongly we hold fast to God's once-for-all revelation of himself in Christ and Scripture, we have to struggle to relate this to the harsh facts of the present situation. Thus revelation and reality belong together as we seek to discern God's will. Consider five such realities.

(1) The End of the Cold War

The most notable change in contemporary reality, which at the same time was the most significant event of the twentieth century and signaled its close, was the dramatic end of the cold war in the late 1980s and early 1990s. Following the relaxation of tension caused by Mr. Gorbachev's proclamation of perestroika (restructuring) and glasnost (openness), event followed event at bewildering speed. In Poland talks between the "Solidarity" leaders and the government led to free elections. Hungary and Austria opened their borders, so that East Germans could cross into freedom. The East German government fell, and Gorbachev refused to intervene. On 9 November 1989 the Berlin Wall was dismantled, symbolizing the collapse of a discredited East European socialism. German reunification followed about a year later. Then in 1991 four of the six Soviet republics voted for independence, communism disintegrated in the Soviet Union, and Gorbachev fell from power. Thus within two years (1989–91) these so-called gentle and peaceful revolutions (apart from some violence in Romania) brought not only political freedom to the Soviet Union and her East European satellites, but also military détente between the United States and the Soviet Union, as both the superpowers turned away from the frantic, competitive arms build-up of the previous era.

Nearly a decade later, however, expectations of peace have proved illusory, and new conflicts have arisen. During the fifty years between 1945 and 1995 there were eighty wars. Yet of these only twenty-eight were "traditional" wars between the regular armies of nation-states, while forty-six were civil or guerrilla wars.

What, then, are the causes of this escalation of violence? Professor Samuel P. Huntington of Harvard, in his book *The Clash of Civilizations and the Remaking of World Order*, develops the thesis that, whereas during the cold war global politics had been "bipolar" (between the two superpowers), after the cold war it has become "multipolar and multi-civilizational."[2] In particular, "in coping with identity crisis, what counts for people are blood and belief, faith and family. People rally to those with similar ancestry, religion, language, values and institutions, and distance themselves from those with different ones."[3] Thus today the important distinctions between people are not so much ideological and political as cultural. Professor Huntington goes on to divide the world into seven or eight major civilizations, whose chief distinctives are religious and which shape "the antagonisms and associations of states."[4]

Robert D. Kaplan, a contributing editor of the *Atlantic Monthly*, develops a similar thesis in his book *The Ends of the Earth*, an expansion of his well-known *Atlantic Monthly* article "The Coming Anarchy" published in February 1994. In it he reflects on his "journey at the dawn of the 21st century," which took him to West Africa and the Nile Valley, to Anatolia and the Caucasus, to the Iranian plateau, Central Asia, the Indian Subcontinent, and Indochina. In so far as any travelogue may be said to have a theme, his is that nation-states with their neat and rigid borders are the artificial creation of colonial powers. "Maps, so seemingly objective, are actually propaganda."[5] They blur the much more fluid realities of ethnicity, which spill over national frontiers. "In the postcommunist world, discontent [is] no longer ideological but religious—in other words cultural."[6]

Both authors are pessimistic, even gloomy, about the future. A global war, involving the core states of the world's major civilizations, Professor Huntington declares, is "highly improbable but not impossible." He even paints a vivid scenario in which the United States, Europe, Russia, and India are aligned against China, Japan, and most of Islam.[7] This is his concluding sentence: "Clashes of civilizations are the greatest threat to world peace, and an international order based on civilizations is the surest safeguard against world war."[8]

Robert Kaplan does not indulge in speculation about the future. But he quotes former UN Secretary-General Perez de Cuellar's statement that the current proliferation of civil wars is "the new anarchy." The fact that in 1993 forty-two countries were engulfed in major conflicts, and thirty-seven others in lesser ones, certainly seems to demonstrate "this anarchic trend."[9] "We are not in control," he concludes, and "the idea that a global élite like the UN can engineer reality from above is . . . absurd." We live in "an age of localized mini-holocausts."[10]

In the light of the changed world situation since the end of the cold war, it is not surprising that Western defense specialists have completely revised their strategy. They are no longer preparing for a single large-scale war with the Soviet Union, but rather for multiple regional conflicts. Nevertheless, while nuclear weaponry remains, so does the fear of its use, either in local conflicts or in crazy acts of terrorism.

(2) International Nuclear Treaties

Before the cold war ended, it was estimated that the two superpowers possessed between them about fifty thousand nuclear warheads, with a total destructive power more than a million times greater than that of the Hiroshima bomb. This stockpile represented such a horrendous situation of "overkill" that George Kennan, in accepting the Einstein Peace Prize in Washington in 1981, called for a "bold and sweeping" initiative, namely, "an immediate across-the-board reduction by 50 percent of the nuclear arsenals now being maintained by the two superpowers." Although his cry went unheeded at the time, in due course it bore fruit.

Ten years later, in 1991, the United States and Russia signed START I (the first "Strategic Arms Reduction Treaty"), which called for a phased reduction of strategic weapons and for the return to Russia of all warheads held by the other republics of the former Soviet Union. START I came into force in 1994. The previous year the United States and Russia signed START II; it banned all land-based ballistic missiles fitted with MIRVs (multiple independently targetable re-entry vehicles), and further reduced strategic nuclear weapons. This treaty was ratified by the United States in 1997, but not yet by Russia. Now that START III talks have begun, however, experts believe that Russia may sign the second and third treaties together. It is true that, strictly speaking, this is not disarmament, since the weapons are not destroyed; but at least they are removed from deployment and so are virtually unavailable.

The Comprehensive Test Ban Treaty is a second international initiative which offers hope. In 1994 the UN's "Conference on Disarmament" commissioned an ad hoc committee to produce a treaty which would ban all further testing of nuclear armaments. This Comprehensive Test Ban Treaty was adopted by the UN's General Assembly in 1996, with 158 votes in favor, 3 against, and 5 abstentions. The three against were Bhutan, India, and Libya. The treaty will not come into force, however, until 49 states have ratified it in their home legislatures. By 31 July 1997 only five states had ratified it. Critics, crying "too little, too late" were proved substantially right when in May 1998 first India, then Pakistan, conducted tests of nuclear devices in blatant disregard of the treaty.

The third initiative relates to nonproliferation. It was as long ago as 1968 that the Nonproliferation Treaty was signed; it called for an eventual, total, global nuclear disarmament. In 1995 the UN decided to extend it indefinitely, and 178 nations pledged themselves to this ultimate goal. Based on it, a movement of over 600 NGOs (nongovernmental organizations) on 6 continents, named "Abolition 2000," is calling for the immediate initiation of negotiations for a phased elimination of all nuclear weapons, beginning in A.D. 2000.

Now that India and Pakistan have carried out tests seven nations are known to have both nuclear weapons and delivery systems—the United States, Russia, Britain, France, China, India, and Pakistan. Israel is almost certainly an eighth member of this deadly club. Doomwatchers are warning that this number may yet increase, which makes movements toward nonproliferation ever more urgent.

In spite of the welcome international efforts described above we still maintain a fearsome level of overkill in our nuclear arsenals. We could take the British Trident program as an example. Britain has ordered a fleet of four nuclear-powered submarines. *Vanguard* was launched in 1994 and *Victorious* in 1995, while *Vigilant* is due in 1999 and *Vengeance* in 2001. Each submarine will carry 16 Trident missiles, with a range of 7,400 kilometers, each of which has 4 to 6 independently targeted nuclear warheads, making a maximum of 96. Since each warhead can deliver a blast of 100 kilotons, and since the Hiroshima bomb is calculated at between 12 and 15 kilotons, each Trident carries between 600 and 800 times the blast of the Hiroshima bomb.[11]

(3) The Consequences of Nuclear War

Probably nothing can bring home to us the ghastly effects of a nuclear explosion more vividly than the eyewitness accounts of what happened at Hiroshima and Nagasaki. Lord Mountbatten quoted one such account shortly before he was himself killed by an act of senseless violence:

> Suddenly a glaring whitish, pinkish light appeared in the sky accompanied by an unnatural tremor which was followed almost immediately by a wave of suffocating heat and a wind which swept away everything in its path. Within a few seconds the thousands of people in the streets in the centre of the town were scorched by a wave of searing heat. Many were killed instantly, others lay writhing on the ground screaming in agony from the intolerable pain of their burns. Everything standing upright in the way of the blast . . . was annihilated . . . Hiroshima had ceased to exist.[12]

That was the result of a single, small atomic explosion. What the consequences of a nuclear war would be like it is impossible to predict with accuracy because of the many imponderables, such as the number of warheads used, the distribution of people in the target zone, the degree of civil defense available, and the climatic conditions at the time. But the U.S. Congress document *The Effects of Nuclear War* (1979) says that "the minimum consequences would be enormous" and gives four escalating case studies. Although these belong to the cold war period, they still provide dramatic illustrations of the horror of a nuclear strike.

A single megaton weapon attack on a single big city like Detroit or Leningrad would mean up to two million dead and a further one million injured. "A very large attack against a range of military and economic targets," in which the Soviet Union struck first and the United States retaliated, would mean the death of up to 77 percent of the American population (or 160 million people) and up to 40 percent of the Russian population (being more scattered in rural areas). These casualties would be the immediate effects (within the first thirty days) of the heat, blast, wind, fire storm, and direct radiation. Many more millions would die of their injuries (since the medical facilities would be completely inadequate) and of epidemics (due to the breakdown of sewerage and the nonavailability of clean water), or would starve or freeze to death during the first winter (because of the collapse of services). A pall of sooty toxic smoke over the devastated area would not only poison many survivors but so completely blot out the warmth and light of the sun as to return the earth to ice age conditions. In the long term cancer would claim many more victims, and both the genetic consequences and ecological devastation would continue for decades and be incalculable.[13]

(4) Conventional Arms Expenditure and Trade

Another contemporary reality is the appalling level of defense expenditure. In 1995, calculated in billions of dollars, the United States spent nearly $278 (3.8 percent of GDP), while the United Kingdom spent just over $34 (3.1 percent of GDP). Russia's total was $82 and China's nearly $32. The global total spent on defense in 1995 was just over $1,173 billion.[14] President Eisenhower once said: "Every gun that is made, every warship launched, every rocket fired, signifies . . . a theft from those who hunger and are not fed, from those who are cold and are not clothed."[15] Although his concept of "theft" may have been more rhetoric than economic reality, he was expressing his sense of outrage over the disparity between expenditure on defense and expenditure on development. How should we correlate the thousands of billions spent on arms with the billion or so people in the world who are destitute?

Arms expenditure raises the related question of arms sales. We may agree that every nation has the right to defend itself against an aggressor, and therefore to purchase arms with which to do so. But how far should former colonial powers get embroiled in civil wars? Can they escape the charge of hypocrisy if they call for peace and fund peace-keeping forces even while arming the protagonists? We have reason to be grateful both that since the end of the cold war "international sales of conventional weapons have declined in value by more than half the average annual level in the 1980s,"[16] and that since 1992 the UN Register of Conventional Arms Transfers has been a voluntary means of recording and so to some degree regulating all conventional arms sales. It is believed that approximately 90 percent of all arms transfers are reported in this way.[17] Nevertheless, the figures remain huge. Calculated in billions of dollars, the sales of conventional weapons in 1995 were $19 by the United States (approaching 50 percent of the total), with the United Kingdom and France next at $7.8 and $7.4, respectively (19.1 percent and 18.1 percent), and with Russia, Germany, and China following to form the top six.[18]

(5) The Havoc of Land Mines

The tragic injuries caused by exploding land mines in many parts of the world have recently aroused public concern, not least through the advocacy of Diana, Princess of Wales. The International Committee of the Red Cross estimates that more than 110 million mines remain in the ground, and that approximately 2 million new mines are laid every year; that the cost of clearing the mines already in the ground would be a minimum of $33 billion; that meanwhile 500 people are killed or maimed by land mines every week; and that in Cambodia one person in 236 is an amputee, whereas in the United States the ratio is one in 22,000.

We may be very thankful, therefore, that the Vietnam Veterans of America Foundation initiated the International Campaign to Ban Land Mines a few years ago, and enlisted the help of the Canadian government, other countries, voluntary organizations, and prominent individuals. In September 1997 an international conference of 50 nations met in Oslo to finalize the terms of a treaty. It calls for (1) a total ban on the future use of all anti-personnel land mines, (2) assistance for land mine victims, (3) the speedy removal of all mines still in the ground, and (4) the destruction of all stockpiles. The Convention to Ban Land Mines was duly signed by 121 countries in Ottawa in December 1997, although the United States was unwilling to sign because the conference was unwilling to exempt either South Korea or three anti-tank weapons with anti-personnel devices. As of August 1998, 129 nations had signed the treaty and 32 had ratified it, bringing the total very close to the 40 ratifications needed to make it binding international law for those who have signed.

Theological and Moral Reflections

Although Christians do not fully agree, and probably have never agreed, about the mind of Christ on war, yet we should neither exaggerate the disagreements among us nor minimize the substantial area in which we are at one. For example, all Christian people affirm that the Kingdom of God inaugurated by Jesus is God's rule of righteousness and peace; that Jesus himself perfectly exemplified in his conduct the ideals of the Kingdom he proclaimed; that the Kingdom community is to hunger for righteousness, to pursue peace, to forbear revenge, to love enemies, in other words, to be marked by the cross; and that in the consummated Kingdom "they will beat their swords into ploughshares and their spears into pruning hooks," for "nation will not take up sword against nation, nor will they train for war any more" (Isaiah 2:4). All this must mean that, as Christians, we are primarily committed to peace and righteousness. True, the quest for peace with justice is much more costly than appeasement. We also admire the loyalty, self-sacrifice, and courage of serving soldiers. Yet we must not glamorize or glorify war in itself, however just we may perceive its cause to be. Some Christians believe that in some circumstances it may be defended as the lesser of two evils, but it could never be regarded by the Christian mind as more than a painful necessity in a fallen world.

Apart from this general biblical background, however, there are three main positions that Christians hold and defend—total pacifism, the just war theory, and relative (or nuclear) pacifism.[19]

(1) The Total Pacifist Position[20]

Pacifists tend to begin with the Sermon on the Mount. At least it is from this part of the teaching of Jesus that many develop their commitment to nonviolence. We are not to resist an evil person, Jesus said. Instead, if he strikes us on the right cheek, we are to turn to him the other also. We are to love our enemies, do good to those who hate us, and pray for those who persecute us. Only so can we qualify as children of our Heavenly Father, for his love is indiscriminate, and he gives the blessings of rain and sunshine to the evil and the good alike. To hate those who love us is the devil's way. To love those who love us and hate those who hate us is the way of the world. If we would follow Jesus, however, and accept the standards of his Kingdom, we must love those who hate us (Matthew 5:38–48; Luke 6:27–36).

Moreover, Jesus practiced what he preached. He exemplified his call to nonresistance. For he resisted neither betrayal nor arrest, neither trial nor sentence, neither torture nor crucifixion. When he was insulted, he did not retaliate. He was the innocent, suffering Servant of the Lord. "He was led like a lamb to the slaughter, and as a sheep before her shearers is silent, so he did not open his mouth" (Isaiah 53:7). He loved those who despised and rejected him. He even prayed for the forgiveness of those who nailed him to the cross.

Thus, pacifists conclude, the teaching and example of Jesus together commit us to the way of nonresistance and nonviolence. For this is the way of the cross, and Jesus calls us to take up our cross and follow him. Moreover, it seems to be historically proven that for two centuries, until the conversion of Constantine, the great majority of Christians refused to serve as soldiers. There is clear evidence that their refusal related to the idolatrous practices associated with life in the Roman army. Pacifists argue that they also perceived war to be incompatible with their Christian obedience. This is not certain.

The pacifist position was adopted by the so-called Radical Reformers of the sixteenth century (the various Anabaptist groups), is preserved by the

"Peace Churches" today (Quakers, Mennonites, United Brethren, etc.), and is also held by considerable minorities in the "historic" Reformation churches.

(2) The "Just War" Tradition[21]

The concept of the "just war" antedates the Christian era and may be traced back both to the "holy wars" of the Old Testament and to some Greek and Roman ethical teaching. The notion was Christianized by Augustine in the fourth century, however, systematized by Thomas Aquinas in the thirteenth, further developed by Francisco de Vitoria in the sixteenth, and endorsed by most of the Reformers. It is held by a majority of Roman Catholics and Protestants today.

It has been stated in various forms, although usually seven conditions have been specified, namely, formal declaration, last resort, just cause, right intention, proportionate means, noncombatant immunity, and reasonable expectation. There is some overlap in these seven criteria, however, and I find it more helpful to reduce them to three, relating to the beginning, the conduct, and the end of a war. Thus, for a war to be "just," first, its cause must be righteous. It must be defensive, not aggressive. Its objectives must be to secure justice or remedy injustice, to protect the innocent or champion human rights. It must be undertaken as a last resort only, after all attempts at negotiation and reconciliation have been exhausted, and then only after a formal declaration (following an ultimatum) by a legitimate authority, not by groups or individuals. Moreover, the intention must be as righteous as the cause. Just causes are not served by unjust motives. So there must be no hatred, no animosity, no thirst for revenge.

Second, its means must be controlled. There must be no wanton or unnecessary violence. In fact, two key words are used to describe the legitimate use of violence in a just cause. One is "proportionate" and the other "discriminate." "Proportionate" signifies that the war is perceived as the lesser of two evils, that the violence inflicted is proportionately less than that which it is intended to remedy, and that the ultimate gains will outweigh the losses. "Discriminate" means that the war is directed against enemy combatants and military targets, and that civilians are immune. We have to concede that the total immunity of noncombatants is impossible to preserve. But in a "just war" the distinction must be preserved and the intentional killing of civilians outlawed. The principle of noncombatant immunity was implicit in the Hague Conventions (1899 and 1907), became explicit in the Geneva Conventions and their Additional Protocol (1949 and 1977), and has been emphatically reaffirmed by the General Assembly of the United Nations (1970).

Third, its outcome must be predictable. That is, like the king in Jesus' little parable who "counted the cost" before going to war (Luke 14:31–32), there must be a calculated prospect of victory, and so of achieving the just cause for which the war was begun.

To sum up, a "just war" is one fought for a righteous cause, by controlled means, with a reasonable expectation of success.

The "just war" theory is only a tradition, however. Can it be commended from Scripture? Some try to do so on the basis of the wars commanded and directed by Yahweh in the Old Testament. But this is a precarious procedure, since these were expressly sanctioned, and no nation can claim today to enjoy Israel's privileged position as a "holy nation," God's special covenant people, a unique theocracy.

A more secure basis is provided by Paul's teaching about the state in Romans 13:1–7, and its context. It is actually embedded in a passage about neighbor-love, since it is preceded by injunctions to love and serve our enemies (12:14–21) and followed by statements that love never harms our neighbor (13:8–10). We are therefore confronted by a difficult exegetical problem. In particular, the end of Romans 12 and the beginning of Romans 13 appear to be in conflict with one another. The first, echoing the Sermon on the Mount, forbids us to repay anybody evil for evil; the second, echoing the Old Testament, describes the state as God's agent for the punishment of evil-doers. The first says that evil-doers are to be served; the second that they are to be punished. How can these instructions be reconciled?

The Peace Churches tend to say that the requirement to love our enemy is primary, that the state's judicial function is incompatible with it, and that therefore the Christian community must keep aloof from the state and have no share in its work. A recent and eloquent advocate of this view is Dale Aukerman in his book *Darkening Valley*, "a biblical perspective on nuclear war." He cannot accept that God "ordained" or "instituted" the state ("God does not consecrate and hallow the civil authorities; such hallowing is reserved for the messianic community"),[22] or that the state could be God's minister, except in a secondary sense. He uses two analogies. As in a collapsing marriage husband and wife accuse each other, and "each is for the other God's agent of retribution," though God is not the author of their quarrel, and as the Assyrian and Babylonian empires were agents of God's judgment, though God was not the author of their arrogant cruelty, so the violence of the civil authorities is not God's intention, yet "they are assigned by God a place . . . a role in the realm of his wrath." This is his conclusion: "Civil authorities in bearing the sword, which represents rule by threatened or inflicted violence, are sinning, going contrary to God's way of love described in the verses immediately before and after the Romans 13:1–7 parenthesis. . . . But in the retributive dynamisms that emerge under God as he sets himself against sin, civil authorities do have their place along with Assyria and the nagging wife."[23]

This exegesis is open to serious criticism, however. The apostle Paul asserts that the governing authorities have been established by God, that he has delegated his authority to them, that therefore in submitting to them we are submitting to him and in rebelling against them we are rebelling against him. Further, "the one in authority" (any official of the state) is "God's servant" to reward the good citizen and punish the evil-doer. In fact, three times Paul repeats that the state's "authority" is God's authority and three times that the state's "ministry" is God's ministry (verses 4a, 4b, and 6). It seems clear to me that these are not grudging concessions that God has "assigned a place" to the state, which when using force to punish evil is nevertheless "sinning," but genuine affirmations that God has "established" the state with his authority and that when exercising its authority to punish evil it is doing God's will. This being so, I cannot say that Christian people should remain insulated from public life; they should rather involve themselves in it, knowing that in doing so they are "ministers of God" just as much as pastors to whom the same expression is applied. There is nothing anomalous about Christians serving in the police force or the prison service, as politicians or magistrates or town councillors. For Christians worship a God who is just and are therefore committed to the quest for justice. The Christian community should not stand aloof from the secular community, but seek to penetrate it for Christ.

Among those who accept the legitimacy of Christian participation in the work of the secular authority are most pacifists who are not members of the Peace Churches. But, like all other Christians, they regard their participation as critical and conditional. For example, they would refuse to obey the state's call to take up arms.

How, then, should we resolve the apparent discrepancy between Romans 12:17–21, with its call for the loving service of enemies, and Romans 13:1–7, with its call for the punishment of evil-doers? We shall begin to perceive the answer when we notice that the contrast between forgiveness and punishment is not only between these paragraphs but is embedded within the first. For the prohibition "do not repay anyone evil for evil" is followed by "I will repay, says the Lord," and the prohibition "do not take revenge, my friends" is followed by "leave room for God's wrath, for it is written: "It is mine to avenge'" (verses 17, 19). So the reason why wrath, revenge, and retribution are forbidden us is not because they are in themselves wrong reactions to evil, but because they are God's prerogative, not ours. Similarly, Jesus himself, when "they hurled insults at him," not only "did not retaliate" but also instead "entrusted himself [and his cause] to him who judges justly" (1 Peter 2:23).

It is better, then, to see the end of Romans 12 and the beginning of Romans 13 as complementary. Members of God's new community can be both private individuals and state officials. In the former role we are never to take personal revenge or repay evil for evil, but rather we are to bless our persecutors (12:14), serve our enemies (12:20), and seek to overcome evil with good (12:21). In the latter role, however, if we are called by God to serve as police or prison officers or judges, we are God's agents in the punishment of evil-doers. True, "vengeance" and "wrath" belong to God, but one way in which he executes his judgment on evil-doers today is through the state. To "leave room for God's wrath" (12:19) means to allow the state to be "an agent of wrath to bring punishment on the wrongdoer" (13:4). This is not to say that the administration of justice should not be tempered with mercy. It should. And state officials should be concerned not only to "punish" evil but to "overcome" it, since retributive and reformative justice should go hand in hand. Nevertheless, what this passage of Scripture emphasizes is that if evil is to be punished (as it deserves to be), then the punishment must be administered by the state and its officials, and not by individuals who take the law into their own hands.[24]

It should be clear, then, that the state's punishing role is strictly limited and controlled. There is no possible justification in Romans 13:1–7 for an oppressive regime to whom the words "law and order" have become a synonym for tyranny. No. The state is God's agent to execute his wrath only on evil-doers, that is, on particular and identifiable people who have done wrong and need to be brought to justice. This implies a threefold restriction on the powers of the state. First, the people the state punishes must be limited to evil-doers or law-breakers. Second, the force used to arrest them must be limited to the minimum necessary to bring them to justice. Third, the punishment given must be limited in proportion to the evil which they have done. All three—the people, the force, and the punishment—must be carefully controlled.

The same principles have to be applied to soldiers as to the police. Indeed, the distinction between them is a comparatively modern one. The enforcement of law, the maintenance of order, and the protection of the innocent, which today are usually the work of the police, were in Paul's day the responsibility of Roman soldiers. Still in our own times there are situations of civil disorder (e.g., during the Mau Mau rebellion in Kenya) in which the army is called in to supplement the police. Whenever this happens, the behavior of soldiers has to be understood as an extended form of police action and regulated accordingly. The British Ministry of Defence, for example, explains existing law relating to security operations by the useful catchphrase "minimum necessary force": "No more force may be used than is both necessary and reasonable in the circumstances. The degree of force can never be reasonable if it is more than that required to achieve the immediate aim"—the main aims being the prevention of crime and the arrest of criminals.

What if the disturber of the peace is not an individual or group but another nation? The argument now is that, by legitimate extrapolation, the state's God-given authority to administer justice includes the restraint and resistance of evil-doers who are aggressors rather than criminals, and so the protection of its citizens' rights when threatened from outside as well as from inside. True, the analogy is not exact. For on the one hand, the state which goes to war is acting as judge in its own cause and not as a third party arbitrator, while on the other the cool judicial procedures of the law court have no parallel in the declaration and conduct of war. These differences are due to the fact that acceptable international justice (in arbitration, intervention, and peace-keeping) is only in its infancy. Nevertheless, the development of the "just war" theory "represented a systematic attempt to interpret acts of war by analogy with "acts of civil government," and so to see them as belonging to "the context of the administration of justice" and as subject to "the restraining standards of executive justice."[25]

Executive justice, however, whether in relation to crime or civil disorder or international warfare, must always be both discriminate action (limiting the people involved to evil-doers who have to be brought to justice) and controlled action (limiting the force used to the minimum necessary to secure this end).

This brings us to the question of whether such a limited justification of the use of force could apply to a war in which nuclear weapons were used (since they appear to be indiscriminate and uncontrolled), and so to the third Christian attitude to war.

(3) Relative or Nuclear Pacifism[26]

The invention of nuclear weapons brought an entirely new dimension to the debate about war. The old categories of conventional wisdom seemed to become as obsolete as the old weapons of conventional warfare. Both scientists and theologians began to call for new and bold thinking. As the Roman Catholic bishops said at the Second Vatican Council, the Church has "to undertake a completely fresh appraisal of war."[27] For everybody knows that if nuclear war were ever to be unleashed, the casualties would be numbered in the hundreds of millions, and could not be limited (as they largely have been in the past, though indeed less this century) to armies confronting one another.

The relevant biblical principle, which we need to evoke and apply, seems to be the great evil of "shedding innocent blood." The importance of "blood" in Scripture is that it is the carrier and so the symbol of life (e.g., Genesis 9:4; Leviticus 17:11; Deuteronomy 12:23). To "shed blood" is therefore to take life by violent means, in other words to kill. But human life, being the life of human beings made in the image of God, is sacrosanct. In the Old Testament the shedding of human blood was strictly forbidden except by specific divine sanction (i.e., in the execution of a murderer and in wars explicitly authorized by God). It is true that in the Mosaic law a small number of other serious offenses (e.g., kidnapping, cursing parents, sorcery, bestiality, idolatry, and blasphemy, see Exodus 21, 22 and Leviticus 24) were punishable by death. But this does not override the principle: "Whoever sheds the blood of man, by man shall his blood be shed, for in the image of God has God made man" (Genesis 9:6). That is, the bloodshedding of murder deserves the bloodshedding of capital punishment. For in the latter case it is the blood of the guilty which is shed. In all other cases, the sin of "shedding innocent blood" has been committed. Hence Abigail's thankfulness that, because David did not avenge himself against Nabal, he did not have "on his conscience the staggering burden of needless bloodshed" (1 Samuel 25:31).

This understanding was enshrined in the Old Testament provision of six "Cities of Refuge," three on each side of the River Jordan, carefully sited to cover the whole country. This arrangement was based on the distinction between murder (intentional killing) and manslaughter (unintentional), and was designed to protect the manslayer from the "avenger of blood" and so prevent the shedding of innocent blood (Numbers 35:9–34; Joshua 20:1–9).

A distinction was made in Old Testament times not only between murder and manslaughter, but also between blood shed in war (which was permissible) and blood shed in peace (which was not). Thus, when Joab killed both Abner and Amasa, the two commanders of Israel's army, David condemned him for "avenging in time of peace blood which had been shed in war," and so bringing upon David's house the guilt of shedding innocent blood (1 Kings 2:5, 31–34, RSV).

Against this background of Old Testament law, the prophets uttered fierce denunciations against Israel. Jeremiah warned them of God's coming judgment because they had forsaken him and profaned Jerusalem. How? They had "burned sacrifices in it" to other gods and "filled this place with the blood of the innocent" (19:4). Thus idolatry and bloodshed were bracketed. No sin against God was worse than worshiping idols. No sin against man was worse than shedding innocent blood. Similarly, Ezekiel described Jerusalem as bringing doom upon herself "by shedding blood in her midst" and "by making idols" (22:1–4; cf. 36:18). Both these prophets coupled worshiping idols and killing the innocent as the two paramount sins.

The same horror over the shedding of innocent blood continues in the New Testament. Judas confessed that he had "betrayed innocent blood" (Matthew 27:4), and when Pilate claimed to be "innocent of this man's blood," the people recklessly responded, "Let his blood be on us and on our children" (Matthew 27:24–25).

The biblical evidence on this matter is an impressively united testimony from the time of the patriarchs through the law and the prophets to the New Testament. Human blood is sacrosanct because it is the life of Godlike human beings. To shed the blood of the innocent is therefore the gravest social sin, whether committed personally in murder or judicially by an oppressive regime. God's judgment fell on Israel in the seventh century B.C. because they were guilty of shedding much innocent blood, and in the first century A.D. because they shed the innocent blood of Jesus Christ. "Hands that shed innocent blood" are among the things which Yahweh is said to hate (Proverbs 6:16–17).

This biblical message must not be evaded. The judicial authority God has given the state, including the use of "the sword" (Romans 13:4), is strictly limited. In the case of the police it is to be used only to arrest criminals and bring them to justice, in the case of the army only to engage in a just war by just means for a just end. In both cases the immunity of the innocent is to be ensured—of law-abiding citizens in peace-time and of noncombatants in war-time. Therefore any unlimited, uncontrolled, or indiscriminate use of force is forbidden. In particular, a distinction has always been recognized in war between combatants and noncombatants, between the army and the civilian population. It is true that the army consists of human beings made in God's image, who may have been conscripted against their will, and who may be entirely innocent of the crimes committed by their government. Nevertheless, if it is legitimate to resist an aggressor nation, it is legitimate to regard its army as its agent in a way that its civilian population is not. This distinction is endorsed both by international law ("the protection of civilian persons in time of war") and by biblical teaching (the prohibition of the shedding of innocent blood). It applies in two ways.

First, the principle of noncombatant immunity condemns the indiscriminate use of "conventional" (i.e., non-nuclear) weapons. For example, the Christian conscience rebels against the "obliteration" or "saturation" bombing of Hamburg, Cologne, and Berlin in 1942 and 1943, and especially of Dresden in 1945. British and American leaders (notably Churchill and Roosevelt) had previously denounced the Nazi bombings of cities as odious and shocking, and the British government publicly announced that it was not part of its policy to bomb nonmilitary targets, whatever the Nazis might do. But the Allies went back on their word, as they had reserved the right to do if Germany did not observe the same restrictions. Allied bombs on Hamburg in 1943 and on Dresden in 1945 created a "fire storm" of unimaginable horror. It was reckoned that about 135,000 people died in two days of raids on Dresden in February 1945 (considerably more than the immediate deaths caused by the atomic bombs dropped on both Hiroshima and Nagasaki); they included thousands of refugees who were fleeing before the Russian advance. I for one am thankful that Bishop George Bell of Chichester had the courage to protest in the House of Lords against this policy. Obliteration bombing "is not a justifiable act of war," he said, and "to justify methods inhumane in themselves by arguments of expediency smacks of the Nazi philosophy that Might is Right." The report of a Church of England commission, *The Church and the Atom* (1948), concurred with his judgment, describing the raids on Dresden as "inconsistent with the limited ends of a just war: it violates the principles of discrimination."[28]

Second, the principle of noncombatant immunity condemns the use of all indiscriminate weapons. Consider "chemical" weapons, that is, poison gas. Its use in World War I was a breach of the 1907 Hague Convention. The 1925 Geneva Protocol bound its signatories (by now nearly every nation) not to be the first to use it. And in World War II no signatory nation broke this pledge, although Italy had used it in Abyssinia in the 1930. Stories about "yellow rain," however, have led to the widespread belief that Soviet troops used it in Afghanistan, and that the communist forces used it in Kampuchea and Laos. Iraq has certainly used it both against the Kurds and in their war with Iran. In January 1989, however, representatives of nearly 150 nations met in Paris for a Conference on Banning Chemical Weapons, and on 29 April 1997 the Chemical Weapons Convention came into force, with 117 signatories. It calls for the complete elimination of all chemical weapons, and is therefore a true disarmament treaty. There is concern, however, that Russia—with the largest stockpile—has not yet signed the treaty (though their own Chemical Weapons Destruction Act will begin to be implemented in 1998), that North Korea, Iran, Libya, and Syria are under suspicion of still producing them, and that the Aum Shinrikyo cult members used a chemical weapon in the Tokyo underground in 1995.

Meanwhile the public needs to understand that modern nerve gases are to the chemist what nuclear weapons are to the physicist. Gas masks would offer no protection, because these gases would penetrate the skin. If they were to be dropped from the air, it is reckoned that twenty civilians would be killed to one combatant, because only combatants would be issued protective clothing.

"Biological" (sometimes called "bacterial") weapons were also included in the renunciations of the 1925 Geneva Protocol. Each nation-signatory undertook not to be the first to use either gas or germs. The Biological Weapons Convention of 1971 went further and called for the abolition of stockpiles, although no verification arrangements were agreed. By July 1996 138 nations had ratified this Convention. But still there is no effective means of ensuring compliance, and about a dozen nations are suspected of possessing secret biological weapons programs.[29]

The third kind of indiscriminate weapon is "atomic" or "nuclear." These three (atomic, biological, and chemical) are sometimes referred to as "ABC" weapons; they surely constitute the most gruesome alphabet ever conceived.

114

The invention and refinement of ABC weapons, especially of nuclear devices, have radically changed the context in which one has to think about the morality of war; they challenge the relevance of the "just war" theory. A war could still have a just cause and a just goal. But at least if macro-weapons were used ("strategic" or "tactical"), there would be no reasonable prospect of attaining the goal (since nuclear wars are not winnable) and the means would not be just, since nuclear weapons are neither proportionate, nor discriminate, nor controlled. Millions of noncombatants would be killed. In a nuclear holocaust much innocent blood would be shed. Therefore the Christian conscience must declare the use of indiscriminate nuclear weapons, and also chemical and biological weapons, immoral. A nuclear war could never be a just war. As President Reagan and Mr. Gorbachev declared in 1985 in Geneva, "A nuclear war cannot be won and must never be fought."

A Christian consensus on this issue seems to be steadily growing. The Second Vatican Council said: "Any act of war aimed indiscriminately at the destruction of entire cities or of extensive areas along with their population is a crime against God and man himself. It merits unequivocal and unhesitating condemnation."[30] The British Council of Churches at its November 1980 Assembly passed the following resolution: "The development and deployment of nuclear weapons has raised new and grave ethical questions for Christians. Because no gain from their use can possibly justify the annihilation they would bring about, and because their effects on present and future generations would be totally indiscriminate as between military and civilians, to make use of the weapons would be directly contrary to the requirements of the so-called just war."[31]

Similarly, the authors of *The Church and the Bomb*, subtitled "Nuclear weapons and Christian conscience," though the unofficial report of a Church of England working party which General Synod did not endorse, have carried many of their readers with them in their theological and moral conclusions: "We must conclude that the use of nuclear weapons cannot be justified. Such weapons cannot be used without harming non-combatants and could never be proportionate to the just cause and aim of a just war."[32] Again, "It is in our view proven beyond reasonable doubt that the Just War theory . . . rules out the use of nuclear weapons. The damage to non- combatants . . . the havoc made of the environment; and the dangers to generations yet unborn; these things make nuclear weapons indiscriminate and nuclear war almost inevitably disproportionate. The evils caused by this method of making war are greater than any conceivable evil which the war is intended to prevent, and they affect people who have nothing to do with the conflict."[33] Again, "We shall have failed wholly in our presentation if we have not made it clear that in our view the cause of right cannot be upheld by fighting a nuclear war."[34]

Evangelical Christians have been slow to catch up with the biblical perspectives of other sections of the Church. In 1980, however, an ecumenical group (with strong evangelical participation) met in the United States, saw a parallel between the nineteenth-century movement to abolish slavery and the need for a twentieth-century movement to abolish nuclear weapons, and issued "The New Abolitionist Covenant." It includes these sentences: "Unlimited in their violence, indiscriminate in their victims, uncontrollable in their devastation, nuclear weapons have brought humanity to an historical crossroads. More than at any previous time in history, the alternatives are peace or destruction. In nuclear war there are no winners."[35] And what these Christian statements affirm about nuclear weapons is equally applicable to chemical and biological weapons. For all three, being indiscriminate in their effects, are indefensible in their use.

The Call for Nuclear Disarmament

The end of the cold war, together with changing popular attitudes during the 1990s, not least the growing Christian consensus, have created a new atmosphere that is more conducive to nuclear disarmament than ever before. Already, as we have seen, some progress has been made in the international treaties that limit nuclear stockpiles. So has the time not now come to move on boldly from the reduction, no-testing, and nonproliferation of nuclear weapons to their complete elimination? Does the comparative success of the campaigns to ban both chemical and biological weapons not give us solid ground for hope that nuclear weapons could be banned as well? Several recent voices have contributed to this hope.

First, former UN Secretary-General Boutros Boutros-Ghali has said that the safest, surest, and swiftest way of dealing with the threat of nuclear arms is to do away with them completely, and that the elimination of all nuclear weapons should be "humanity's great common cause."[36]

Second, the Canberra Commission on the Elimination of Nuclear Weapons was established as an independent commission by the Australian government in November 1995. Its brief was to propose practical steps toward a world free of nuclear weapons, while at the same time maintaining international stability and security.

The Canberra Commission's "statement" begins by describing the present situation, namely, that (a) any use of nuclear weapons would be "catastrophic"; (b) nuclear weapons pose "an intolerable threat to all humanity and its habitat"; (c) the "extraordinary time of deep antagonism" in which nuclear arsenals were built up has passed; (d) if the peoples of the world were "more fully aware" of the danger and consequences of nuclear weapons, "they would reject them"; (e) the present situation, in which only a handful of states possess nuclear weapons, is "highly discriminatory and thus unstable"; and (f) the threats of "nuclear proliferation and nuclear terrorism" are growing. In the light of these things, the opportunity now exists, "perhaps without precedent or recurrence," to take a new initiative:

> The members of the Canberra Commission call upon the US, Russia, the UK, France and China to give the lead by committing themselves, unequivocally, to the elimination of all nuclear weapons. Such a commitment would propel the process in the most direct and imaginative way. All other governments must join this commitment and contribute to its fulfilment.

Third, in July 1996 the International Court of Justice (the world's highest judicial body), meeting in The Hague, in response to requests from the UN General Assembly and the WHO, ruled by 8 votes to 7 that "the threat or use of nuclear weapons would generally be contrary to the rules of international law applicable in armed conflicts, and in particular the principles and rules of humanitarian law."

Many people were disappointed both that the adverb "generally" made the ruling ambiguous and that the judgment was carried only by the casting vote of the chairman. On the other hand, the Court also reached a unanimous agreement as follows: "There exists an obligation to pursue in good faith and bring to a conclusion negotiations leading to nuclear disarmament in all its aspects under strict and effective international control."

The fourth encouragement came in December 1996 from a distinguished international group of more than sixty generals and admirals. Identifying themselves as "military professionals" who had devoted their lives to the national security of their countries and peoples, they expressed their conviction that nuclear weapons "represent a clear and present danger to the very existence of humanity." They went on to appeal for urgent action:

> First, present and planned stockpiles of nuclear weapons are exceedingly large and should now be greatly cut back;
> Second, remaining nuclear weapons should be gradually and transparently taken off alert. . . .
> Third, long-term international nuclear policy must be based on the declared principle of continuous, complete and irrevocable elimination of nuclear weapons.

How to proceed to eventual abolition, they concede, cannot at present be foreseen. It will necessitate a procedure of surveillance, inspection, and, where necessary, forcible intervention. But a movement toward the creation of a world free of nuclear weapons must begin now. "The end of the cold war makes it possible. The dangers of proliferation, terrorism and a new nuclear arms race render it necessary."

These four statements, emanating from such different circles (political, legal, and military) are very impressive. At the same time, we cannot claim that there is a universal consensus on the possession and use of nuclear weapons. It is necessary to consider, therefore, the questions which are being asked and the qualifications which are being proposed.

Questions and Qualifications

First, some are maintaining that the distinction between combatants and noncombatants is obsolete. That is, modern war is total war, and there are no noncombatants any longer. The nation's whole population is sucked into the war effort. Every taxpayer is helping to finance it. Even people in civilian jobs are thereby releasing others for military service. Therefore, since everybody is involved, the use of indiscriminate weapons is legitimate.

In reply, we agree that the old, clear-cut distinction between a country and its small professional army no longer applies, and that certainly everybody engaged in the manufacture, deployment, or use of weapons may be regarded as a combatant. Nevertheless, there are still some categories, like elderly people, little children, and the physically and mentally sick, who should be guaranteed noncombatant immunity, for to kill such people would clearly be to shed innocent blood.

It will not do to quote Old Testament examples of universal slaughter, since in such cases we are specifically told that the guilt was universal too. They were, therefore, not "indiscriminate" judgments. Before the Flood "The LORD saw how great man's wickedness on the earth had become, and that every inclination of the thoughts of his heart was only evil all the time" (Genesis 6:1). Sodom and Gomorrah would have been spared if only ten righteous people could have been found there (Genesis 18:32), while the Canaanites' practices were so depraved and detestable that the land itself is said to have "vomited out its inhabitants" (e.g., Leviticus 18:25).

If the universal judgments of the Old Testament supply no precedent for indiscriminate warfare, what about the Old Testament principle of corporate solidarity or responsibility? God described himself as "punishing the children for the sins of the fathers to the third and fourth generations" of those who hated him (Exodus 20:5), and the humiliated survivors of the destruction of Jerusalem complained: "Our fathers sinned . . . and we bear their punishment" (Lamentations 5:7). Does not this divine action, it is asked, justify the slaughter of the innocent with the guilty in war? No. The principle was exemplified in God's dealings with his people as a nation; it was not transferred to the lawcourts, where guilt had to be established. If therefore we are right that a moral defense of the "just war" is possible only if it can be seen as an extension of the administration of justice, then the distinction between the innocent and the guilty must somehow be preserved.

Second, it is pointed out that not all nuclear weapons are indiscriminate. During the immediate postwar years and during the Dulles era of the 1950s the Allied policy was indeed to threaten "massive retaliation." But the 1960s brought nuclear stalemate, and in 1962 U.S. Defense Secretary Robert McNamara developed the "counter-force" concept, namely, that retaliation would be limited to the destruction of the enemy's military installations, not cities. The key expressions became "flexible response" and "graduated response," which (it is claimed) could be contained. Apart from this, during the past two decades both "tactical" and "theater" (as opposed to intercontinental or "strategic") weapons have become so sophisticated that they could hone in on precise targets with incredible accuracy. And the Enhanced Radiation Weapon or "neutron bomb" can immobilize a single tank by killing its crew. So, as the processes of miniaturization and precision targeting continue, nuclear weapons will become increasingly discriminate in their effects, and their use cannot be given a blanket condemnation. That is the argument.

There is plainly some cogency in this reasoning. The less indiscriminate weapons become, the less unacceptable they are. There might conceivably, therefore, be a situation in which it would be morally permissible to use a very limited nuclear weapon, even though there would be some degree of radioactive fallout and some noncombatants would probably be killed. It would have to be a situation of the utmost urgency, in which the only alternative would be the worse evil of surrender to a godless regime.

But before the Christian conscience could depart from its absolute renunciation of nuclear weapons, it would need to be convinced that the use of a limited weapon would almost certainly be effective and cause the enemy to back off. For the alternative is the grave risk of escalation by the losing side. It is true that not all experts consider escalation inevitable. Michael Quinlan claims that "escalation is not an inexorable scientific process; it is a matter of human decision."[37] Yet this is the most hazardous speculation. He admits that we do not know what would happen, because (mercifully) we have had no experience of this situation. I think the American Roman Catholic bishops were wiser in their Pastoral Letter to express their "extreme scepticism about the prospects for controlling a nuclear exchange, however limited the first use might be."[38] Similarly, the Public Hearing on Nuclear Weapons and Disarmament, organized in Amsterdam in 1981 by the World Council of Churches, reported: "The weight of the evidence convinces us that the risks are too great, and that there is no moral justification for believing that a limited nuclear war could remain limited."[39]

The majority of experts and commentators are predicting that once the nuclear threshold or "firebreak" has been passed, escalation could not be halted. "The Church and the Bomb is fully justified in drawing attention to the central importance of 'escalation.' It is a metaphor drawn from the moving staircase and implies that once embarked upon the bottom step you can neither get off nor turn back, nor is there any emergency stop button."[40]

In the Roman Catholic study *Nuclear Deterrence—Right or Wrong?* Roger Ruston quotes Lord Cameron as agreeing that "in any battlefield use of nuclear weapons the risk of escalation must be immensely high." Roger Ruston's conclusion is that all uses of nuclear weaponry "would very probably result in mass slaughter of innocent people."[41]

The Palme Report (1982) is even stronger: "We on the Commission are firmly of the mind that there would be virtually no likelihood of limiting a nuclear war, once begun."[42] Therefore, they urge nations "to maintain a clear nuclear threshold . . . a clear distinction between nuclear and conventional weapons" and "to abstain from deploying weapons which blur the distinction by appearing to be more 'usable.'"[43]

If the risk of escalation is as great as these quotations indicate, then the only way of safety is to ensure that the nuclear threshold is never crossed.

The third question which people ask nuclear pacifists is this: If the use of nuclear weapons would be evil, must not their retention as a deterrent be declared equally evil? Supposing we agree that the use of macro-nuclear weapons, being agents of indiscriminate destruction, would be immoral, and that the risk of escalation is too great to justify the use of micro-weapons, does that not mean that all Christians should be committed to unilateral nuclear disarmament? No, not all relative (or nuclear) pacifists are unilateralists. For there is a moral distinction among possession, threat, and use.[44] It is probably true that if an action is immoral, then the active threat to perform it is immoral too. But the possession of nuclear weapons is more a conditional warning than an aggressive threat. Indeed, since the intention behind possession is not to encourage use but to deter it, possession cannot be pronounced as immoral as use.

Shall we then renounce use but defend possession? This seems to be the conclusion to which we are coming. Of course we can immediately see its logical inconsistency. For the effectiveness of a deterrent depends on the skill (technical) and the will (moral and political) to use it if necessary, and on the belief of the enemy that we intend to do so. A deterrent lacks credibility if the enemy knows we would never use it, and if it lacks credibility it loses its power to deter. So "retaining possession, renouncing use," though morally defensible, seems practically self-defeating. We are caught between the ineffective and the immoral, or rather between a moral stance which is ineffective and an effective deterrent which (if used) would be immoral, and so between principle and prudence, between what is right and what is realistic. Professor Wolfhart Pannenberg has put his finger on this tension. He writes about "the conflict . . . between two different ethical attitudes: an ethics of conviction that adheres to the purity of moral principles, and an ethics of responsibility that feels obliged to consider the consequences that might follow from the decision embraced."[45]

Speaking for myself, however, I am not willing to be forced to choose between Christian idealism and Christian realism, if I may use these terms loosely. Nuclear pacifists are certainly idealists, who perceive clearly and refuse to compromise the principle that the use of weapons of indiscriminate destruction would be immoral. But in clinging to this ideal, we must also face the realities of evil in our fallen world and of the current situation which reflects it. How then can we reconcile the ideal and the reality? Is there any escape from the dilemma which I have expressed as "immoral to use, prudent to keep"?

1. I accept the argument that immediate unilateral disarmament might well make nuclear war more rather than less likely. It might tempt an enemy to exploit our self-imposed weakness. They might either bully us into surrender by using nuclear missiles without fear of retaliation (in which case we have precipitated use by others through forswearing use ourselves) or blackmail us by threatening to use them (in which case our renunciation will have encouraged an enemy takeover). The question is how to prevent the use of nuclear weapons by both sides and at the same time preserve our freedom. It seems to be safer therefore, and more consistent with both ideal and reality, to retain a nuclear deterrent while developing the search for a disarmament that is mutual, progressive, and verifiable.

2. The retention of a deterrent whose weapons it would be immoral to use can be morally justified only as a temporary expedient. As Pope John Paul II said in June 1982 to the UN Second Special Session on Disarmament, the nuclear deterrent "may still be judged morally acceptable," but only if it is seen "certainly not as an end in itself, but as a step on the way towards a progressive disarmament."[46] This should increase the urgency with which the quest for effective disarmament proposals is pursued.

3. Within the framework of bilateral disarmament there is a place for imaginative unilateral initiatives, which Pope John Paul II has called "audacious gestures of peace." Some were earlier taken by the West without being reciprocated (e.g., the American removal from Europe in 1979 of a thousand nuclear warheads, although to be sure, they had long been obsolete). Yet more could surely have been taken without

undue danger. Whoever the perceived enemy may be, we should have the courage to declare a "no first use" commitment.

4. Whether or not our conscience can accept a distinction between limited and unlimited nuclear weapons, we should be able to agree that the latter should be renounced and abolished as soon as possible. Professor Keith Ward, for example, who on the moral principle that we may "commit an evil act (one causing harm) in order to prevent a much greater evil" thinks that the use of a limited nuclear weapon might in an extreme situation be the lesser of two evils, nevertheless declares that "all-out nuclear war must . . . stand unequivocally condemned. . . . It is morally unjustifiable." "It is therefore imperative," he adds, "to dismantle the apparatus which makes all-out war possible,"[47] and to retain only "a limited nuclear deterrent," indeed the minimum necessary to deter. Nuclear "superiority" is entirely unnecessary; nuclear "sufficiency" is enough. Moreover, because of the enormous "overkill" of the superpowers' arsenals, to reduce them further would not appear to entail unacceptable risk. And such a reduction might well be the impetus which is needed to accelerate the downward spiral of disarmament on both sides.

5. Meanwhile the deterrent must somehow remain credible. If the use of nuclear weapons would be immoral, we cannot threaten their use. Yet if we want the deterrent to deter, we cannot bluff either. The only alternative seems to be to cultivate uncertainty. We might say to a perceived enemy, "We believe that the use of weapons of indiscriminate destruction would be both crazy and immoral. We are determined not to use them. We are sure you do not want to use them either. Yet if you attack us, you may provoke us to act against both our reason and our conscience. We beg you not to put us in that position."

This brings us to the fourth question which is addressed to relative (nuclear) pacifists: Would not an enemy takeover be a greater evil even than nuclear war?

The scenario that is frequently envisaged and greatly feared is that we and our allies, threatened with defeat by an invading army equipped with superior conventional weapons, would be tempted in self-defense to resort to nuclear weapons, and so would plunge the world into nuclear war. "Would that not be justified?" we are asked. Can we seriously envisage the possibility that we would allow our country to be overrun and subjugated? For, if we anticipate the worst that might happen, then the freedom we have come to accept as indispensable to our quality of life would be brutally suppressed. Churches would be closed and Christians harassed. Atheism would be taught in our schools, and the Christian education of children prohibited. Dissidents would be arrested, and without a fair trial consigned to prison, a labor camp, or a psychiatric hospital. The whole hateful apparatus of oppression would be installed. We would find ourselves enslaved. Millions would die. The long dark night of the world would have begun.

Would not such an evil be literally "intolerable," worse even than the evil of nuclear war? True, the evil of subjugation would be perpetrated by the atheistic aggressor, not by us. Yet if it could be avoided by some moral action on our part, and we do not take action, we would become accomplices in the evil. If something could be done, then to do nothing is to do evil. On the other hand, if the "something" which could be done to prevent a takeover is a resort to nuclear war, we are back with the original question: Which is the greater evil?

Nuclear pacifists, however, are concerned about moral principle, not prudential balance. Our position is this: to start (or share in starting) a nuclear war would be a moral evil of such magnitude that no situation could ever justify it, not even the fear that we ourselves would otherwise be subjugated or destroyed. How can we hope to preserve our values by violating them? Would it not be better to live under an oppressive regime, with all the suffering and slavery that would involve, than be responsible for destroying the whole of human civilization? It would be appalling indeed to allow millions of people to be deprived of liberty; but would we be prepared to incinerate millions in order to prevent it happening? Would it not be better to suffer injustice ourselves than inflict it on others?

In the end, then, we have to decide which blessing we value the more: social freedom, though at the cost of losing our moral integrity by starting a nuclear war; or moral integrity as a nation, though at the cost of losing our social freedom by allowing our country to be overrun. If this might one day be the option before us, I hope we should know which to choose. It would be better to suffer physical defeat than moral defeat; better to lose freedom of speech, of assembly, even of religion, than freedom of conscience before God. For in his sight integrity is yet more valuable than liberty.

Christian Peace-Making

Jesus spoke of both war and peace. On the one hand, he warned us of "wars and rumours of wars"; on the other, he included in his characterization of the citizens of God's Kingdom the active role of peace-making. He pronounced his peace-making followers both blessed by God and the children of God (Matthew 5:9). For peace-making is a divine activity. God has made peace with us and between us through Christ. We cannot claim to be his authentic children unless we engage in peace-making too.

What practical peace-making initiatives are possible for us to take?

(1) Christian Peace-Makers Must Recover Their Morale

There are two tendencies in today's Church which undermine Christian morale. Both must be firmly repudiated.

The first is the tendency to trivialize the nuclear horror. We need to watch our vocabulary. Robert W. Gardiner has given examples of the "ingenious rhetoric" we use to reduce the awfulness of nuclear war. A projectile which destroys millions but deposits little fall-out is called "a clean bomb"; weapons of mass destruction are given "diminutive and affectionate labels" like "nukes"; "Bambi" is the name of a missile (i.e., "Don't be afraid of nuclear missiles, they're really cute, harmless little things"); and as for "nuclear umbrella," what could be "more suggestive of the safe, ordinary world of daily living than an umbrella?"[48] We might add the "nuclear club," since a "club" is normally a place of comfort, privilege, and convivial fellowship, not an association of nations whose common denominator is the possession of lethal weaponry.

The second tendency which undermines morale is to be so pessimistic about the future as to acquiesce in the general mood of helplessness. But both indifference and pessimism are inappropriate to the followers of Jesus. We need to recover our sense of indignation about the excessive nuclear stockpile and resolve to join others in seeking to reduce it further. As Dr. David Owen has written in his Introduction to Common Security, the Palme Commission Report, "Governments do respond to popular feeling. They can be influenced, particularly if the pressure is coming from a broadly based public opinion."[49]

(2) Christian Peace-Makers Must Pray

Please do not reject this exhortation as a piece of pietistic irrelevance. For Christian believers it is nothing of the sort. Irrespective of the rationale and the efficacy of praying, we have been commanded to do it. Jesus our Lord specifically told us to pray for our enemies. Paul affirmed that our first duty when we assemble as a worshiping congregation is to pray for our national leaders, so that "we may live peaceful and quiet lives in all godliness and holiness" (1 Timothy 2:2). Yet today "often the pastoral prayer in public worship is brief and perfunctory; the petitions are so unimaginative and stale as to border on 'vain repetitions'; and the people doze and dream instead of praying."[50] There is a great need to take seriously the period of intercession in public worship, and to pray for rulers and governments, peace and justice, friends and enemies, freedom and stability, and for deliverance from a nuclear conflagration. The living God hears and answers the sincere prayers of his people.

(3) Christian Peace-Makers Must Set an Example as a Community of Peace

God's call to us is not only to "preach peace" and to "make peace" but also to embody it. For his purpose, through the work of his Son and his Spirit, is to create a new reconciled society in which no curtains, walls, or barriers are tolerated, and in which the divisive influences of race, nationality, rank, and sex have been destroyed. He means his Church to be a sign of his Kingdom, that is, a model of what human community looks like when it comes under his rule of righteousness and peace. An authentic Kingdom community will then challenge the value system of the secular community and offer a viable alternative. We can hardly call the world to peace while the Church falls short of being the reconciled community God intends it to be. If charity begins at home, so does reconciliation. We need to banish all malice, anger, and bitterness from both church and home, and make them instead communities of love, joy, and peace. The influence for peace of communities of peace is inestimable.

(4) Christian Peace-Makers Must Contribute to Confidence Building

During the cold war there was considerable debate in the West about whether the Soviet Union's aggressive postures were a symptom of imperialism or of paranoia. Whichever interpretation was correct, each superpower certainly perceived the other as a threat. This is why one of the most important sections of the "Final Act" (1975) of the Helsinki Conference on Security and Co-operation in Europe (CSCE) was the "Document on Confidence-Building Measures" ("CBMs"), designed to remove the fear of sudden attack. In order to eliminate the causes of tension, build trust, and so contribute to the strengthening of peace and security in the world, the participating states agreed (1) to give each other notice twenty-one days in advance of major military maneuvers and movements; (2) to exchange observers at such maneuvers; and (3) to promote exchanges among their military personnel. The follow-up CSCE in Stockholm (1986) went further. Participants agreed (1) to share with each other their annual calendar of military activities, (2) to allow each other on-site "challenge inspections"; and (3) to prohibit large-scale troop movements unless announced a year or more in advance.

But there is no reason why the valuable concept of "CBMs" should be restricted to specifically military matters. In every situation in which people feel threatened, our Christian response should be to seek to remove fear and build confidence. CBMs should include cooperation in commerce, industry, culture, and service to the developing world. Tour groups and student exchanges are particularly valuable. For personal contacts break down caricatures and help people to discover one another as human beings. It is even more important for Christians to travel, to serve, and to share, so that they may find one another as brothers and sisters in Christ.

(5) *Christian Peace-Makers Must Promote Public Debate*

Peace movements will contribute to peace-making only if they succeed in stimulating informed discussion. There is always need for a fresh debate with fresh questions. Are nuclear arsenals a deterrent any longer? Is "moral possession, immoral use" a viable stance or totally self-contradictory? Are we shut up to the straight choice between nuclear deterrence and unilateralism, or are there "alternative defence policies"?[51] Would the build-up of "conventional" armies make it safer for nuclear arsenals to be reduced, or can both be reduced simultaneously? Would it ever be justifiable to buy national defense at the cost of millions of civilian lives? Which is the more important in the end: national integrity or national security? Such questions—and many more—need to be raised and debated.

Every Christian is called to be a peace-maker. The Beatitudes are not a set of eight options, so that some may choose to be meek, others to be merciful, and yet others to make peace. Together they are Christ's description of the members of his Kingdom. True, we shall not succeed in establishing Utopia on earth, nor will Christ's Kingdom of righteousness and peace become universal within history. Not until he returns will swords be beaten into plowshares and spears into pruning hooks. Yet this fact gives no possible warrant for the proliferation of factories for the manufacture of swords and spears. Does Christ's prediction of famine inhibit us from seeking a more equitable distribution of food? No more can his prediction of wars inhibit our pursuit of peace. God is a peace-maker. Jesus Christ is a peace-maker. So, if we want to be God's children and Christ's disciples, we must be peace-makers too.

6

Our Human Environment

In June 1992 over 25,000 people assembled in Rio de Janeiro for the United Nations Conference on Environment and Development. Popularly known as the "Earth Summit," this gathering of more than one hundred heads of state with representatives of other governments, of the scientific community, and of special interest groups is thought to have been the largest conference ever held. For in this post–cold war age it is environmental rather than nuclear destruction which has become for many the greatest threat to the human race.

Environmental studies are a comparatively recent development. Only in 1970 did the British government create a Department of the Environment with a Secretary of State in charge of it, whose responsibilities also included housing, transport, and local government. Words like "ecology," "habitat," "conservation," and "pollution" have not long been part of our everyday vocabulary. One of the most notable features of the 1980s was the rapid, almost worldwide, growth of the "green movement."

Public awareness of the critical dangers we face increased, in particular, on account of a series of four disasters: (1) the leak of poisonous gases from a chemical plant at Bhopal (1984), which killed more than two thousand Indians and blinded or injured over two hundred thousand more; (2) the catastrophic accident at the nuclear power plant at Chernobyl (1986), which released a huge radioactive cloud over Europe, whose full lethal effects will not be known for years; (3) the release of 30 tons of agricultural chemicals by firemen fighting a blaze at the Sandoz factory in Switzerland (1986), which seriously polluted the Rhine and killed millions of fish; and (4) the grounding of the tanker *Exxon Valdez* in Prince William Sound (1989), which caused

127

the spillage of 10 million gallons of crude oil and the consequent devastation of Alaskan coastline and wildlife.

In 1988 Jonathon Porritt, director of Friends of the Earth, wrote that "Green ideas have moved decisively from the fringes of society . . . into the mainstream," so that now "there is really no area of social or political concern that hasn't been touched in one way or another by the coming of the Greens."[1] In 1992 this statement seemed validated in the United States when Senator Al Gore's book *Earth in the Balance,* dealing with a host of environmental issues, was published. Vice president at the time of this writing, he has taken serious environmental concern into the second highest office in the country.

It is remarkable how quickly a dedicated, campaigning minority succeeded in alerting the general public to green concerns. Nearly everybody nowadays seems to be apprehensive about the destruction of the Amazonian rainforest, the depletion of the ozone layer, the greenhouse effect, and the slaughter of whales, elephants, and seals. Previously indifferent politicians have become obliged to add green issues to their agendas. Corporations have departments specializing in the ecological aspects of their businesses. Most cars on the road use lead-free petrol, and emissions laws are being tightened. In addition, householders are becoming "green consumers," using environmentally friendly products, eating "natural" or "organic" foods, and encouraging the recycling of paper, glass, and metals.[2]

There seem to be four main areas of widespread environmental concern which help to explain this rise in public awareness. They should be seen in relation to one another.

Reasons for Environmental Concern

First, population growth. It has been known for centuries that world population is growing. Only since World War II, however, has the accelerating growth rate been clearly perceived and the potential for disaster in the aftermath of an unchecked population explosion predicted. It is said that in the year A.D. 1800 there were about a billion people on earth. By 1900 this had doubled to 2 billion, and by 1974 doubled again to 4 billion. In 1996 the total reached nearly 6 billion, and the United Nations predicts that world population will approach 8 billion by the year 2015.

Out of 4 billion people in the 1980s, one-fifth of them (800 million) were destitute, and it is being anxiously asked how more than 7 billion people can possibly be fed thirty-five years later. This is a special problem in the developing world, where 90 percent of population growth is taking place. The earth cannot sustain a larger population which, owing to poverty and even starvation, is forced to use its resources with only short-term gain in mind, often making long-term destruction inevitable. But this is not just a Third World problem. In Britain the population is growing at the comparatively slow rate of 116,000 people per year. However, each new Briton uses more than 30 times the amount of fossil fuel consumed by the average Bangladeshi. Thus, it takes a population growth of 3.39 million Bangladeshis to equal the environmental impact of just over 100,000 Britons.[3] This figure helps put population growth into context. It is not growth per se that is the problem, for the earth could sustain many more people; it is rather the environmentally unfriendly way in which we live. The wealthy consume too much and are wasteful, while the poor are preoccupied with their immediate survival, rather than with the long-term care of the planet.

There are varying opinions even among Christians about the extent of the population problem and what should be done in response to it. In his Grove booklet entitled *Population Growth and Christian Ethics* (1995) Roy McCloughry, who presented a paper at the 1994 UN International Conference on Population and Development in Cairo, argues that the population problem is primarily neither economic nor environmental but moral, because it is basically about relationships. He pleads for "a positive vision for human life," in which (1) human beings are seen to have an intrinsic value because they are made in God's image; (2) access to education, especially by women and children, enables them to develop their full potential and to enjoy a quality of life compatible with their human dignity; and (3) the limiting and spacing of children is determined not by coercive governments but by the free decision of the parents.[4] Any discussion of population must begin by reaffirming the dignity of all human life, and the rights of human beings to live out their full potential.

The second cause for concern is resource depletion and loss of biodiversity. It was the so-called Club of Rome which in 1972 drew the world's attention to the finite nature of the earth's resources. Until then Western leaders had confidently been predicting an annual growth rate of 4 percent. Now continuous growth and finite resources were seen to be incompatible. And that was still a year before the first oil price shock. It was E. F. Schumacher who in 1973 popularized the unpalatable truth in his famous book *Small Is Beautiful,* subtitled "a study of economics as if people mattered." He wrote of "the failure to distinguish between income and capital where this distinction matters most . . . namely the irreplaceable capital which man has not made, but simply found." His first example of this "natural capital" was fossil fuels: "Fossil fuels are not made by men; they cannot be recycled. Once they are gone they are gone for ever." His other example was "living nature" (the plankton of the oceans, the green surface of the earth, clean air, etc.), much of which was being destroyed by pollution. "If we squander our fossil fuels, we threaten civilization," he wrote, "but if we squander the capital represented by living nature around us, we threaten life itself." The folly of "the modern industrial system," he continued, is that it "consumes the very basis on which it has been erected. To use the language of the economist, it lives on irreplaceable capital, which it cheerfully treats as income."[5]

Since Schumacher and the Club of Rome brought the dangers of resource depletion to the discussion table, conversation has also centered on the related problem of loss in biodiversity. Biodiversity is a term that, according to Sir Ghillean Prance, director of the Royal Botanic Gardens at Kew, encapsulates "the diversity of species of living organisms on earth, the genes or genetic information which they contain and the complex ecosystems in which they live."[6] Estimates for the number of different living species on earth range from 5 million to 50 million, with conservative estimates generally around the 10 million mark.[7] Each species contains a unique genetic code and lives in a certain habitat, often requiring very specific conditions for life. Extinction is a daily part of normal life in a world where species exist in a surprising amount of flux. The concern in the biodiversity discussion, however, is not simply with the natural extinction of species, but with the rate at which human intervention in the natural environment has accelerated those extinctions. Ecologists believe that because of human impact on the environment the current rate of extinction is between 1,000 and 10,000 times the natural rate, representing twenty to fifty species every day![8] The reason why scientists are worried about the loss of biodiversity is not only that individual species become extinct, but that when they do, the delicate balance of their ecosystem is disturbed. And when a so-called keystone species becomes extinct, large-scale problems are quickly encountered. A well-known example is the near extinction of sea otters off the West Coast of the United States. Stephen Schneider, a professor in biological sciences at Stanford University, describes what happened. "After their decline, a major disturbance propagated through the offshore marine community. Sea urchins, normally a principal food for otters, multiplied rapidly and in turn decimated the kelp forests leading to biologically impoverished, desert-like stretches of sea floor known as sea-urchin barrens. Only after controversial political pressures to restore the otter were successful did the urchin populations decline, the kelp grow back, and a new community of fish, squid, and lesser organisms reestablish themselves."[9]

A third reason for concern is waste disposal. An increasing population brings an increasing problem of how to dispose safely of the undesirable by-products of production, packaging, and consumption. A glaring example occurred in 1987 when the so-called garbage barge left Long Island, New York, and spent six months searching for a port that would take its 3,000 plus tons of garbage. Having been declined entry to numerous ports in the United States and elsewhere, the barge eventually returned to New York, where the problem had begun.

In January 1994 the British government published an extensive report entitled *Sustainable Development: The UK Strategy.* It recommended a four-fold "hierarchy of waste management," namely, "reduction," "reuse," "recovery (including recycling and energy recovery)," and "disposal without energy recovery by incinerator or landfill." The last of these options, although the commonest, is the least environmentally productive. It is still unavoidable, however, whenever "the environmental costs of recycling waste, in terms of energy consumption and emissions, are higher than for disposal." Clearly the best option in the hierarchy is to reduce the waste which we produce and so have to dispose of.

A fourth major environmental concern, which has been at the forefront of discussion since the 1980s, is our damaged atmosphere, owing to a combination of the twin problems of ozone depletion and global warming. Both are the result of atmospheric pollution, to which most of us contribute every day, often without even realizing it.

The depletion of the protective ozone layer exposes us to ultraviolet radiation, which causes skin cancers and upsets our immune system. In consequence, the discovery in 1985 of a continent-sized hole in the ozone over the Antarctic caused widespread public alarm. By 1991 this hole had reached a record size, extending over 21 million square kilometres, and by 1993 the concentration of Antarctic ozone was the lowest ever registered. The neighboring countries of Argentina and Chile, Australia, and New Zealand have been reporting damage to animals and vegetation as well as to humans, and by the mid-1990s serious ozone depletion was recorded in the more temperate regions of the northern hemisphere as well.[10]

Soon after the discovery of the Antarctic ozone hole, its cause was traced to chlorofluorocarbons (CFCs), chemicals that are used in aerosol propellants, air conditioners, and refrigerators. Recognizing the gravity of the crisis, the United Nations Environmental Programme took action. The Montreal Protocol (1987) called for the halving of CFC use by 1999, while amendments in 1991 and 1992 resolved that industrialized nations should phase out CFCs completely by 1996 and nonindustrialized nations by 2006. The cooperation of many countries in securing this agreement is a great encouragement.

The issue of global warming is a different, though related, problem.[11] The warmth of the earth's surface (which is essential for the planet's survival) is maintained by a combination of the radiation it absorbs from the sun and the infrared radiation it emits into space. This is the so-called greenhouse effect. Atmospheric pollution by so-called greenhouse gases, methane, nitrous oxide, and especially carbon dioxide (nearly 50 percent of the total) results in reducing the emission and so increasing the earth's surface temperature.

Scientists are not agreed about the seriousness of the human contribution to the greenhouse effect. Nor is the public's reaction uniform. It ranges from the fear of an imminent catastrophe to a dismissal of the threat as a fiction. There is general agreement, however, that by the year 2100 the average global temperature is likely to rise between 1 and 5 degrees centigrade. Even a one-degree increase would be ten times the average rate of temperature change since the last ice age. The long-term effects could include substantial climatic changes, the thermal expansion of the oceans, the flooding of many islands, port cities, and low-lying countries like Bangladesh, the drying out of pre-viously fertile regions, and the regional extinction of plants that cannot adjust to the changes. As with ozone depletion, so with global warming, it is urgent to reduce the human augmentation of the problem.

In December 1997 negotiators from all over the world met in Kyoto, Japan, to discuss setting limits and reducing greenhouse gas output. After eleven days of intense debate and multiple compromise by all sides those attending reached a tentative agreement. Thirty-eight industrialized nations, includ-ing the United States, the EU, Russia, and Japan, all agreed to reduce emis-sions to 6 to 8 percent below 1990 levels by 2008. Developing countries are not required to meet these same requirements, but have been given the option to comply and receive technological and material aid in return. As part of reaching their individual reduction goals the industrialized nations are able to "trade" emissions between themselves. Thus, if the EU, having pledged to reduce emissions to 8 percent below 1990 levels, were to achieve a 12 per-cent reduction, they could then sell the surplus reduction to another country that had been unable to reach its own goal. The country buying the surplus would then be able to apply it toward its own reduction goal. In this way, a potential for economic incentive was worked into the reduction process.

Very few people are happy with the treaty. Environmentalists say it has done far too little to curb emissions, while business and industry advocates, especially in the United States, claim it will create economic turmoil if applied. There are no mechanisms in place by which to enforce or even monitor com-pliance, and the treaty faces uphill battles in many legislatures before it is rat-ified. Buenos Aires, Argentina, hosted a follow-up conference in 1998 to work out details of enforcing the treaty, and to cover issues not fully examined in Kyoto. It is at least encouraging that governments have come together and begun the process of seeking to reduce greenhouse gas emissions. This is an achievement which many thought impossible.

These four major reasons for concern—population growth, resource depletion and loss of biodiversity, waste disposal, and atmospheric dam-age—are integrally related to one another and together constitute a single "interlocking global crisis." This expression was used in Our Common Future, the official report of the 1987 UN World Commission on Environ-ment and Development. The central notion of the report was that the vari-ous environmental, development, and energy problems which plague the world are all aspects of the same crisis, whose solution lies in "sustainable development." This was reaffirmed at the 1992 Earth Summit in Rio, and given sweeping endorsement in *Agenda 21: A blueprint for action for global sustainable development into the 21st century*. One of the official papers to come out of Rio, *Agenda 21* is a wide-ranging document which has been adopted by 178 governments. It sets environmental, development, and economic goals covering a whole spectrum of human and national activities. It does not have the power of a fully legal document, but it has been called "international soft law," meaning that it carries moral authority and that all nations should adhere to it to the best of their ability. Although the term "sustainable development" has been variously interpreted, it was defined in *Our Common Future* as development which "meets the needs of the present without compromising the ability of future generations to meet their own needs."[12] Indeed the intergenerational responsibility implicit in the word "sustainable" has been captured in the popular expression "not cheating on our kids."

The Biblical Perspective

The biblical approach to the environmental issue is to ask this basic question: To whom does the earth belong? It is deceptively elementary. For how shall we reply? The first answer is straightforward. It is given in Psalm 24:1: "The earth is the LORD's, and everything in it." God is its Creator, and so by right of creation is also its owner. But this is only a partial answer. Here is Psalm 115:16: "The highest heavens belong to the LORD; but the earth he has given to man." So then, the balanced biblical answer to our question is that the earth belongs to both God and man—to God because he made it, to us because he has given it to us. Not, of course, that he has handed it over to us so completely as to retain neither rights nor control over it, but that he has given it to us to rule on his behalf. Our possession of the earth is leasehold, therefore, not freehold. We are only tenants; God himself remains (in the most literal sense) the "landlord," the Lord of all the land.

This double truth (that the earth is both his and ours) is spelled out more fully in Genesis 1 and 2. In several verses of Genesis 1 the word "earth" occurs:

Verse 10: "God called the dry ground 'earth.'"

Verses 11, 12: "Then God said, 'Let the earth produce vegetation' ... And it was so. The earth produced vegetation."

Verse 24: "And God said, 'Let the earth produce living creatures' ... And it was so."

Verse 26: "Then God said, 'Let us make man in our image . . . and let them rule . . . over all the earth.'"

Verse 28: "God blessed them and said to them, '. . . fill the earth and subdue it.'"

We may legitimately make three affirmations from this biblical material. First, God has given us dominion over the earth. We note the two divine resolves of verse 26, "Let us make man in our image" and "let them have dominion over the earth." We note also the two divine actions in which his resolves were expressed: "So God created man in his own image" and "God . . . said to them, '. . . fill the earth and subdue it'" (verses 27–28). Thus from the beginning human beings have been endowed with a double uniqueness: we bear the image of God (consisting of rational, moral, social, and spiritual qualities that make it possible for us to know God) and we wield dominion over the earth and its creatures.

Indeed, our unique dominion over the earth is due to our unique relation with God. God arranged an order, even a hierarchy, of creation. He set human beings midway between himself as Creator and the rest of the creation, animate and inanimate. In some ways we are one with the rest of nature, being a part of it and having the status of creatures. In other ways we are distinct from nature, having been created in God's image and given dominion. Biologically, we are like the animals. For example, we breathe like them ("a living being," Genesis 1:21, 24 and 2:7), eat like them (1:29–30), and reproduce like them ("be fruitful and increase," 1:22, 28). But we also enjoy a higher level of experience, in which we are unlike the animals and like God: we are able to think, choose, create, love, pray, and exercise dominion. This is our intermediate position between God and nature, between the Creator and the rest of his creation. We combine dependence on God with dominion over the earth. Gerhard von Rad comments: "Just as powerful earthly kings, to indicate their claim to dominion, erect an image of themselves in the provinces of their empire, where they do not generally appear, so man is placed upon earth in God's image as God's sovereign emblem."[13]

Generally speaking, human beings have obeyed God's command to fill the earth and subdue it. At first progress was slow, as they graduated from food-gathering to farming. They learned to cultivate the soil, to protect cultivated areas from marauding animals, and to use the earth's produce to feed, clothe, and house themselves and their families. Next they learned to domesticate animals, and to harness them to their service, in order to make their labor lighter and to bring them pleasure as well. Then they learned the secrets of power which God had locked up inside the created world—the power of fire and water, later that of steam, coal, gas, and oil, and now that of uranium, the atom, and the mighty silicon chip.

In all this, in human research, discovery, and invention, in biology, chemistry, physics, and other spheres, and in all the triumphs of technology, human beings have been obeying God and exercising their God-given dominion. There is no question (at least in principle) of their having behaved like Prometheus, who stole fire from the gods. In their progressive control of the earth, they have not been invading God's private sphere and wresting power from him, still less imagining that they have stopped up the gaps in which God used to lurk, so that they can now dispense with him. It is foolish to draw these deductions. Human beings may not have known it or humbly acknowledged it, but in all their research and resourcefulness, far from usurping God's prerogatives or power, they have been exercising the dominion God gave them. Developing tools and technology, farming the land, digging for minerals, extracting fuels, damming rivers for hydroelectric power, harnessing atomic energy—all are fulfillments of God's primeval command. God has provided in the earth all the resources of food, water, clothing, shelter, energy, and warmth which we need, and he has given us dominion over the earth in which these resources have been stored.

Second, our dominion is a cooperative dominion. In exercising our God-given dominion, we are not creating the processes of nature, but cooperating with them. It is clear from Genesis 1 that the earth was made fruitful before man was told to fill and subdue it. It is true that we can make the earth more fruitful. We can clear, plow, irrigate, and enrich the soil. We can put plants under glass to catch more of the sun. We can manage the soil by rotating our crops. We can improve our stock by selective breeding. We can produce hybrid grains with a fantastic yield. We can mechanize our reaping and threshing by using huge combine harvesters. But in all these activities we are merely cooperating with the laws of fruitfulness that God has already established. Moreover, the "painful toil" which we experience in agriculture, because of God's "curse" upon the ground (Genesis 3:17), only modifies and does not override our continuing care of the soil under God's "blessing" (Psalm 65:9ff.).

True again, we are controlling and even accelerating things artificially. But it is an artificial control of essentially natural processes. It is humans cooperating with God. It is a recognition that what God gives is "nature"; what we do with it is "culture" or "cultivation."

True, God has humbled himself to need our cooperation (that is, he needs us to subdue the earth and till the soil). But we must also humble ourselves to acknowledge that our dominion over nature would be entirely fruitless if God had not made the earth fruitful, and if he did not continue to "give the increase."

This combination of nature and culture, of human helplessness and human prowess, of resources and labor, of faith and work, throws light on the recent fashion of declaring that "man has now come of age" and that (in our newly acquired adulthood) we can dispense with God. The truth is that humankind has come of age technologically. We have developed extraordinary expertise in taming, controlling, and using nature. In this respect we are lords, as God meant and told us to be. But we are also children in our ultimate dependence on the fatherly providence of God, who gives us sunshine, rain, and fruitful seasons. E. F. Schumacher quotes Tom Dale and Vernon Gill Carter in this respect: "Man, whether civilized or savage, is a child of nature—he is not the master of nature. He must conform his actions to certain natural laws if he is to maintain his dominance over his environment."[14]

Third, our dominion is a delegated and therefore a responsible dominion. That is, the dominion we exercise over the earth does not belong to us by right, but only by favor. The earth "belongs" to us not because we made or own it, but because its Maker has entrusted its care to us.

This has important consequences. If we think of the earth as a kingdom, then we are not kings ruling our own territory, but viceroys ruling it on the king's behalf, since the king has not abdicated his throne. Or if we think of the earth as a country estate, then we are not the landowners, but the bailiffs who manage and farm it on the owner's behalf. God makes us, in the most literal sense, "caretakers" of his property.

God's continuing ownership and caring supervision of the earth (indeed of the universe) is asserted many times in Scripture. We have already considered the assertion of Psalm 24:1 that "the earth is the LORD's." This includes all living things which inhabit the earth: "every animal of the forest is mine, and the cattle on a thousand hills. I know every bird in the mountains, and the creatures of the field are mine" (Psalm 50:10–11). In the Sermon on the Mount Jesus extended the divine dominion further—from the largest to the smallest of creatures. On the one hand, God makes "his sun" to rise (it belongs to him), and on the other he feeds the birds, and he clothes the lilies and the grass of the field (Matthew 5:45; 6:26, 28, 30). He thus sustains the whole of his creation; in committing it to us, he has not renounced responsibility for it.

This must be the reason why even Canaan, "the land of Israel," did not belong to Israel. True, it was "the promised land" because God had promised to give it to Abraham's descendants, and did in fact do so. Yet individuals owned land only as representatives of their tribe. No one was allowed to transfer land outside the tribe (Numbers 36:5ff.), nor to sell it to anyone in perpetuity. Every fifty years, in the Year of Jubilee, all land was to revert to its original owner. God was teaching that the land was still his, and that no human being had freehold rights. True, property rights were acknowledged, so that not only theft but also covetousness were forbidden in the law. Nevertheless, the proprietors were to remember two fundamental truths. First, they were only temporary residents: "The land must not be sold permanently, because the land is mine and you are but aliens and my tenants" (Leviticus 25:23).

Second, they must not keep all the produce of the land for themselves but provide for their needy neighbor out of it. As Professor Martin Hengel has put it, "The right to property was in principle subordinated to the obligation to care for the weaker members of society."[15] It is interesting that Pope John Paul II summed up the Christian tradition on this matter in similar terms. In his Encyclical on "Human Work" (1981) he distanced himself from both Marxist "collectivism" and liberal "capitalism." In the latter case, he explained, the question is how "the right to ownership or property is understood." He continued: "Christian tradition has never upheld this right as absolute and untouchable. On the contrary, it has always understood this right within the broader context of the right common to all to use the goods of the whole creation: the right to private property is subordinated to the right to common use, to the fact that goods are meant for everyone."[16]

If therefore our dominion over the earth has been delegated to us by God, with a view to our cooperating with him and sharing its produce with others, then we are accountable to him for our stewardship. We have no liberty to do what we like with our natural environment; it is not ours to treat as we please. "Dominion" is not a synonym for "domination," let alone "destruction." Since we hold it in trust, we have to manage it responsibly and productively for the sake of both our own and subsequent generations.

The Conservation Debate

Trusteeship includes conservation. The greatest threat to humankind may prove in the end to be not a wartime but a peacetime peril, namely, the spoliation of earth's natural resources by human folly or greed. All life on earth is dependent on the biosphere, the narrow layer of water, soil, and air in which we live. Yet our record in conserving it, especially in the twentieth century, is not good.

Vast areas of America, Africa, and Asia, once fertile agricultural land, are now through misuse irrevocable deserts or dustbowls. Worldwide, deserts have increased by 150 percent during the past hundred years, so that almost 50 percent of the earth's surface is now desert or semi-desert. The Aral Sea, once the most productive fishing site in central Asia and the fourth largest inland sea in the world, is now at half its volume of thirty years ago. A poorly conceived irrigation scheme to channel water away from the rivers that feed the sea resulted in its virtual drying out. In some places the coast has moved 30 miles, replaced by a desert of sand and salt deposits.[17] In spite of well-publicized concern over the destruction of the rainforests, each year ten trees are being cut down for every one replanted, which has resulted in the total loss of half the tropical rainforests in the world.[18] Deforestation, among other results, leads to severe soil erosion. It is estimated that 25 billion tons of topsoil are lost each year. Soil has been so abused in parts of the world that 11 percent of the world's vegetated soil is now beyond recovery. This is an area the size of China and India.[19] Some of this destruction of the environment undoubtedly happens as a result of human ignorance (e.g., the early dustbowls). Nevertheless, the Church of England's Board for Social Responsibility were not exaggerating when they said that "despoiling the earth is a blasphemy, and not just an error of judgment, a mistake."[20] It is a sin against God as well as humankind.

At the same time, not all Christians have accepted the responsibility which Scripture lays upon us; some have even used the Genesis story to excuse their irresponsibility. Gavin Maxwell, author of books on otters, especially *Ring of Bright Water*, once wrote how he lost two lovely otter cubs he had brought back from Nigeria: "A Minister of the Church of Scotland, walking along the foreshore with a shotgun, found them at play by the tide's edge and shot them. One was killed outright, the other died of her wounds in the water. The minister expressed regret, but reminded a journalist that 'the Lord gave man control over the beasts of the field.'"[21] As Professor C. F. D. Moule rightly comments, "a crime against sense and sensibility cannot be defended by the appeal to mere texts."[22]

To be sure, the biblical texts have been variously interpreted. In the Middle Ages, for example, Thomas Aquinas taught that animals exist entirely for human pleasure and profit, whereas Francis of Assisi treated them as his equals, his brothers and sisters. It was Jeremy Bentham, however, at the end of the eighteenth century, who first maintained that animals have rights, because they are sentient creatures that feel pain. In our day Dr. Peter Singer, professor of philosophy at Monash University, Melbourne, has gone much further. In his controversial book *Animal Liberation*,[23] although he concedes that there are differences between humans and animals, he yet argues for the extension of the "basic principle of equality" to animals (or rather to "non-human animals," as he calls them). He rejects what he calls "speciesism" as vigorously as he rejects racism and sexism. He defines it as "a prejudice or attitude of bias in favor of the interests of members of one's own species and against those of members of other species."[24] In consequence, the presupposition that "the human animal" has the right to rule "over other animals" is in his opinion "now obsolete."[25]

This is an extreme overreaction, however. We cannot possibly surrender the fundamental truth that human beings alone of all God's creatures are made in his image and are given a responsible dominion over the earth and its creatures. It is more meaningful, therefore, to speak of our responsibilities to and for animals than of rights possessed by animals themselves.

Since God created them (Genesis 1), since he shows his concern for them by giving them life, food, and shelter (Psalm 104), and since Jesus spoke of their intrinsic "value" (Matthew 10:31; 12:12), we too must be committed to their welfare. The Bible is quite clear on this point. According to the law, the benefits of the Sabbath rest were to be enjoyed by animals as well as humans (Exodus 20:10). According to the Wisdom literature, "a righteous man cares for the needs of his animals" (Proverbs 12:10).

Anxious public debate continues, not least among Christians, about the application of these biblical principles to such practices as vivisection, intensive farming, the shipping and slaughter of animals for food, their domestication for work and play, and the keeping of pets. Christians should protest against all perceived cruelty to animals, and campaign for their humane treatment in all circumstances, asking ourselves whether each practice is consonant with their value (as God's creatures) and with our responsibility (as God's stewards).[26]

What about the Genesis texts, however? Are we sure that we have interpreted them correctly? Or are the critics of Christianity right in saying that these verses are to blame for contemporary ecological irresponsibility? For example, the American historian Lynn White, of the University of California, Berkeley, has written: "Christianity . . . not only established a dualism of man and nature, but also insisted that it is God's will that man exploit nature for his proper ends. . . . Christianity bears a huge burden of guilt."[27] More outspoken still is Ian L. McHarg. He is a Scot who spent his childhood between the ugliness of Glasgow and the beauty of the Firth of Clyde and the Western Highlands and Islands. He became a town planner, an ecologist, and the founder and chairman of the Department of Landscape Architecture and Regional Planning at the University of Pennsylvania. In 1969 he wrote that the Genesis story, "in its insistence upon dominion and subjugation of nature, encourages the most exploitative and destructive instincts in man rather than those that are deferential and creative. Indeed, if one seeks license for those who would increase radioactivity, create canals and harbors with atomic bombs, employ poisons without constraint, or give consent to the bulldozer mentality, there could be no better injunction than this text" (i.e., Genesis 1:26, 28). "When this is understood," he continues, "the conquest, the depredations and the despoliation are comprehensible."[28] For God's affirmation about man's dominion was "also a declaration of war on nature." And he concludes with these words: "Dominion and subjugation must be expunged as the biblical injunction of man's relation to nature."[29]

In his Dunning Trust lectures in 1972–73 Ian McHarg further extended his assault. He traced Western man's attitude to the natural world to "three horrifying lines" in Genesis 1 about the dominion which God gave to man. "Dominion is a non-negotiating relationship," he said. "If you want to find one text of compounded horror which will guarantee that the relationship of

man to nature can only be destruction, which will atrophy any creative skill
... which will explain all of the destruction and all of the despoliation accomplished by western man for at least these 2,000 years, then you do not have to look any further than this ghastly, calamitous text."[30]

Ian McHarg uses very intemperate language to state his case. Some misguided people (for example, Gavin Maxwell's minister) may have tried to defend their irresponsible use of Genesis 1. But it is absurd to call this text "horrifying," "ghastly," and "calamitous," and then attribute to it two millennia of Western man's exploitation of the environment.

A much more temperate judgment is supplied by Keith Thomas, the Oxford University social historian. In his *Man and the Natural World*, he provides meticulously thorough documentation for changing attitudes toward nature in England between 1500 and 1800.[31] His theme is that at the beginning of this period, "human ascendancy" was taken for granted. People accepted "the long- established view ... that the world had been created for man's sake and that other species were meant to be subordinate to his wishes and needs."[32] Gradually, however, this "breathtakingly anthropocentric" interpretation of the early chapters of Genesis was discarded.[33] It is true that some Christians did use the grant of "dominion" over the creatures as a mandate even for such cruel sports as bear-baiting and cock-fighting.[34] But Dr. Thomas also writes that Genesis 1 cannot be blamed for ecological problems, since (a) they exist in "parts of the world where the Judaeo-Christian tradition has had no influence," (b) Genesis also contains a "distinctive doctrine of human stewardship and responsibility for God's creatures," and (c) other parts of the Old Testament clearly inculcate care for the animal creation.[35] In fact, he concedes that "the modern idea of the balance of nature ... had a theological basis before it gained a scientific one. It was belief in the perfection of God's design which preceded and underpinned the concept of the ecological chain, any link of which it would be dangerous to move."[36] So let us look at the Genesis text again.

It is true that the two Hebrew words used in Genesis 1:26 and 28 are forceful. The verb translated "have dominion" means to "tread" or "trample" on, so that the paraphrase in Psalm 8 is "you have put all things under his feet." It is often used in the Old Testament of the rule of kings. The other verb, "subdue," was used of subduing enemies in warfare and of bringing people into subjection or bondage as slaves. So man was commanded to rule the creatures of the sea, sky, and earth (verse 26) and to enslave the earth, bringing it into subjection (verse 28). Ian McHarg is right, then? No, he is not. It is an elementary principle of biblical interpretation that one must not establish the meaning of words by their etymology alone, but also and especially by the way they are used in their context. What I have written earlier about this biblical instruction is germane to the interpretation of these texts. We have seen that the dominion God has given us is delegated, responsible, and cooperative; that it is intended to express the same sustaining care of the environment as its Creator's; and that, far from exploiting the earth and its creatures, we are to use them in such a way as to be accountable to God and to serve others. We have no liberty to do what Ian McHarg did in one of his lectures, namely, to set Genesis 1 and 2 in opposition to each other as if Genesis 2 taught "cultivation" and Genesis 1 "destruction." On the contrary, the two passages interpret each other. The dominion God has given humankind is a conscientious and caring stewardship which involves the husbanding of the earth's resources. It would be ludicrous to suppose that God first created the earth and then handed it over to us to destroy it.

Contemporary Awareness

Certainly our generation is taking environmental responsibility more seriously than our immediate predecessors did. Scientists are emphasizing the delicate balance of nature. God has established in nature almost unbelievable powers of recuperation and regeneration, and in particular a cycle for the renewal of energy (from sun to plants to animals to bacteria to earth, and back to plants again). It is an example of what Barbara Ward called "the most majestic unity" of our planet. It is due to natural laws that produce a "dynamic equilibrium of biological forces held in position by checks and balances of a most delicate sort."[37] "They are so intricate," commented Dr. John Klotz, the American conservationist, "that they could not have developed by chance."[38] But if we despoil the green surface of the earth, or destroy the plankton of the oceans, we will quickly reach the point of no return in the recycling process. Our immense modern scientific knowledge teaches us "one thing above all," wrote Barbara Ward, namely, the "need for extreme caution, a sense of the appalling vastness and complexity of the forces that can be unleashed, and of the eggshell delicacy of the agents that can be upset."[39]

There have been a number of encouragements in recent years. Yet there is also a sense that in some ways the environment has passed out of the international spotlight. Nations have been slow to conform to goals set at Rio. Bureaucracy and red tape clutter the path, and many large environmental organizations are bogged down in fund-raising and bureaucracy of their own. So there remains room for more innovation and personal involvement. Only one percent of the land area of the earth is under cultivation. If only a cheaper and more efficient way to desalinate salt water could be invented, many of the world's deserts could be irrigated and made to blossom like the rose. The sea, which covers two-thirds of the planet's surface, has vast riches in terms of fish protein (not to mention oil, gas, and mineral deposits). Yet we have still not learned to farm the oceans; we are still at the stage of primitive hunter-gatherers, and are guilty of overfishing too. Enormous sums of money have been invested in the space program; I am not convinced, however, that we have a clear mandate to land people on the moon, let alone the other planets of our solar system, before we have completed our God-given task of filling and subduing the earth.

Have Christians a distinctive contribution to make to the ecological debate? Yes, we believe both that God created the earth, entrusting its care to us, and that he will one day re-create it, when he makes "the new heaven and the new earth." For "the whole creation has been groaning as in the pains of childbirth right up to the present time." Its groans are due to its "bondage to decay" and its consequent "frustration." In the end, however, it will come to share in "the glorious freedom of the children of God." That is, its bondage will give place to freedom, its decay to glory, and its pain to the joy of a new world being born (Romans 8:19–22). These two doctrines, regarding the beginning and the end of history, the Creation and the Consummation, have a profound effect on our perspective. They give us an appropriate respect for the earth, indeed for the whole material creation, since God both made it and will remake it.

In consequence, we must learn to think and act ecologically. We repent of extravagance, pollution, and wanton destruction. We recognize that human beings find it easier to subdue the earth than they do to subdue themselves. Ronald Higgins's book *The Seventh Enemy* is significant in this respect. For the first six "enemies" are the population explosion, the food crisis, the scarcity of resources, environmental degradation, nuclear abuse, and scientific technology. The seventh enemy, however, is ourselves, our personal blindness and political inertia in the face of today's ecological challenge. That is why the subtitle of the book is "The Human Factor in the Global Crisis." The human race needs a new self-awareness and fresh vision, a reawakening of its moral and religious capabilities.[40] But is this possible? Yes, Christians are convinced it is. One of the particular merits of the late Professor Klaus Bockmuhl's booklet *Conservation and Lifestyle* is that he goes beyond the "Christian criteria" for environmental responsibility to the "Christian motives." And in his conclusion he presses the challenge home: "What is sought from Christians is the motivation for selfless service, which once distinguished the Christian heritage. We should be pioneers in the care of mankind. . . . We should show whence the power and perspective for such a contribution come. We are charged to give an example." We have to "reawaken the heart of the gospel ethic."[41] We may be thankful that there are now a number of Christian organizations working specifically in the area of care for creation. Among them are the International Evangelical Environmental Network, the A Rocha Trust, the Au Sable Institute, and the Christian Society of the Green Cross.[42]

At the root of the ecological crisis is human greed, what has been called "economic gain by environmental loss." Often it is a question of competing commercial interests (though some multinational corporations have an environmental department). It is only logical that the consumer should pay the cost of production without pollution, whether in increased prices or (through a government subsidy to the manufacturer) in increased taxes. Christians should not grudge this, if it is the cost of responsible, ecological stewardship.

A crucial aspect of the economic problems in ecological stewardship is the race for industrialization occurring in the Third World. As developing countries struggle to raise their standards of living, the environment is often given less priority than the more immediate problems of undernourishment, disease, and poverty. This is understandable, and these deeper issues must be addressed if we are ever to make headway in preserving and enhancing the natural environment. Furthermore, to insist on the protection of tropical forests in the Third World, if we are unwilling to reduce carbon dioxide output in our own countries, is rank hypocrisy. We must also be willing both to share technologies which can help curb natural destruction and to create economic benefits for environmentally safe business practices. While the vast disparity between wealth and poverty remains, Christians are bound to have an uneasy conscience. We should strenuously avoid all wastefulness and greed, not only out of solidarity with the poor but also out of respect for the living environment.

7

North–South
Economic Inequality

Opinions differ as to what is the principal problem confronting humanity today. For decades following World War II it was the arms race and the fearful specter of nuclear war. With the end of the cold war, the major global concern became the environment. Now, however, according to the World Bank, "development is the most important challenge facing the human race."[1] Indeed, development and the environment are closely related.

In 1964, at the first United Nations Conference on Trade and Development (UNCTAD), the representatives of Third World countries formed themselves into the "Group of 77" (which has now grown to over 130) in order to promote their economic concerns. Then in 1973, at a meeting of nonaligned countries in Algiers, the concept was formulated of a New International Economic Order (NIEO). This urgent call for a radical restructuring of the world economy in the interests of developing nations was doubtless a flexing of Third World muscle immediately after the quadrupling of the price of oil by the OPEC countries. It also expressed the resolve of countries that had recently obtained their political independence to gain their economic independence as well.

The following year (1974), to the jubilation of many and the chagrin of some, the General Assembly of the United Nations endorsed the call for an NIEO, and published a few months later a "Charter of Economic Rights and Duties of States." This recognized the propriety of NIEO demands, for example, for more direct aid and better credit facilities, for the right to regulate (even nationalize) multinational corporations, for the removal of trade barriers to create more favorable trade terms, and for more adequate representation in international decision-making structures like the IMF (International Monetary Fund). But little progress was made to implement these proposals. The next two UNCTADs—in Nairobi (1976) and Manila (1979)—repeated the cry for more credit, aid, trade, power, and stability of commodity prices, but the Third World delegates were disappointed that little if anything had been achieved. Then in 1980, at the threshold of the third Development Decade, the Brandt Commission offered new hope in its report entitled *North–South: A Programme for Survival*.

The Brandt Commission Reports

On any showing *North–South* is a remarkable book. Even its critics (to whom I will come later) concede that it was a great achievement to produce a unanimous report by eighteen distinguished independent leaders from five continents and from different political backgrounds after two years' work; that the Commission had the courage to draw the world's attention to the need for radical action on a global scale; and that it presented its challenge with an unusual combination of reason and passion. In his personal introduction Herr Willy Brandt, the former West German Chancellor, expressed his conviction "that the two decades ahead of us may be fateful for mankind."[2]

The Brandt report was published nearly twenty years ago (in 1980). But it still speaks with relevance today, although its statistics need, of course, to be updated. World population will grow to roughly 8 billion by the year 2015, with five-sixths of people living in the Third World.[3] In spite of three decades of development, with some genuine improvements in economic growth, public health, life expectancy, and literacy, still about a quarter of the world population is condemned to absolute poverty.[4] Half the population of the developing world lives on diets which lack essential calories, and every two seconds a child dies of hunger or disease.[5] The Third World has about 80 percent of the world's population, but subsists on less than 20 percent of the world's income.[6] It is essential to know these basic statistics; our Christian thinking has to be grounded in reality.

The Brandt Commission saw its task as relating to "international development issues." It is important, therefore, to be aware of its understanding of "development." The report emphasizes that "the prime objective of development is to lead to self-fulfillment and creative partnership in the use of a nation's productive forces and its full human potential."[7]

So, "development" is much more than "relief" or "aid." Relief is still necessary in emergency situations. Aid is also often needed, especially as a "pump-priming" operation, although it can both demean people (if it is

146

offered in a patronizing way) and make them more rather than less dependent. Development, on the other hand, does not increase dependence: it aims to end it. Also, true development is wider than mere economic growth; it includes dimensions of human experience which are of great concern to Christians. This is why the "Wheaton 83" Conference of the World Evangelical Fellowship preferred "transformation" to "development," since the transformation Christians desire to promote embraces both individuals and communities, and both the material and the spiritual spheres of human life.

The Villars Statement on Relief and Development (1987) saw "relief and development" as "an expression that recognizes two biblical principles. Relief refers to the insistence in both Testaments that the people of God must help the hungry and the oppressed. Development stems from the biblical vision of a people exercising their proper stewardship of God's gifts—of societies that are productive, healthy and governed justly. Together relief and development envision substantial improvement in economic and human well-being."[8]

At the same time, social transformation is often resisted by a selfish elite who have vested interests in maintaining the status quo. Vishal Mangalwadi, who founded the Association for Comprehensive Rural Assistance (ACRA) in 1976, and has been involved ever since in serving India's rural poor, soon discovered that this reactionary element was the basic cause of continuing poverty. People "starve, suffer and die because the powerful have other priorities," he writes. Indeed, when he became convinced that "poverty was planned and perpetuated by powerful people," his emphasis changed "from development to reform."[9]

Toward the development goal the Brandt Commissioners called for an immediate "Emergency Programme: 1980–85." I summarize it in only the barest outline:

1. A large-scale transfer of resources to developing countries.
2. An international energy strategy.
3. A global food program.
4. A start on some major reforms in the international economic system, including the creation of a new "World Development Fund," greater Third World participation in existing international economic institutions, the stabilization of exchange rates and commodity prices, greater access to world markets in more favorable terms, and more regulation of transnational corporations.[10]

How did the Commissioners imagine that the nations of the North could be persuaded to share their resources, skills, and power on such a massive scale? They certainly referred to a sense of "human solidarity and a commitment to international social justice."[11] But this was not their main thrust.

147

Instead, they wrote, the "principle of mutuality of interest has been at the centre of our discussions."[12] That is, "North and South depend on each other in a single world economy," and now that they are "increasingly aware of the interdependence, they need to revitalize the dialogue to achieve specific goals, in a spirit of partnership and mutual interest rather than of inequality and charity."[13]

Critics have not questioned the evident sincerity of the Commissioners, although they have tended to call the report "visionary" and "romantic," failing to take sufficient account of human selfishness, and they have drawn attention to the report's emphasis on the distribution of wealth, without a logically prior concern for its creation.

Professor Brian Griffiths (now Lord Griffiths) in his 1980 London Lectures, published as *Morality and the Market Place*, developed a still more fundamental criticism, which I mentioned in Chapter 4. He is a reluctant critic, because he too is deeply disturbed that "hundreds of millions of our fellow human beings who like us have been created in the image of God . . . live in conditions of appalling deprivation."[14] His main criticism is of the report's omissions. Why did the Commissioners fall into the trap of generalizing about "the South" or "the Third World"? Why did they not probe the embarrassing question of why some Third World countries are developing much faster than others? The different pace of development is not due just to the disparity of available natural resources. The reason is deeper than that. For the causes of Third World poverty concern people, Griffiths argues, and their political, economic, and cultural behavior. The political factors include mismanagement, the expulsion of racial minorities, extravagance, and corruption on the part of governments and their leaders. Then there is the economic system which they choose and operate. But above all there is the cultural factor, that is, the profound effect of people's cultural background on their motives, thoughts, aspirations, and actions.

As a matter of fact, the Brandt Commission did not altogether ignore the cultural factor:

> No matter how enlightened the plans for the economic and social betterment of people's conditions, they will achieve little unless in parallel the battle is fought at the same time in both North and South, to liberate people from outworn ideas, from the grip of narrowly conceived national interests, and from the passions and prejudices inherited from the past. A new international economic order will need men and women with a new mentality and wider outlook to make it work, and a process of development in which their full capacities flourish.[15]

But Griffiths rightly seized on Willy Brandt's own assertion, on behalf of the Commission: "We take it for granted that all cultures deserve equal respect, protection and promotion."[16] "While all cultures deserve respect," Griffiths responded, "they do not all deserve equal protection and promotion." On the contrary, how can we wish to "protect and promote" cultures which actively hinder development, for example by inculcating a spirit of fatalism and apathy? He continues:

> If we really wish to understand the origins of poverty in Third World countries, I believe we are driven back to an examination of the culture of different countries and to asking basic questions. Why is it that in some societies individual human beings have the views of the physical world, of the importance of work, and the sense of self-discipline which they do? Why is it that in other societies they do not? . . . Personally, I find it impossible to answer these questions satisfactorily in purely economic terms. It is at this point that economic analysis needs a religious dimension. . . . To the extent that any culture contains Judaeo-Christian values, then surely those facets of that culture deserve especial protection and promotion.[17]

Brian Griffiths's main criticism, then, of the Brandt Commission's recommendations is that "they totally ignore the relationship between economic structures and economic philosophy. . . . Cultures express values which shape institutions and motivate people—some of which . . . promote wealth and justice and liberty, and others of which do not."[18]

So then, "culture is central to the whole process [of development]," Dr. Herbert Schlossberg has written, "and central to culture is the religious vision that informs the culture."[19] It makes a huge difference to the quality and speed of development whether people are characterized by fatalism or confidence, indolence or industry, corruption or integrity, whether they believe the world is ruled by malign spirits who resent any interference with nature or by a good Creator who tells them to transform it, and whether they think of the future in terms of endless reincarnations or of personal accountability to the Judge of all the earth. If the causes of poverty are spiritual as well as material, the remedies must be also. "The most effective means of spreading economic development, therefore," Schlossberg continues, "is a full-orbed mission program"—that is, preaching and teaching the gospel in its fullness.[20] For, as the Villars Statement put it, "the work of Christian relief and development . . . must involve spiritual transformation, setting people free from destructive attitudes, beliefs, values and patterns of culture."[21]

The 1981 London Lectures in Contemporary Christianity, given the year after those by Brian Griffiths, took the form of a symposium published under the title *The Year 2000 A.D.*[22] One of the contributors was Donald Hay of Oxford University. Most of his essay was concerned with motivation for development. He pointed out that the Brandt Commissioners tried to induce the North to take action (1) by "arguments from doom" (that otherwise world war, eco-

149

logical disaster, or economic collapse are inevitable) and (2) by "arguments from mutual economic interests." These two sets of arguments he found neither convincing nor fully Christian. In their place he restated "the Christian moral argument," which is not compassion but justice, especially "justice in the access to resources,"[23] that is, to the resources of education, technology, land, and "a culture based on hope and not despair about the possibilities for economic development."[24] By contrast, the North had "used its power to determine North-South economic relations to its own advantage."[25]

The publication of the Brandt Commission report, in spite of the criticisms, brought high hopes that at last some action would be taken to redress the North–South economic imbalance. The immediate outcome was minimal, however, and the nations of the North appeared preoccupied with their own economic problems.

So in 1983 the Brandt Commission issued its second document, a memorandum entitled *Common Crisis*.[26] In his introduction Herr Willy Brandt was even more impassioned than before. Three years had elapsed since the publication of *North–South*. Meanwhile, some of the Commissioners' worst fears had been confirmed. The prospects for economic recovery had deteriorated rapidly. Further decline could "cause the disintegration of societies and create conditions of anarchy in many parts of the world." So Willy Brandt and his colleagues felt it necessary "to present an urgent and up-to-date version of our original Emergency Programme,"[27] in the hope of breaking the deadlock and averting economic collapse.

They summarized their proposals under five headings:

1. Finance (making more money available to promote recovery).
2. Trade (increasing world trade by resisting protectionist pressures).
3. Food (raising food and agricultural production, to make nations more self-sufficient).
4. Energy (creating a new energy agency to increase energy production).
5. Negotiation (improving the negotiating process between North and South).

I do not think Brandt II contained any proposals of substance that were not in Brandt I. It was the same medicine, though perhaps the mixture was stronger, and certainly the tone of the doctors' appeal was more urgent.

Debt and Development

Looking back, it is evident that the 1980s, which had been proclaimed as the Third Development Decade, did not live up to their name. True, there was much idealism. A notable example was Bob Geldof, the Irish pop star who, outraged by television pictures of starving children in Ethiopia, touched the compassion of millions of young people. He did more than raise money (£8 million through Band Aid, £100 million through Live Aid, and more through Sport Aid and later efforts); he raised the issue of development in the public consciousness, produced educational resources for schools, and sought to generate political change by his "punk diplomacy."[28] The tragedy is that, in spite of this kind of widespread goodwill, the development process actually went into reverse during the 1980s, disastrously in Africa, seriously too in Latin America, though less so in Asia. During the 1980s and early 1990s the income gap between rich and poor nations widened at a pace faster than it had done in more than three previous decades.[29]

One of the major reasons for this is the debt burden which many Third World countries continue to bear, following the massive lending of the 1970s. Although, of course, in principle all contracts should be kept and debts repaid, one wonders if the present situation does not fall under the Old Testament condemnation of usury. It certainly gives the appearance of the exploitation of the poor through extortionate money-lending by the rich. In 1996 alone Third World debt grew by 7.2 percent. The debt crisis cannot be attributed in a simplistic way to mismanagement and extravagance by unscrupulous governments and their elite supporters. It is mainly due to factors over which the country's leaders have little if any control—the worldwide recession of the early 1980s, rising interest rates in the lending countries, crippling inflation in the borrowing countries, and the instability—in some cases collapse—of commodity prices. So the debts have increased even while the ability to repay them has decreased.

Moreover, whenever the banks have stopped making fresh loans, while the repayment of old debts has continued, the net flow of money has been out of the Third World instead of into it. For every dollar of aid that goes into the Third World three dollars are paid out in debt repayments. Between 1990 and 1993 debt servicing cost sub-Saharan Africa more than $13 billion, and this was only half of what they needed to pay in order to keep up. As a result, the debts were rolled over and overall debt doubled during this period.[30] Some countries are now paying over half their annual earnings in the servicing of their national debt. A few owe even more in debt repayment and interest than their total income from exports. It is surely unjust that the world's poorest countries should have to stagger under this heavy load; in most cases the lender nations could easily afford more generous rescheduling arrangements, and even remissions.

I am thankful that under Britain's RTA ("Retrospective Terms Adjustment") twenty-one of the poorest countries (whose per capita GNP was below £300) had by 1985 had their debts cancelled by the conversion of loans into grants, at the cost of nearly £1 billion. At the same time, in rescheduling and cancellation arrangements it is morally wrong for the North to compel debtor governments to reduce their public expenditure on social programs like education, health, and employment, since it is the poor who suffer most from such cuts. Critics claim that this is often what happens under the Structural Adjustment Programs initiated by the World Bank and the IMF's stabilization policies, both of which are aimed at long-term structural change of unproductive economic practices. "UNICEF estimates that the total additional annual cost of meeting basic human needs for health, education, nutrition . . . for everyone in Sub-Saharan Africa is only around $9 billion," a sum which could easily be found if governments were not struggling to service their debts.[31]

In 1990, at Keele University, Martin Dent decided that there could be a practical way forward in the debt crisis. With the help of others he founded the Jubilee 2000 Campaign. Inspired by the Old Testament jubilee legislation (Leviticus 25), by which every fifty years debts were cancelled and slaves freed, and by the vision of 2,000 million people enjoying a debt-free entry into the new millennium, he called for a one-off cancellation of debt to the world's poorest countries by the year 2000. What began as a simple grassroots concern has exploded into a worldwide movement with groups in dozens of countries supporting the initiative. It is sponsored in the United Kingdom by many different organizations including Tearfund and Christian Aid. If the initiative meets its stated goals, forty-seven nations will have their foreign debt remitted by the year 2000.[32]

Important fresh thinking in the development debate was contributed by the UN's World Commission on Environment and Development (chaired by Mrs. Gro Harlem Brundtland, at that time prime minister of Norway), whose report, *Our Common Future*, was published in 1987. Characterized by the same urgent tone as the Brandt reports, it called for the integration of the world's environmental and developmental problems (since economics and ecology are inseparable) and for the cooperation of all nations in solving them. It popularized the notion of "sustainable development," defining it as "development that meets the needs of the present (in particular, the essential needs of the poor) without compromising the ability of future generations to meet their own needs."[33] The definition combines "two key concepts"—meeting needs and setting limits. It thus promotes development and protects the environment simultaneously. Sustainable development became the hallmark of the 1992 United Nations Conference on the Environment and Development in Rio de Janeiro, where details of the interplay between the environment and development were more thoroughly worked out (see Chapter 6).

The decade of the 1990s has been marked by a continuous questioning and reformulating of the basic ideas of development. Paul P. Streeten, director of the World Development Institute, has said, "Development must be redefined as an attack on the chief evils of the world today: malnutrition, disease, illiteracy, slums, unemployment and inequality."[34] Alternatively, the same concerns may be expressed more positively. Whereas traditional economics has been concerned mainly with the growth and allocation of resources, development economics is concerned to improve a population's quality of life. Development then becomes a multidimensional vision. In particular, the "three core values of development" are defined as (1) "sustenance" or the ability to meet one's basic needs (i.e., food, health, and shelter), (2) "self-esteem" or the ability to be a person (with the dignity that comes from education and employment), and (3) "freedom from servitude" or the ability to make choices (economic, social, and political).[35]

In 1990 the United Nations Development Program launched its now-annual publication, the *Human Development Report*, which provides essential insight into the advances and retreats of the development movement.[36] The Human Development Index (HDI) was created and is now a useful tool in analyzing the extent to which people are being genuinely helped by the development movement. Based on three general goals of development, the HDI takes into account "longevity" measured by life expectancy at birth, "knowledge" measured by adult literacy and mean years of schooling, and "standard of living" measured by real per capita income adjusted by cost of living and other factors that differ between countries. By looking at facts and figures beyond simple economic growth, the Human Development Index puts a human face on poverty; it helps us to evaluate development in terms of how it affects people in all areas of life.

This especially concerns women. In spite of the designation of 1975 as International Women's Year, and 1976–85 as the Decade for the Advancement of Women, much development has been "gender-blind." That is, it has not noticed that women have been undervalued, disadvantaged, and denied an equal share in the benefits of development. For example, more than 70 percent of the population's poorest people are women and children, and of the estimated one billion illiterate adults in the world, more than 60 percent are women. These and other imbalances have led some researchers to speak of the "feminization" of poverty.[37] But if development has to do with human potential, and if men and women have the same potential as human beings created in God's image, no further argument is necessary to secure gender equality. Now, therefore, development is becoming increasingly gender-sensitive, alert to women's rights in law and politics, in access to literacy and education, in paid as well as voluntary work, and so in the personal dignity which these things promote. Alongside the HDI (Human Development Index) there is now a GDI (Gender-related Development Index), and the search is on for GEMs (Gender Empowerment Measures).[38]

In spite of many failures during the final three decades of the twentieth century, there has been an encouraging increase in international concern for the poor and the oppressed. As a result, many different aid, trade, relief, and development organizations have come into existence, and the United Nations itself has a number of independent programs devoted to aspects of development. Yet we must not allow the quest for social justice to be smothered by politics or bureaucracy. A sobering example of the attempted manipulation of the Third World by the First World took place at the United Nations Conference on Human Settlements (known as Habitat II) in Istanbul in June 1996. Designed to address issues of sustainable urban development in the Third World, it descended into a battle over "reproductive health," which is liberal language for abortion on demand. Third World countries resisted the political agenda of the European and North American pro-abortion lobby. As a result of their stubbornness, a courageous speech by John Gummer (then British Secretary of State for the Environment), and the support of pro-life nongovernmental organizations present, the Third World majority radically modified the pro-abortion vocabulary of some conference resolutions, reaffirmed the family as a cornerstone of society, and left no room for universal abortion on demand.

It is certainly legitimate to conclude this section of the chapter on a note of optimism. At the World Summit for Social Development, held in Copenhagen in 1995, nearly all the nations of the world committed themselves to the goal of eradicating severe poverty during the early decades of the third millennium. What progress has been made since then?

At the launch of the eighth *Human Development Report* in June 1997 some stirring words were spoken by Richard Jolly, the report's main author and special adviser to the administrator of the United Nations Human Development Program:

> The dramatic record of poverty reduction in the twentieth century shows that we should raise our sights, not downsize our vision, for human development. . . . The resources needed to eradicate poverty are a mere fraction of resources available. . . . This is a moment of extraordinary hope for people across the world. The nations of the world must reach out, not retreat. . . . Eradicating absolute poverty in the first decades of the twenty-first century is feasible, affordable and a moral imperative.[39]

Not being an economist or development expert,[40] I lack the expertise to comment either on what shape a "New International Economic Order" should take, or on the specific proposals of the Brandt, Brundtland, and other reports. What I do feel able to do, however, is to offer some biblical thoughts as justification for continuing to seek global economic and environmental cooperation. It is another case of struggling to clarify the principles involved, while leaving the framing of policies to those who have the necessary training, knowledge, and influence. It seems to me that two fundamental biblical principles apply to this issue.

The Principle of Unity

The first is the principle of unity, namely, that the planet earth is one, and the human race is also one. Yet this double unity does not control our behavior. Instead, the basic human predicament is that "the Earth is one but the world is not."[41] So nothing is more important than that the two unities God has created should permeate our consciousness.

Some claim that it was Buckminster Fuller, the famous inventor of the geodesic dome, who first coined the term "Spaceship Earth." Others attribute the first use of the expression to Ambassador Adlai Stevenson. It is certainly true that, during the last speech he made before the Economic and Social Council in Geneva on 9 June 1965, he referred to the earth as "a little spaceship" on which we are all traveling together, "dependent on its vulnerable supplies of air and soil." The following year the economist Barbara Ward took up the theme in her book *Spaceship Earth,* and a few years later elaborated it with René Dubos in *Only One Earth.*[42] Published in preparation for the 1972 United Nations Conference on the Human Environment in Stockholm, and subtitled "the care and maintenance of a small planet," the book is addressed to the question of how the growing human population can husband the planet's limited resources, for the common good, and neither exploit, nor waste, nor destroy them. The last chapter, "Strategies for Survival," ends on a rueful note. Governments have paid lip-service to the notion of planetary interdependence by setting up a whole variety of United Nations agencies to develop worldwide strategies. But these international institutions "are not backed by any sense of planetary community and commitment. . . . The planet is not yet a centre of rational loyalty for all mankind." Yet such a shift of loyalty is possible, and could well be awakened within us by "a profound and deepening sense of our shared and interdependent biosphere." After all, the human race has continually enlarged its allegiance—"from family to clan, from clan to nation, from nation to federation." So why should it not take the final, logical step? "Today, in human society, we can perhaps hope to survive in all our prized diversity, provided we can achieve an ultimate loyalty to our single, beautiful and vulnerable Planet Earth."[43] Christians will want to modify this statement, in that our ultimate loyalty is to God the Creator, who has both made the earth and entrusted it to our care.

This is a clear biblical vision. "The earth is the Lord's and everything in it, the world, and all who live in it" (Psalm 24:1). I have already quoted this verse in reference to the environment: the earth belongs to God. Now we take note that those who live in it belong to him too. For God has created a single people (the human race) and placed us in a single habitat (the planet earth). We are one people inhabiting one planet. Moreover, these two unities (planet and people) are closely related to one another. For God said, "Be fruitful, and increase in number; fill the earth and subdue it" (Genesis 1:28). Thus the one people were to populate and tame the one earth, in order to harness its resources to their service. There was no hint at the beginning of the partitioning of the earth or of rivalry between nations. No, the whole earth was to be developed by the whole people for the common good. All were to share in its God-given riches. This principle of "distributive justice" still applies today.

But this divine purpose has been frustrated by the rise of competitive nations who have carved up the earth's surface and now jealously guard its mineral deposits and fossil fuels for themselves. Of course the Bible (realistic book that it is) recognizes the existence of nations, indicates that their developing histories and territorial frontiers are ultimately under God's sovereign control, welcomes the cultural diversity (though not all the cultural practices) they have created, and warns us that "nation will rise against nation" until the end. But it does not acquiesce in this international rivalry. On the contrary, it tells us that the multiplicity of mutually hostile nations with mutually incomprehensible languages is a consequence of God's judgment on man's disobedience and pride (Genesis 11).

The Bible also indicates that one of God's major purposes in redemption will be to overcome the enmity that separates nations and to reunite the human race in Christ. So, immediately after the Tower of Babel episode, God promised through Abraham's posterity to bless all the peoples of the earth (Genesis 12:1–3); he predicted through the prophets that all nations would one day "flow" like rivers to Jerusalem (e.g., Isaiah 2:2); the risen Jesus told his followers to go and make disciples of all the nations (Matthew 28:19); the Holy Spirit came upon "all flesh," the nineteen national groups Luke mentions representing the known world (Acts 2:5–11, 17); Paul describes the accomplishment of Christ's cross in terms both of the abolition of the dividing wall of hostility between Jew and Gentile and of the creation out of the two of "one new man" or a single new humanity (Ephesians 2:14–15); and the vision of the redeemed before God's throne is of a countless multitude "from every nation, tribe, people and language" (Revelation 7:9). It would be impossible to miss this strand of internationalism which appears right through the biblical revelation.

So then, we cannot evade our responsibility to the world's poor people on the ground that they belong to other nations and are no concern of ours. The English tend to exhibit a particularly unpleasant kind of national pride. When we travel on the European continent, we express surprise that other people do not talk our language, and even annoyance that they expect us to learn theirs. We also have an obnoxious habit of dismissing foreigners with contemptuous epithets. It is enough to call somebody a "wog," "hun," "dago," "frog," "chink," or "yank"; this puts him or her beyond the pale of our respect. It should go without saying, however, that Christians should have repented of such conceited attitudes. The main point of the Parable of the Good Samaritan is its racial twist. It is not just that neighbor-love ignores racial and national barriers, but that in Jesus' story a Samaritan did for a Jew what no Jew would ever have dreamed of doing for a Samaritan.

"Patriotism" is good and right. It is a legitimate love for the fatherland to which in God's providence we belong. But Sir Alfred Duff Cooper was grievously wrong when he remarked (I think in the early 1950s) that "the love of one's country should be like all true love—blind, prejudiced, and passionate." I hope he had his tongue in his cheek, for what he was describing was not "patriotism" but "nationalism," namely, a blinkered and exaggerated loyalty to "my country, right or wrong." It is nationalism, not patriotism, which leads to the framing of trade policies which benefit us at the expense of developing nations. Nationalism is incompatible with the perspective of the Bible and the mind of Christ. We Christians should seek to become more committed internationalists by reading about other countries, visiting them if possible, welcoming overseas visitors into our homes, learning a second language, and making friends with people of other cultures. These things will enrich our own lives. They will also symbolize our resolve to affirm the biblical principle of unity (one planet, one people), to develop a global perspective, and to recognize everybody's unavoidable interdependence.

Is this a starry-eyed concept? Perhaps Christians can by God's grace become internationalists, since the biblical vision of human unity is very clear. But can we expect this of people who do not profess faith in Jesus Christ? Are not elected governments obliged to consider the national interest first? Otherwise they will not be reelected. In his useful introduction to the problems of international aid and trade, *Trade, Justice and the Wealth of Nations,* Duncan Munro points out that the expression "the family of nations," though helpful, is misleading, since "there is harmony of interests in family life, which nations cannot share. . . . The family, with its close knit bond between members . . . is capable of considerable self-sacrifice. . . . The nation, however, is incapable of love." International relationships have to be based on justice instead. "But," he continues, "the moral philosophers are right in saying that there is no logical necessity for men to choose to act justly on the basis of nature alone." Only the Christian gospel can supply the necessary motivation.[44]

Duncan Monro is justified in drawing our attention to the differences between the nuclear (or extended) family and the family of nations. Yet we must not acquiesce too readily in the distinction. People do recognize that they belong to the worldwide human family. And there is in all human beings, even since the Fall, a basic sense of compassion and justice that can influence their individual and collective behavior. There is certainly a very widespread concern in the West to help the developing nations and to eradicate poverty. Let me quote Barbara Ward again, this time from her book *Progress for a Small Planet*. She saw the contemporary world as living in an "unsteady interregnum between imperial ages which may be dying and a planetary society which struggles to be born." The "chief new insight of our century," she claimed, is the "inescapable physical interdependence" of all human beings.[45] Can this lead to a real cooperation for survival? She commends the theory of "a global compact based upon the application to the planetary community of certain of the basic principles which govern and harmonize domestic society,"[46] namely, the redistribution of wealth by taxation not charity. Could we not apply this domestic model to the planet? Ward asks. The first step would be a commitment of the rich nations to giving 0.7 percent of their GNP to the Third World, rising to one percent, together perhaps with indirect taxation on international travel. Yet only the Netherlands succeeds in attaining this goal, with "Official Development Assistance" (ODA) regularly over one percent. Other developed countries are lagging behind, and some have actually reduced their ODA in the last decade. Thus Britain's ODA decreased from 0.34 percent in 1984 to 0.31 percent in 1994. The United States' ODA dropped in the 1970s from 0.31 percent to the low figure (excluding military assistance) of 0.20 percent in 1989, and further dropped to 0.15 percent in 1994.[47] We are ready to pay taxes in our own country, Ward argues, because we are one nation, so should we not be willing to pay an international tax because we are one world?

The Principle of Equality

I move now from the first biblical principle (unity) to the second (equality). Consider the following teaching of the apostle Paul in 2 Corinthians 8:8–15:

> I am not commanding you, but I want to test the sincerity of your love by comparing it with the earnestness of others. For you know the grace of our Lord Jesus Christ, that though he was rich, yet for your sakes he became poor, so that you through his poverty might become rich. And here is my advice about what is best for you in this matter: last year you were the first not only to give but also to have the desire to do so. Now finish your work, so that your eager willingness to do it may be matched by your completion of it,

158

according to your means. For if the willingness is there, the gift is acceptable according to what one has, not according to what he does not have. Our desire is not that others might be relieved while you are hard pressed, but *that there might be equality*. At the present time your plenty will supply what they need, so that in turn their plenty will supply what you need. Then *there will be equality*, as it is written: "He that gathered much did not have too much, and he that gathered little did not have too little."

The two references to the goal of equality have been italicized in the text, so that we do not overlook them. Yet we need to see them in the whole context of Paul's instruction about the collection for the poor Judean Christians which he is organizing in the Greek churches.He begins by assuring them that his teaching is not a command but a test; he is seeking evidence of the genuineness of their love (verse 8). So their giving is to be voluntary. Not in the sense that it is optional (because they are under obligation to share with their more needy Christian brothers and sisters), but in the sense that it is spontaneous and free (an expression of their love for the poor, rather than mere obedience to the apostle).

That leads Paul straight to Christ, and to a sublime statement of his spontaneous grace (verse 9). He grounds his mundane appeal for the disadvantaged on the theology of the Incarnation, and the gracious renunciation which it entailed. He makes two references to wealth, and two to poverty. Christ had been rich, but he became poor; not as a meaningless gesture of asceticism, but "for your sakes," namely, that through his poverty you might become rich. That is to say, because of our poverty he renounced his riches, so that through his poverty we might share them. It was a renunciation with a view to a certain equalization. Moreover, both his concern to end our poverty and his decision to renounce his riches were expressions of his "grace" (verse 9), as similar action on our part will be of our "love" (verse 8). For grace is free, undeserved love.

To his exhortation that they should prove their love Paul adds some practical advice as to how to do so. They should now complete what a year previously they desired and began to do. For desiring and doing must go together, according to their means (verses 10–12). Christian giving is proportionate giving, and is acceptable according to what one has, provided that the willingness is there. Paul is not wanting them to relieve the needs of others by putting themselves in want, for that would be merely to reverse the situation, solving one problem by creating another. No, his desire is rather "that there might be equality" (verse 13). He puts the affluence of some alongside the want of others, and then calls for an adjustment, that is, an easing of want by affluence (verse 14). Twice he says that this is with a view to *isotēs*, which normally means "equality," but can also mean "fairness" or "justice." Finally (verse 15), he appeals to an Old Testament quotation about manna. God provided enough for everybody. Larger families gathered a lot, but not too much, for they had nothing over; smaller families gathered only a little, but not too little, for they had no lack. Each family had enough, because they collected according to need, not greed.

Let me try to sum up these instructions, in the reverse order, applying them to the world situation today. (1) God has provided enough for everybody's need (adequate resources in sun and rain, earth, air, and water); (2) any great disparity between affluence and want, wealth and poverty, is unacceptable to him; (3) when a situation of serious disparity arises, it ought to be corrected by an adjustment, in order to secure "equality" or "justice"; (4) the Christian motive for desiring such "justice" is "grace," loving generosity, as in the case of Jesus Christ who, though rich, became poor, so that through his poverty we might become rich; (5) we are to follow his example in this, and so prove the genuineness of our love. Just how a worldwide equalization could or should be effected is another question. Economists differ. A massive transfer of aid is not necessarily the long-term solution. Whatever the method, however, the motivation for seeking equality or fairness is love.

It may be objected by some that Paul's instructions related to an equalization within the household of God, Gentile Christians from Greece coming to the aid of Jewish Christians in Judea, and that we have no liberty to extend its application from the Church to the world. But I cannot accept this limitation. The "poor" for whose sake the rich Christ impoverished himself were unbelieving sinners like us. Besides, the principle that grave disparity should be evened out sounds like a universal truth. And when Paul wrote "as we have opportunity, let us do good to all people, especially to those who belong to the family of believers" (Galatians 6:10), the purpose of his "especially" was not to exclude unbelievers, but to remind us that our first responsibility is to our Christian brothers and sisters.

I need now to interpret Paul's teaching with an important qualification: the "equality" he sets before us as a goal is relative rather than absolute. He is not recommending a total "egalitarianism," by which all people become precisely the same, receiving an identical income, living in an identical home with identical furniture, wearing identical clothes, and developing an identical lifestyle. For the living God is not the Lord of drab uniformity but of colorful diversity. True, he made us equal in dignity and worth (for we all share his life and bear his likeness). True also, he gives the blessings of sunshine and rain to all humankind indiscriminately (Matthew 5:45). But he has not made us equal in ability. On the contrary, by creation we differ from one another—intellectually (we have different IQs), psychologically (our temperaments vary), and physically (some are handsome, others plain, some are strong, others weak). And the new creation extends this disparity. For although we are "all one in Jesus Christ" (Galatians 3:28), equally

160

God's children, justified by his grace through faith, and although we have all received the same Holy Spirit to indwell us, yet Christ by his Spirit bestows on us different spiritual gifts, whose value differs according to the degree to which they build up the Church.[48]

Personal and Economic Deductions

How then can we put together what we find in the Bible—this unity and diversity, this equality and inequality? Two answers may be given. First, there is the question of our personal economic lifestyle. Is there any criterion by which to decide at what level we should choose to live and how much difference we should permit between ourselves and others in our neighborhood? It is a question which all missionaries have to face, especially when they go from an affluent situation to a developing country. The Willowbank Report was helpful on this topic: "We do not believe that we should 'go native,' principally because a foreigner's attempt to do this may not be seen as authentic but as play-acting. But neither do we think there should be a conspicuous disparity between our lifestyle and that of the people around us. In between these extremes, we see the possibility of developing a standard of living which expresses the kind of love which cares and shares, and which finds it natural to exchange hospitality with others on a basis of reciprocity, without embarrassment."[49] This strikes me as a very practical rule of thumb. The moment I am embarrassed either to visit other people in their home or to invite them into mine, because of the disparity between our lifestyles, something is wrong. The inequality has broken the fellowship. There needs to be an equalization in one or other direction, or both. President Nyerere applied this challenge to the building of a Tanzanian state in which "no man is ashamed of his poverty in the light of another's affluence, and no man has to be ashamed of his affluence in the light of another's poverty."[50]

Second, this principle can help us in our thinking about North–South economic inequality. Since we all have equal worth (despite our unequal capacity), it must be right to secure equal opportunity for each person to develop his or her God-given potential for the common good. We cannot abolish all inequalities, nor even (because of the diversity of creation) attempt to. It is inequality of privilege we should seek to abolish, in order to create equality of opportunity. For millions of people are unable to develop their human potential. This Christians see to be the real scandal. It is not only an offense to human beings, since they are frustrated and unfulfilled, but also to their Creator who bestowed his gifts on them to be developed and used in service, not to be wasted. Let me comment briefly on equality of opportunity in education, responsibility, and trade.

Education must surely come first. Nearly 23 percent of the world's adult population cannot read. In Africa only 67 percent of primary-school-aged children are enrolled in school, and the average dropout rate for students enrolled in primary school in Africa and Asia is 54 percent.[51] We should therefore support every program that seeks equality of educational opportunity. Universal education is probably the shortest route to social justice, for it develops people's social awareness, and thus gives them the understanding and the courage to take hold of their own destiny. This is the process of "conscientization," an ugly word popularized by Paolo Freire of Brazil.

Second, the developing nations should be given equality in international responsibility. The International Monetary Fund, the World Bank, and the General Agreement on Trade and Tariffs were all set up as a result of the Bretton Woods conference in 1944, more than twenty years before the first meeting of UNCTAD at which for the first time representatives of Third World countries had a forum of their own. It would seem to be elementary justice (and the Brandt Report argues for it) that developing countries should be given a greater say in these international institutions which control so much of their economic life. Those affected by decisions made should have a share in the decision-making.

Third, I come to the controversial area of international trade. Many are nowadays calling for "trade not aid." They are understandably disillusioned that much aid has either financed the wrong things (e.g., prestigious buildings instead of genuine development which creates jobs, increases exports, and helps the poor) or been squandered by incompetence or corruption. And they are further frustrated because it is usually thought unacceptable to lay down conditions for the giving of aid. Yet Brandt I and II continue to call for a massive transfer of resources, and it seems to me the duty of givers or lenders (not least because, in the case of a government or bank, it is not their money which is being transferred) to ensure that it is used for the development purposes for which it is given.

Brandt also pleads for less protectionism and more favorable trade terms. Indeed, in principle it is widely acknowledged that justice demands this. It is also recognized, however, that genuine equality in trade is hard to achieve, since the developing nations come to the negotiating table and the marketplace as unequal partners, with unequal bargaining powers. This is partly because (before industrialization) the products they have to offer are limited by their geography, and partly because they lack the resources (the capital, technology, and skill) to be able to diversify their exports. Probably two-thirds of the world comes to the international markets disadvantaged in these and other ways.

It is perhaps equality of opportunity in these three areas (education, responsible decision-making, and trade) which would ensure, more than anything else, a fairer distribution of the world's wealth.

The present situation of North–South inequality ("a gap so wide that at the extremes people seem to live in different worlds")[52] is not God's fault (for he has provided ample resources in earth and sea), nor is it the fault of the poor (since they were mostly born into it, though some government leaders are to blame for corruption and for incompetence), nor is it necessarily our fault (although our colonial forefathers may have had a share in creating it). We become personally culpable only if we acquiesce in its continuance. In Jesus' story of the Rich Man and Lazarus there is no hint that the rich man was responsible for the poor man's plight. The rich man was guilty, however, because he ignored the beggar at his gate, did nothing about his destitution, failed to use his affluence to relieve the poor man's need, and acquiesced in a situation of gross economic inequality that had dehumanized Lazarus and which he could have remedied. The pariah dogs who licked the poor man's wounds showed more compassion toward him than the rich man. The rich man went to hell not because he had exploited Lazarus, but because of his scandalous indifference and apathy (Luke 16:19–21).

Our temptation is to use the complexity of macro-economics as an excuse to do nothing. We need to pray that God will call more of his people to develop new international economic policies, work for political solutions, and give their lives in the field of Third World development, practical philanthropy, and evangelism. But these are the callings of only some.

All of us, however, can feel what Jesus felt—the pangs of the hungry, the alienation of the poor, the indignities of the "wretched of the earth." Ultimately, the inequalities between North and South are neither political nor economic but moral problems. Until we feel moral indignation over worldwide social injustice, and compassion for worldwide human suffering, we are not likely to act. What action can we take? We can begin by informing ourselves. As Lazarus lay at the rich man's gate, so the Third World lies at ours. The rich man could not plead ignorance; nor can we. We should ensure that our daily paper has adequate Third World coverage, and perhaps subscribe to a magazine devoted to Third World needs or join the World Development Movement. We could make friends with somebody from a developing country and perhaps do short-term service in a Third World situation. Self-education of this kind may lead to political agitation. It will also undoubtedly affect our pocket. Those who read this book will all be comparatively rich; they could not afford to buy it otherwise. We should be thankful for the good things God has given us, but also remember the biblical principles of unity and equality. Then we shall give generously to both world development and world evangelization. Our personal commitment to a simpler lifestyle will not of course solve the world's economic problems. But it will be an important symbol of Christian obedience, of solidarity with the poor, and of our share in the grace of Jesus Christ which induced him to empty himself and take the form of a servant.

8

Human Rights

"Whoever wishes to live a quiet life," Leon Trotsky is said to have remarked, "should not have been born in the twentieth century." In this at least he was right.

Human Rights Violations

This century has been characterized both by violence and by violations of human rights.[1] In the two World Wars approximately 60 million people were killed. Six million Jews were exterminated in the "Holocaust" of Hitler's concentration camps and gas chambers. Millions of dissidents were also liquidated by Stalin in his Siberian labor camps. According to Solzhenitsyn, 65 million Russians were killed by their own leaders after 1923. Idi Amin's reign of terror from 1971 to 1979 cost the lives of between half and three-quarters of a million Ugandans, and under President Milton Obote at least 200,000 of his tribal enemies were murdered in the Loweru Triangle. The ruthless killings by the Khmer Rouge between 1975 and 1979 under their leader Pol Pot, carried out under the sick illusion of "purifying" and "transforming" Cambodian society, constituted nothing less than genocide; for 3 million Cambodians died by execution, disease, or starvation, which was almost half the country's population. In the 1970s Latin America was home to widespread political and ideological oppression with thousands of "disappearances," killings, and arrests in Argentina, Uruguay, Chile, and, in the 1980s, Peru. These countries were not alone.

In Ethiopia between 1983 and 1985 more than a million died, while approximately 3 million people were displaced. After years of segregation and repression under the racist apartheid regime South Africa held its first nonracial national elections in April 1994. This was a triumphant moment for human rights supporters around the world, but only after many years of abuses. During the years 1963 to 1988 thousands died in political violence, many while in detention or police custody, mostly in mysterious circumstances, of whom the best known was Steve Biko, the leader of the "Black Consciousness" movement, who died in 1977. Only recently have his killers confessed to the Truth and Justice Commission the blatant injustices surrounding his (and others') detention and death.

In 1989 we witnessed the unbelievably brutal suppression of the spontaneous democracy movement in China, in which the People's Liberation Army massacred their own unarmed compatriots. Many participants in this movement remain imprisoned or detained to this day.

But in 1989 there was also a glimmer of hope. With the fall of the Iron Curtain many in the West thought we were witnessing the dawn of an era of relative freedom and security for people around the world, as democratic forms of government began to take root in formerly oppressive situations. And this indeed was the case in many Latin American countries, whose records of human rights abuses have steadily improved in the years since. Little did we know that in spite of some improvements, the world was about to embark on a decade of widespread human rights abuses, massive continued exploitation of women and children, the reemergence of blatant genocide, and a growing persecution of Christians.

In Central Africa we have seen ethnic and tribal disputes erupt into what has been described as the "systematic planned and condoned" killing of half a million Tutsis in Rwanda in 1994 alone.[2] Moreover, a majority of the Rwandan killings were carried out with clubs or machetes against unarmed citizens, many of whom had gathered together in churches for protection.[3] The story is much the same in the Balkans, where "ethnic cleansing" (a horrible expression) led to severe repression, death, and "disappearance." Two top Bosnian Serb leaders, Radovan Karadzic and Ratko Mladic, are accused of having personally seen to the executions of 8,000 Muslims in Serbian territory. It will be some years before we can know the exact number of civilian deaths in this conflict.

Women and children, victims of longstanding abuse, have emerged as a priority concern in the human rights community during recent years. It is estimated that over a million children are forced into prostitution each year. Two hundred million children are regular laborers in Asia alone.[4] Child slavery is not uncommon in India and Sudan.[5] Street children are regularly killed and abused by police in Colombia, Brazil, Bulgaria, India, Guatemala, Kenya, and Turkey.[6] Female genital mutilation is still widespread in various parts of Africa.[7]

Christians too have been increasingly oppressed in certain parts of the world, and are killed each year by governments or mobs because of their faith. They are especially persecuted in Egypt, Sudan, Iran, Indonesia, and China, where kidnapping into slavery, torture, and church burning are reported to have taken place.

In such a list of atrocities we run the risk of selective indignation, as if the human rights violations are being perpetrated only by militant ethnic groups, corrupt police, and evil dictators. We British need, therefore, to remember with shame that in 1978 the European Court of Human Rights in Strasbourg ruled that the interrogation methods used briefly in 1971 on fourteen IRA terrorist suspects by the Royal Ulster Constabulary violated Article 3 of the European Convention on Human Rights. Although the Court cleared Britain of Irish government charges that these techniques amounted to "torture," it nevertheless described them as "inhuman and degrading treatment." The British government accepted the Court's ruling, set up a review committee, and implemented the committee's recommendations.

There are many other ways in which human beings are being oppressed. The United Nations Commission on Human Rights receives about twenty thousand complaints every year. There has been, and in some cases still is, the unjust treatment of minorities, for example, of Asians in East Africa, Indians in Brazil, aborigines in Australia, untouchables in India, Kurds in Turkey, Iran, and Iraq, Jews in the former Soviet Republics, Palestinians in Israel, Native Americans in Canada and the United States, Inuit (Eskimos) in Canada, and, perhaps one should add, Roman Catholics in Northern Ireland. There is the plight of refugees, hostages, and the victims of terrorists, and the human degradation caused by illiteracy, racism, poverty, hunger, and disease. Worse than all these, however, is the continuing use of torture, in spite of its universal condemnation. Dr. Emilio Castro has written correctly: "Torture kills the human in the torturer, and crushes the personality of the one tortured."[8]

Concern for Human Rights

Alongside the violation of human rights, even while abuses and outrages have increased, there seems to have been a corresponding growth in the recognition of rights and in concern for their safeguarding. In a sense this is not new. Being self-conscious creatures, human beings have doubtless thought about themselves and their identity, their duties, and their rights, from the beginning. So the concept has had a very long history. Plato and

Aristotle wrestled with the notions of freedom and justice, while Thomas Aquinas and other medieval theologians christianized the thought of the Greeks in terms of "natural rights." Britain looks back gratefully to the Magna Carta, which King John was induced to sign in 1215, and which King Henry III reissued ten years later. Among its provisions were the guarantees of freedom for the Church and of fair trial by one's peers. Another milestone in British history was the Bill of Rights (1688–89), which made the Crown subject to Parliament.

America and France look back to their revolutions toward the end of the eighteenth century as the time when constitutional rights were secured for their citizens. The American Declaration of Independence (1776), drafted by Thomas Jefferson, affirmed as "self-evident" that "all men are created equal" and that they "are endowed by their Creator with certain inalienable rights," especially the rights to "life, liberty, and the pursuit of happiness." Similar language was used in France's Declaration of the Rights of Man and of Citizens, which was promulgated by its National Assembly in 1789. It speaks of man's "natural, imprescriptible and unalienable rights" or "the natural, inalienable and sacred rights of man." This Declaration was eloquently defended by Thomas Paine in his celebrated book *The Rights of Man* (1791). I shall quote from it presently.

Yet it was World War II, with the horrors of Hitler's savagery and of Japan's brutality, which brought human rights to the top of the world's agenda. In June 1941 President Roosevelt made his famous State of the Union address, in which he looked forward to the emergence of "a world founded upon four essential freedoms"—freedom of speech and expression, the freedom of every person to worship God in his own way, freedom from want, and freedom from fear—after each of which he added the words "everywhere in the world."[9]

The United Nations organization was established in 1945. The preamble to its charter reads: "We, the people of the United Nations," are determined "to reaffirm faith in fundamental human rights, in the dignity and worth of the human person, the equal rights of men and women and of nations large and small." Article 1 speaks of international cooperation "in promoting and encouraging respect for human rights and for fundamental freedoms for all without distinction as to race, sex, language or religion." Article 55 goes further and says that the United Nations shall promote "universal respect for, and observance of, human rights and fundamental freedoms for all without distinction as to race, sex, language or religion."

The following year the United Nations established the Human Rights Commission, under the chairmanship of President Roosevelt's widow, Eleanor, charged with the task of preparing a Universal Declaration of Human Rights as the first element in the international Bill of Rights which it had been commissioned to produce. Its preamble affirms that "recognition of the inherent dignity, of the equal and inalienable rights, of all members of the human family, is the foundation of freedom, justice and peace in the world." Article 1 declares that "all human beings are born free and equal in dignity and rights." Article 2 adds that "everyone is entitled to all the rights and freedoms set forth in the Declaration, without distinction of any kind, such as race, colour, sex, language, religion, political or other opinion, national or social origin, property, birth or other status." The first part of the Declaration covers political and civil rights, and the second part economic, social and cultural rights. It was adopted by the UN General Assembly in Paris on 10 December 1948, though not all nations ratified it.

Writing of the late 1940s, while the draft Declaration was being prepared, the late Dr. Charles H. Malik, who belonged to the Christian community of Lebanon, and was later to become president of the UN General Assembly, wrote:

> We believed that nothing was more needful in a world that had just emerged from a most devastating war—devastating not only physically, economically, politically, but above all morally, spiritually, humanly—than to recapture and reaffirm the full integrity of man. We loved man and thought him to be wonderful, and we wanted him to be fully himself, enjoying his inherent dignity and freedom, and yet as we looked around, we found only caricatures of humanity—men deprived of their material needs, oppressed by the ideas with which they interpreted themselves and the world, distorted by the arbitrary laws of their governments, warped by the customs and convictions of their societies, diminished and disfigured in their human stature. . . . Therefore we set about inquiring how much . . . we could define and protect what belonged to the essence of man. I never worked harder, I never had a surer sense of self-confidence, I never pulsated with a deeper existential joy, than in those memorable days.[10]

The adoption of the Universal Declaration was only the beginning. The European Convention for the Protection of Human Rights (1950) was followed by the creation of the European Commission on Human Rights (1953) and of the European Court of Human Rights (1958). In 1961 Amnesty International was founded. In 1966 the two International Covenants (one on economic, social, and cultural rights, and the other on civil and political rights) were published. 1968 was the International Year for Human Rights. And in 1973 the Helsinki Conference on Security and Co-operation in Europe was held, whose final Act (1975) included a section on "The Respect of Human Rights and Fundamental Freedoms." The following year (1976) the two International Covenants came into effect, and so the long dreamed-of International Bill of Human Rights became a reality.

And yet, in spite of half a century of developing standards for human rights, their promotion and protection have been fading as issues of public concern in the West. Although governmental and nongovernmental human rights organizations continue to work tirelessly for the oppressed worldwide, the general public seems to be losing interest in the plight of others. The Chicago Council on Foreign Relations and the Gallup Organization, in a recent poll of Americans, show that support for the promotion of human rights around the world has declined 25 percent between 1990 and 1997.

This, then, is the paradoxical situation (a Universal Declaration of Human Rights, a widespread violation of them, and a growing public apathy) in which Christians need to ask some basic questions. How is it that human beings have any rights? Whence did they acquire them? Have Christians anything distinctive to contribute to continuing debate and action about human rights? It may be good to begin our answers with Thomas Paine. For, although he was a deist and therefore far from being an orthodox Christian, his father was a Quaker and his mother an Anglican, so that he was still Christian enough in his outlook to know that the rights of man go back to the creation of man. He wrote in 1791:

> The error of those who reason by precedents drawn from antiquity, respecting the rights of man, is that they do not go far enough into antiquity. They do not go the whole way. They stop in some of the intermediate stages of an hundred or a thousand years. . . . But if we proceed on, we shall at last come out right; we shall come to the time when man came from the hand of his Maker. What was he then? Man. Man was his high and only title, and a higher cannot be given him.[11]

Thomas Paine was correct. The origin of human rights is creation. Human beings have never "acquired" them. Nor has any government or other authority conferred them. We have had them from the beginning. We received them with our life from the hand of our Maker. They are inherent in our creation. They have been bestowed on us by our Creator.

This is an important principle to understand as the relativistic, secular worldview of our postmodern era threatens to leave the traditional human rights community with little ground to stand on in absolute support of human rights. Gary Haugen, former director of the United Nations' genocide investigation in Rwanda and current president of the International Justice Mission, sums up the problem:

> The truth is, the secular human rights movement is philosophically committed to cultural relativism, and it is simply a matter of time before repression finds comfort in the moral vacuum. Since World War II, the traditional human rights community has taken a courageous stand for justice out of a passionate moral intuition that is rooted, consciously or not, in the Judaeo-Christian commitment to ethical absolutes. The human rights activists of the

nineties, however, are the children of a secular philosophy of moral relativism, multi-culturalism, and radical pluralism. Consequently, when push comes to shove in the new disorderly world of the next century, the international human rights movement may find it increasingly difficult to navigate its way without a moral compass, to avoid moral confusion, or to avoid being captured by the political fashion of the day.[12]

Christians are called to provide that moral compass. The nature of human rights depends on the nature of the human beings whose rights they are. Fundamental, therefore, to human rights is the question of what it means to be human. Since the Bible focuses on the divine purpose for human beings, it has much to say on this topic. Three words seem to summarize it—"dignity," "equality," and "responsibility."

Human Dignity

The dignity of human beings is asserted in three successive sentences in Genesis 1:27–28, which we have already examined in relation to the environment. First, "God created man in his own image." Second, "Male and female he created them." Third, "God blessed them and said to them, '. . . fill the earth and subdue it.'" Human dignity is here seen to consist of three unique relationships which God established for us by creation, which together constitute a large part of our humanness, and which the Fall distorted but did not destroy.

The first is our relationship to God. Human beings are God-like beings, created by his will in his image. The divine image includes those rational, moral, and spiritual qualities which separate us from the animals and relate us to God. In consequence, we can learn about him from evangelists or teachers (it is a basic human right to hear the gospel); come to know, love, and serve him; live in conscious, humble dependence upon him; understand his will and obey his commands. So then, all those human rights we call the freedom to profess, practice, and propagate religion, the freedom of worship, of conscience, of thought, and of speech, come under this first rubric of our relationship to God. It is striking that even the deistic leaders of the American and French Revolutions knew this instinctively and referred to the "Supreme Being" from whom human rights are ultimately derived.

The second unique capacity of human beings concerns our relationship to one another. The God who made humankind is himself a social being, one God comprising three eternally distinct modes of personhood. He said: "Let us make man in our image," and, "It is not good for the man to be alone." So God made man male and female, and told them to procreate. Sexuality is his creation, marriage is his institution, and human companionship is his purpose. So then, all those human freedoms which we call the sanctity of sex, marriage, and family, the right of peaceful assembly, and the right to receive respect, whatever our age, sex, race, or rank, come under this second rubric of our relationship to each other.

Our third distinctive quality as human beings is our relationship to the earth and its creatures. God has given us dominion, with instructions to subdue and cultivate the fruitful earth, and rule its creatures. So then, all those human rights we call the right to work and the right to rest, the right to share in the earth's resources, the right to food, clothing, and shelter, the right to life and health and to their preservation, together with freedom from poverty, hunger, and disease, come under this third rubric of our relationship to the earth.

In spite of the oversimplification, we may sum up what is meant by human dignity in these three ways: our relationship to God (or the right and responsibility of worship), our relationship to each other (or the right and responsibility of fellowship), and our relationship to the earth (or the right and responsibility of stewardship)—together of course with the opportunity which our education, income, and health provide to develop this unique human potential.

Thus all human rights are at base the right to be human, and so to enjoy the dignity of having been created in God's image and of possessing in consequence unique relationships to God himself, to our fellow human beings, and to the material world. Christians have something important to add to this, namely, that our Creator has also redeemed or re-created us, at great personal cost, through the incarnation and atonement of his Son. And the costliness of God's redeeming work reinforces the sense of human worth which his creation has already given us. William Temple expressed this truth with his customary clarity:

> There can be no Rights of Man except on the basis of faith in God. But if God is real, and all men are his sons, that is the true worth of every one of them. My worth is what I am worth to God; and that is a marvellous great deal, for Christ died for me. Thus, incidentally, what gives to each of us his highest worth gives the same worth to everyone; in all that matters most we are all equal.[13]

Our value depends then on God's view of us and relationship to us. As a result of this, human rights are not unlimited rights, as if we were free to be and do absolutely anything we like. They are limited to what is compatible with being the human person God made us and meant us to be. True freedom is found in being our true selves as authentic human beings, not in contradicting ourselves. That is why it has been essential to define "human being" before defining "human rights." This principle will also help to guide us when we come to the demands for "feminine rights" and "gay rights." The question these demands pose is how far feminism and homosexual practices are compatible with the humanness God has created and intends to safeguard.

There is no situation in which it is permissible to forget the dignity of human beings by creation, and their consequent right to respect. Convicted criminals may justly be deprived of their freedom during a period of imprisonment. But the right to incarcerate does not imply the right to inflict solitary confinement on prisoners, or to treat them inhumanly in other ways. I am thankful for the work of Prison Fellowship International, founded by Charles Colson after his personal experience of the brutalizing effects of incarceration. Prison Fellowship now has more than one hundred thousand volunteers working in over seventy-five countries with inmates who have been deprived of liberty by a court, but may not be deprived of other rights. "I was in prison," Jesus said, "and you visited me."

Human Equality

The tragedy is that "human rights" have not always meant "equal rights." The good gifts of the Creator are spoiled by human selfishness. The rights God gave to all human beings equally, easily degenerate into my rights on which I insist, irrespective of the rights of others or of the common good. So the history of the world has been the story of conflict between my rights and yours, between the good of each and the good of all, between the individual and the community. Indeed, it is when human rights are in conflict with one another that we are presented with a difficult ethical dilemma. It may be the tension between the rights of the mother and her unborn child when an abortion is being considered; or between an individual landowner's right to property and peace on the one hand, and the community's need on the other for a new motorway or airport; or between the freedom of speech and assembly which a civil rights group claims for its demonstration and the freedom which the local inhabitants claim not to have their quiet disturbed or their patience exhausted.

The conflict of rights regularly envisaged in the Bible, however, takes a rather different form. Its emphasis is that no powerful individuals may impose their will on the community, and that no community may violate the rights of an individual or minority. The weak and vulnerable were carefully protected by the Mosaic law. Far from exploiting them, God's people were to be the voice of the voiceless and the champion of the powerless, including their enemies. Paul Oestreicher has put it well:

> When the electrodes are turned on, the torture victim suffers equally when the "security" think they are saving free enterprise from the revolution or the revolution from reaction. . . . My own commitment is neither to liberalism nor to Marxism, but to a curious idea put about by a carpenter turned dissident preacher in Palestine that the test of our humanity is to be found in how we treat our enemies. . . . A society's maturity and humanity will be measured by the degree of dignity it affords to the disaffected and the powerless.[14]

The equality of human beings is clearly expressed in the familiar Authorized Version words, "no respect of persons." It is a misleading phrase, because of course persons must at all costs be respected. But what the original Greek expression means literally is "no acceptance of faces." In other words, we must show "no partiality" (NIV) in our attitude to other people, and give no special deference to some because they are rich, famous, or influential. The biblical authors insist much on this. Moses declared, for example: "The LORD your God is God of gods and Lord of lords, the great, the mighty, the terrible God, who shows no partiality. . . ." Therefore Israelite judges were to show no partiality either, but rather give justice "to the small and to the great alike" (Deuteronomy 10:17; 1:16–17; cf. 16:18, 19).

The same emphasis occurs in the New Testament. God is the impartial Judge. He does not regard external appearances or circumstances. He shows no favoritism, whatever our racial or social background may be (e.g., Acts 10:34; Romans 2:11; 1 Peter 1:17). Jesus was once described (perhaps in flattery, but still with accuracy) in these terms: "Teacher, we know you are a man of integrity. You are not swayed by men, because you pay no attention to who they are" (Mark 12:14). That is, he neither deferred to the rich and powerful, nor despised the poor and weak, but gave equal respect to all, whatever their social status. We must do the same.

I rather think the best illustration of this principle is to be found in the Book of Job. It is Job's final appeal for justice, after his three comforters have at last stopped their unfair, unkind, untrue accusations. Job clings to his innocence, while at the same time acknowledging that God is a just judge. If he has broken God's laws (by immorality, idolatry, or oppression), then indeed let God's judgment fall upon him. He continues: "If I have denied justice to my servants, when they had a grievance against me, what will I do when God confronts me? What will I answer when called to account? Did not he who made me in the womb make them? Did not the same One form us both within our mother?" (Job 31:13–15). Job continues in a similar vein with reference to the poor and needy, widows and orphans. We

174

have equal rights because we have the same Creator. Both the dignity and the equality of human beings are traced in Scripture to our creation.

This principle should be even more obvious in the New Testament community, since we have the same Savior also. Paul regulates the behavior of masters and slaves to each other by reminding both that they have the same heavenly master, and that "there is no favoritism with him" (Ephesians 6:9; cf. Colossians 3:25). James seeks to banish class distinctions from public worship by urging that there must be no "favoritism" between rich and poor among believers in Jesus Christ (2:1–9). Yet the same truth is self-evident among unbelievers. Our common humanity is enough to abolish favoritism and privilege, and to establish equal status and rights. All human rights violations contradict the equality we enjoy by creation. "He who oppresses the poor shows contempt for their Maker" (Proverbs 14:31). If God shows, and if we should show, a "bias to the poor" (as is now often claimed), and if such bias is not an infringement of the "no favoritism" rule, it must be justified either because society as a whole is biased against them, or because they have no one else to champion them.

The fact that "there is no favoritism with God" is the foundation of the biblical tradition of prophetic protest. The prophets were courageous in denouncing tyranny in leaders, especially in the kings of Israel and Judah. The fact that they were monarchs, and even "the Lord's anointed," did not make them immune to criticism and rebuke. To be sure, due respect was to be shown to rulers because of their office, but any attempts on their part to convert authority into tyranny or rule into despotism were to be strenuously resisted. David was the best known of all the kings of Israel, but that gave him no warrant to kill Uriah and steal his wife Bathsheba; God sent the prophet Nathan to rebuke him. When Ahab was king in Samaria, his wife Jezebel thought his power was absolute. "Do you now govern Israel?" she asked contemptuously, when she found him sulking because Naboth had refused to sell him his vineyard. God sent Elijah to denounce Ahab's later murder of Naboth and seizure of his property. Jehoiakim was king of Judah in the seventh century B.C., yet he had no right to build himself a luxurious palace by forced labor. "Woe to you," cried Jeremiah. "Does it make you a king to have more and more cedar?" The prophet then reminded him of his father Josiah. "He did what was right and just, so all went well with him. He defended the cause of the poor and needy, and so all went well. . . . But your eyes and your heart are set only on dishonest gain, on shedding innocent blood and on oppression and extortion." No one would lament him when he died, Jeremiah added; he would have the burial of a donkey, and would be dragged away and thrown outside the gates of Jerusalem.[15]

In our day dictators try to defend arbitrary arrest and detention, and even imprisonment or execution without public trial, on the ground of "national security." One wonders how a biblical prophet would react. Protest or denunciation within the country concerned would doubtless cost the prophet his life. But at least from outside the kind of work which Amnesty International undertakes is consistent with biblical precedent, and with the recognition that with God "there is no favoritism." Human rights are equal rights.

Human Responsibility

Christians often cringe when the conversation turns to human rights. For it smacks of one person asserting his or her rights against another person, and so of conflict. It seems also to encourage selfishness. It overlooks the fact that human beings have duties and responsibilities as well as rights. Solzhenitsyn has called recently for this balance to be redressed. "During these 300 years of Western Civilization, there has been a sweeping away of duties and an expansion of rights. But we have two lungs. You can't breathe with just one lung and not with the other. We must avail ourselves of rights and duties in equal measure."[16] Let me try, then, to clarify the relationship between rights and responsibilities.

The Bible says much about defending other people's rights, but little about defending our own. On the contrary, when it addresses us, it emphasizes our responsibilities, not our rights. We are to love God and to love our neighbor. These primary requirements comprise our whole duty; for "all the Law and the Prophets hang on these two commandments," Jesus said (Matthew 22:40). In fact, what the Bible contains, as Dr. Christopher Wright has written, is a "Universal Declaration of Human Responsibilities" (especially in terms of loving God and neighbor), not of human rights.[17] Indeed, the Bible goes further and links them. It emphasizes that our responsibility is to secure the other person's rights. We must even forgo our own rights in order to do so.

Of this responsible renunciation of rights Jesus Christ is the supreme model. Although eternally "in very nature God," he "did not consider equality with God something to be grasped, but made himself nothing, taking the very nature of a servant, being made in human likeness" (Philippians 2:6–7). Throughout his life he was a victim of abuses of human rights. He became a refugee baby in Egypt, a prophet without honor in his own country, and the Messiah rejected by the religious establishment of his own people to whom he had come. He became a prisoner of conscience, refusing to compromise in order to secure his release. He was falsely accused, unjustly condemned, brutally tortured, and finally crucified. And throughout his ordeal he declined to defend or demand his rights, in order that by his self-sacrifice he might serve ours.

"Let this mind be in you, which was also in Jesus Christ," wrote Paul. And Paul practiced what he preached. He had rights as an apostle (the right to marry, the right to receive financial support). But he renounced them for the sake of the gospel, in order to become everybody's slave and so serve their rights (see, e.g., 1 Corinthians 9).

The renunciation of rights, however unnatural and idealistic it may seem, is an essential characteristic of God's new society. In the world outside people assert their own rights and exercise authority. "Not so with you," Jesus said. On the contrary, in his community those aspiring after greatness must become servants, the leader the slave, and the first last. For love "is not self-seeking," Paul wrote. And this fundamental stance, learned from Jesus, applies in every situation. For example, believers should not prosecute one another, especially in an unbelieving court. Christian litigation was a scandal in Corinth; it still is in India, Pakistan, Sri Lanka, and other countries. Christians should at the very least settle their own disputes. Better still, "Why not rather be wronged? Why not rather be cheated?" Is not this the way of Christ? Another first-century application was to Christian slaves with cruel masters. What if they were unjustly beaten? They must bear it patiently, following in the footsteps of Jesus, who did not retaliate, but entrusted himself and his cause to the just Judge of all.[18] This last point, that the nonretaliation of Jesus was accompanied by a commitment of himself to God, is an important addition. To renounce rights is not to acquiesce in wrongs. The reason we do not judge is that this is God's prerogative, not ours (Romans 12:19). Besides, Christ is coming back, and then all evil will be judged, and justice finally and publicly vindicated.

Here then is a Christian perspective on human rights. First, we affirm human dignity. Because human beings are created in God's image to know him, serve one another, and be stewards of the earth, therefore they must be respected. Second, we affirm human equality. Because human beings have all been made in the same image by the same Creator, therefore we must not be obsequious to some and scornful to others, but behave without partiality to all. Third, we affirm human responsibility. Because God has laid it upon us to love and serve our neighbors, therefore we must fight for their rights while being ready to renounce our own in order to do so.

Two main conclusions follow. First, we have to accept that other people's rights are our responsibility. We are our brother's keeper, because God has put us in the same human family and so made us related to and responsible for one another. The law and the prophets, Jesus and his apostles, all lay on us a particular duty to serve the poor and defend the powerless. We cannot escape this by saying they are not our responsibility. To quote Solzhenitsyn again, "There are no internal affairs left on this globe of ours. Mankind can be saved only if everybody takes an interest in everybody else's affairs."[19] We need then to feel the pain of those who suffer oppression. "Remember those in prison as if you were their fellow prisoners, and those who are maltreated as if you yourselves were suffering" (Hebrews 13:3). In order to do this, we may need to inform ourselves more thoroughly about contemporary violations of human rights.[20] Then whatever action we may believe it right to take, we need to ensure that the methods we use do not infringe the very human rights we are seeking to champion.

Second, we have to take more seriously Christ's intention that the Christian community should set an example to other communities. I am not thinking only of our Christian conduct at home and work, in which as husbands and wives, parents or children, employers or employees we are to be submissive to one another out of reverence for Christ (Ephesians 5:21). I am thinking particularly of the life of the local church, which is meant to be a sign of God's rule. The Church should be the one community in the world in which human dignity and equality are invariably recognized, and people's responsibility for one another is accepted; in which the rights of others are sought and never violated, while our own are often renounced; in which there is no partiality, favoritism, or discrimination; in which the poor and the weak are defended, and human beings are free to be human as God made them and meant them to be.

An exciting new initiative in the United States provides an excellent example of how Christians can become involved in defending the rights of others. In November 1994 a study was commissioned to examine the need for "a specialized Christian ministry that could help people overseas who suffer injustice and abuse in circumstances where local authorities cannot be relied upon for relief."[21]

Eighteen months of extensive research and consultation provided overwhelming evidence that overseas Christian workers all over the world were regularly observing human rights abuses in situations where the local authorities could not be counted on to provide relief. It also showed that the existence of a faith-based ministry with the professional expertise to document human rights abuses and to intervene on behalf of victims without putting missionaries and their agencies in compromising positions was not only a welcome idea but an absolute need. It was in response to this that the International Justice Mission was founded and has begun to work with overseas ministries to support the rights of all people, Christian and non-Christian, in the face of abuse and oppression. Most recently, the IJM's attention has been drawn to cases of child sexual exploitation in Asia, land expropriations in Latin America, and detentions without charge or trial in Africa. In such cases, the IJM is seeking to bring to bear professional expertise in documenting the abuses and securing appropriate relief for the victims.

Initiatives like this indicate to the world that Christians take seriously our commitment to the needs and rights of others.

Notes

1 Involvement: Is It Our Concern?

1. *Evangelism and Social Responsibility: An Evangelical Commitment*, The Grand Rapids Report, in John Stott (ed.), *Making Christ Known*, "Historic mission documents from the Lausanne movement 1974–1989" (Paternoster, 1996; Eerdmans, 1997), p. 179.

2. The adjective "evangelical" is used in different ways by different people, but in this book it denotes those Christians who, as heirs of the Reformation, emphasize Scripture as having supreme authority in the Church and the cross of Christ as being the only ground of salvation.

3. G. M. Trevelyan endorsed the opinion of the French historian Elie Halevy that evangelical religion in England "was the chief influence that prevented our country from starting along the path of revolutionary violence," *English Social History* (Longmans, Green, 1942), p. 477. See also W. E. H. Lecky, *A History of England in the Eighteenth Century*, vol. VI (Longmans, Green, 1919), p. 376.

4. J. Wesley Bready, *England: Before and After Wesley* (Hodder & Stoughton, 1939), pp. 11, 14.

5. ibid. p. 126.

6. ibid. p. 405.

7. ibid.

8. ibid. p. 327.

9. ibid. p. 316.

10. Ernest Marshall Howse, *Saints in Politics*, "The "Clapham Sect" and the growth of freedom" (George Allen & Unwin, 1953), p. 26. See also Kenneth Hylson-Smith, *Evangelicals in the Church of England 1734–1984* (T. & T. Clark, 1989), Chapter 5.

11. Howse, *Saints in Politics*, p. 27.

12. Georgina Battiscombe, *Shaftesbury*, "A biography of the 7th Earl 1801–1885" (Constable, 1974), p. 334.

13. Quoted by David O. Moberg in *The Great Reversal*, "Evangelism versus social concern" (1972; Scripture Union, 1973), p. 184. For an account of evangelical social work in Britain in the nineteenth century, see also Kathleen Heasman, *Evangelicals in Action* (Geoffrey Bles, 1962).

14. Donald W. Dayton, *Discovering an Evangelical Heritage* (Harper & Row, 1976), pp. 15–24. See also Timothy L. Smith, *Revivalism and Social Reform*, "American Protestantism on the eve of the Civil War" (1957; John Hopkins University Press, 1980).

Dr. Smith begins his preface by saying that Thomas Paine, if he had visited New York in 1865, would have been amazed to discover that "the emancipating glory of the great awakenings had made Christian liberty, Christian equality and Christian fraternity the passion of the land" (p. 7).

15. Dayton, *Discovering an Evangelical Heritage*, p. 25.

16. From an article by Donald W. Dayton in *The Post-American* (March 1975).

17. From the Introduction by R. Pierce Beaver in Samuel Escobar and John Driver, *Christian Mission and Social Justice* (Herald, 1978), pp. 7–9.

18. See also George Marsden, *Fundamentalism and American Culture* (Oxford University Press, 1980), pp. 85–93.

19. Michael Cassidy, *The Passing Summer*, "A South African pilgrimage in the politics of love" (Hodder & Stoughton, 1989), pp. 253–54.

20. Walter Rauschenbusch, *Christianity and the Social Crisis* (Macmillan, London, 1907).

21. ibid. pp. 391–400.

22. ibid. p. 357.

23. ibid. p. 65.

24. ibid. p. xiii.

25. ibid. p. 149.

26. ibid. p. 420.

27. ibid. p. 210.

28. ibid. p. 380.

29. Walter Rauschenbusch, A *Theology for the Social Gospel* (1917; Macmillan, New York, 1918).

30. ibid. p. 1.

31. ibid. p. 131.

32. ibid. p. 142.

33. ibid. p. 145.

34. George Marsden, "An Overview," in Michael Cromartie (ed.), *No Longer Exiles* (Ethics and Public Policy Center, Washington DC, 1993), p. 14.

35. Moberg, *The Great Reversal*, pp. 53–57.

36. The National Evangelical Anglican Congress (ed. Philip Crowe), Keele 67 (Falcon, 1967), para. 20.

37. Stott (ed.), *Making Christ Known*, p. 185.

38. ibid. p. 196.

39. ibid. pp. 197–98.

40. Dr. Edward Norman, *Christianity and the World Order* (Oxford University Press, 1979).

41. Stott (ed.), *Making Christ Known*, p. 202.

42. Tom Sine, *The Mustard Seed Conspiracy* (Word, 1981), pp. 69–71.

43. I think it was Dr. Carl F. H. Henry who coined this phrase. See his autobiography, *Confessions of a Theologian* (Word, 1986), p. 257.

44. John Gladwin, *God's People in God's World*, "Biblical motives for social involvement" (InterVarsity Press, 1979), p. 125.

45. H. J. Blackham, *Humanism* (Penguin, 1968). He writes: "Humanism is the human case and the human cause, an age-old conviction about the human case . . .

which will induce men and women . . . to espouse the human cause with head and heart and with two hands" (p. 9).

46. Sir Julian Huxley (ed.), *The Humanist Frame* (George Allen & Unwin, 1961), p. 47.

47. Summarized from Sir Frederick Treves, *The Elephant Man and other Reminiscences* (Cassell, 1923). For a thoroughly researched account of the whole affair, see Michael Howell and Peter Ford, *The True History of the Elephant Man* (Penguin, 1980).

48. Quoted by Charles Smyth in Cyril Forster Garbett (Hodder & Stoughton, 1959), p. 106.

49. A. R. Vidler, *Essays in Liberality* (SCM, 1957), pp. 95–112. Dr. Vidler contrasted it with "unholy worldliness," which is "to conform uncritically and complacently to the standards and fashions that prevail" (p. 96).

50. A. N. Triton, *Whose World?* (InterVarsity Press, 1970), pp. 35–36.

51. CARE, Jubilee Trust, Tearfund, and the Institute for Contemporary Christianity (among others) all sponsor groups which seek to blend Christian thought on specific issues with action. See M. A. Eden and E. C. Lucas, *Being Transformed* (Marshall, 1988), especially Appendix 3; and Roy McCloughry, *The Eye of the Needle* (InterVarsity Press, 1990).

2 Complexity: Can We Think Straight?

1. William Temple, *Citizen and Churchman* (Eyre & Spottiswoode, 1941), p. 82.

2. ibid. p. 83.

3. ibid. p. 84.

4. William Temple, *Christianity and the Social Order* (Penguin, 1942), p. 29.

5. ibid. p. 31.

6. Harry Blamires, *The Christian Mind* (SPCK, 1963), p. 70.

7. ibid. p. 43.

8. ibid. p. 3.

9. ibid. p. 50.

10. David W. Gill, *The Opening of the Christian Mind*, "Taking every thought captive to Christ" (InterVarsity Press, U.S., 1989), pp. 65–75 and 91. See also Arthur Holmes, *Contours of a World View* (Eerdmans, 1983) and Oliver R. Barclay, *Developing a Christian Mind* (InterVarsity Press, 1984).

11. Theodore Roszak, *Where the Wasteland Ends*, "Politics and transcendence in post-industrial society" (1972; Anchor, 1973), pp. xxi and 67.

12. J. S. Whale, *Christian Doctrine* (1941; Fontana, 1957), p. 33.

13. Reinhold Niebuhr, *The Children of Light and the Children of Darkness* (Nisbet, 1945), p. vi.

14. Sine, *The Mustard Seed Conspiracy*, p. 70.

15. Temple, *Christianity and the Social Order*, p. 54.

16. *The Lausanne Covenant*, para. 15. See Stott (ed.), *Making Christ Known*, p. 49.

17. C. E. M. Joad, *The Recovery of Belief* (Faber & Faber, 1952), p. 82.

18. From *The Essence of Security*, quoted by Gavin Reid in *The Elaborate Funeral* (Hodder & Stoughton, 1972), p. 48.

19. Whale, *Christian Doctrine*, p. 41.

20. Os Guinness, *Fit Bodies, Fat Minds* (Hodder & Stoughton, 1994), p. 105.

3 Pluralism: Should We Impose Our Views?

1. Peter Brierley and Heather Wright (eds.), *UK Christian Handbook* 1996/1997, p. 240.

2. ibid. p. 23.

3. ibid. pp. 281–84.

4. ibid.

5. ibid. p. 283.

6. The standard work on the Inquisition is still H. C. Lea, *A History of the Inquisition of the Middle Ages*, 3 vols. (1887; Macmillan, 1906). Bernard Hamilton gives a briefer account in *The Medieval Inquisition* (Edward Arnold, 1981).

7. John Kobler, *Ardent Spirits,* "The rise and fall of prohibition" (Michael Joseph, 1974), pp. 216–17.

8. Richard Gutteridge, *Open Thy Mouth for the Dumb,* "The German Evangelical Church and the Jews 1870–1950" (Basil Blackwell, 1976).

9. ibid. p. 48.

10. ibid. p. 128.

11. ibid. p. 181.

12. ibid. p. 268.

13. ibid. p. 298.

14. ibid. p. 299.

15. ibid. p. 304.

16. Abraham Lincoln concluded his famous *Gettysburg Address* (1863) with the resolve "that this nation, under God, shall have a new birth of freedom, and that government of the people, by the people, for the people, shall not perish from the earth." He seems to have borrowed this definition of democracy from the Rev. Theodore Parker, who used it in a speech in Boston in 1850.

17. O. R. Johnston, *Who Needs the Family?,* "A survey and a Christian assessment" (Hodder & Stoughton, 1979), pp. 43–46.

18. J. D. Unwin, *Sex and Culture* (Oxford University Press, 1934), pp. 411–12 and 431–32.

19. See, for example, Hugh Arthur, *Sex and Society* (Presbyterian Church of England, 1969): "There is no doubt, physiologically and psychologically speaking, that whereas for men intercourse is a pleasure and an end in itself, it is a pleasure and a beginning for a woman . . . the basic feminine sexual need really is security."

20. Temple, *Christianity and the Social Order*, p. 59.

21. Reinhold Niebuhr, *Moral Man and Immoral Society* (Scribner's, 1932; revised ed., 1960), pp. xi and xx.

22. John R. Lucas, *Democracy and Participation* (1975; Pelican, 1976), p. 10. Also recommended is Reinhold Niebuhr, *The Children of the Light and the Children of the Darkness* (Nisbet, 1945). He wrote it eighteen months before the end of World War II, in which he saw "bourgeois civilization" collapsing before the onslaught of Nazi barbarism. He subtitles his book "A vindication of democracy and a critique of its traditional defenders." His faith in democracy was not the blind optimism of liberals who, having no conception of original sin, held a "fatuous and superficial view of man" (p. 15). It was rather that democracy is the best way to resolve the tension

between the individual and the community, self-interest and the common good, freedom and order.

23. John V. Taylor, *Enough is Enough* (SCM, 1975), pp. 64 and 114.

4 Alienation: Have We Any Influence?

1. From his Inaugural Address to students on 28 April 1972, when installed as rector of Glasgow University.

2. K. S. Latourette, *History of the Expansion of Christianity* (Eyre & Spottiswoode, 1945), vol. 7, pp. 503–4.

3. Charles W. Colson, *Kingdoms in Conflict*, "An insider's challenging view of politics, power and the pulpit" (William Morrow/ Zondervan, 1987), e.g., pp. 238, 253–64, 371. Fran Beckett, in her book *Called to Action* (Fount, 1989), emphasizes the responsibility of each church to get to know its local community and to mobilize teams to serve the needs it has discovered.

4. Nikolai Berdyaev, *The Destiny of Man* (Geoffrey Bles, 1937), p. 281.

5. Temple, *Christianity and the Social Order*, p. 27.

6. Sine, *The Mustard Seed Conspiracy*, p. 113.

7. Matthew 5–7. I try to develop this exposition in *The Message of the Sermon on the Mount*, "Christian counter-culture" (InterVarsity Press, 1978).

8. *Evangelism and Social Responsibility*, in Stott (ed.), *Making Christ Known*, p. 200.

9. Colson, *Kingdoms in Conflict*, p. 327.

10. Quoted in Ronald J. Sider, *Exploring the Limits of Non-Violence* (Spire, 1988), p. 70. See also Dr. Isabelo Magalit, "The Church and the Barricades," in *Transformation*, April–June 1986.

11. Colson, *Kingdoms in Conflict*, p. 333.

12. *Evangelism and Social Responsibility*, in Stott (ed.), *Making Christ Known*, p. 182.

13. ibid. p. 183.

14. Brian Griffiths, *Morality and the Market Place*, "Christian alternatives to capitalism and socialism" (Hodder & Stoughton, 1982), p. 69.

15. *North–South*, "A programme for survival," the report of the Independent Commission on International Development Issues under the chairmanship of Willy Brandt (Pan Books, 1980), p. 25.

16. Griffiths, *Morality and the Market Place*, pp. 148–49.

17. ibid. pp. 154–55.

18. Alexander Solzhenitsyn, *One Word of Truth* (Bodley Head, 1972), pp. 22–27.

19. *Speech* by Sir Keith Joseph in Birmingham, October 1974.

20. John Howard Yoder, *The Politics of Jesus* (Eerdmans, 1972), pp. 111 and 157.

21. *Evangelism and Social Responsibility*, in Stott (ed.), *Making Christ Known*, p. 189.

22. Dom Helder Camara, *Spiral of Violence* (1970; Sheed & Ward, 1971), p. 69.

23. Dom Helder Camara, *The Desert is Fertile* (Sheed & Ward, 1974), p. 3.

24. Camara, *Spiral of Violence*, p. 43.

25. Dom Helder Camara, *Race Against Time* (Sheed & Ward, 1971), pp. vii–viii.

26. ibid. p. 17.

27. Sine, *The Mustard Seed Conspiracy*, pp. 11–12.

28. Harper & Row, 1985.

5 Wars and Rumours of Wars

1. Albert Einstein, in a telegram asking prominent persons for funds for the Atomic Scientists' Emergency Committee, cited in the *New York Times*, 25 May 1946.

2. Samuel Huntington, *The Clash of Civilizations and the Remaking of World Order* (Simon & Schuster, 1997), p. 21.

3. ibid. p. 126.

4. ibid. p. 29.

5. Robert D. Kaplan, *The Ends of the Earth*, "A journey at the dawn of the 21st century" (Random House, 1996; Papermac, 1997), p. 5.

6. ibid. p. 134.

7. Huntington, *The Clash of Civilizations*, pp. 312–16.

8. ibid. p. 321.

9. Kaplan, *The Ends of the Earth*, pp. 8, 9.

10. ibid. p. 436.

11. *SIPRI Yearbook* 1997 (Stockholm International Research Institute, 1997), pp. 398–99.

12. From Earl Mountbatten's "The Final Abyss?" speech, May 1979, published in *Apocalypse Now?* (Spokesman Books, 1980), p. 11.

13. See also *The Long-Term Consequences of Nuclear War* (1983), the report of an international conference sponsored by thirty-one groups. Two imaginative scenarios, written by military men, were published in 1978. *World War 3*, "A military projection founded on today's facts," edited by Brigadier Shelford Bidwell (Hamlyn, 1978) predicted that in 1983 the Third World War would start "as a result of some intolerable provocation" (p. xiii), e.g., the invasion of West Germany by Soviet tanks to prevent her from becoming a nuclear power. The last chapter is entitled "Doomsday" and describes the final, total devastation. *The Third World War* by General Sir John Hackett, assisted by top-ranking American and German generals (Sidgwick & Jackson, 1978), calls itself "A future history." It also describes an invasion of West Germany by Soviet tanks, though in 1985, which steadily escalates until first Birmingham and then in retaliation Minsk are obliterated by nuclear missiles. This time, however, the final holocaust is averted by the uprising against the Soviet Union of her satellites.

The ghastly consequences of a nuclear explosion are factually described by Donald B. Kraybill in *Facing Nuclear War* (Herald Press, 1982) and in *Common Security* (the Palme Commission Report, 1982), pp. 49–70.

14. International Institute for Strategic Studies, *The Military Balance 1996/1997* (Oxford University Press, 1996), pp. 306–11.

15. From an address entitled "The Chance for Peace," delivered on 16 April 1953. See *Public Papers of the Presidents of the United States: Dwight Eisenhower, 1953* (Washington, DC: U.S. Government Printing Office, 1960), p. 182.

16. *The Military Balance 1996/1997*, p. 273.

17. ibid. p. 289.

18. ibid. p. 273.

19. For a debate among eight Christian thinkers, who assess the arguments for and against these three positions, see Oliver R. Barclay (ed.), *Pacifism and War*, "When Christians Disagree" series (InterVarsity Press, 1984). Similar ground is covered in

Robert G. Clouse (ed.), *War: Four Christian Views* (InterVarsity Press, U.S., 1981). See also J. Andrew Kirk (ed.), *Handling Problems of Peace and War* (Marshall Pickering, 1988).

20. For recent statements of the pacifist position, see Jean Lasserre, *War and the Gospel* (E.T. James Clarke, 1962), Ronald J. Sider, *Christ and Violence* (Herald Press, Canada, 1979), and Ronald J. Sider and Richard K. Taylor, *Nuclear Holocaust and Christian Hope* (InterVarsity Press, U.S., 1982).

21. The theory of the "just war" is carefully argued in two books by Paul Ramsey: *War and the Christian Conscience* (Duke University Press, 1961) and *The Just War* (Scribner's, 1968). For more recent statements of the "just war" position, see Arthur F. Holmes in Clouse (ed.), *War: Four Christian Virtues*, pp. 120–21; *The Church and the Bomb* (Hodder & Stoughton, 1982), pp. 81–98; and *The Challenge of Peace: God's Promise and Our Response*, the U.S. Bishops' Pastoral Letter (CTS/SPCK, 1983), pp. 24–32. For a similar position based on the justice of God, see Jerram Barrs, *Peace and Justice in the Nuclear Age* (Garamond Press, 1983).

22. Dale Aukerman, *Darkening Valley*, "A biblical perspective on nuclear war" (Seabury, 1981), Chapter 15, p. 95.

23. ibid. pp. 92–94.

24. It needs to be added that in some emergency situations when no policeman is present, it may be right for a citizen to intervene in a fight, protect an innocent person against assault, or arrest a burglar. But in such cases the citizen is temporarily constituting himself an arm of the law; he is not acting as a private individual, nor is he justified in feeling personal animosity or taking personal revenge.

25. Oliver O'Donovan, *In Pursuit of a Christian View of War*, Grove Booklet on Ethics No. 15 (Grove Books, 1977), pp. 13–14. This booklet is a valuable inquiry into the legitimacy of the analogy between domestic justice and warfare.

26. Dana Mills-Powell (ed.), *Decide for Peace*, "Evangelicals against the bomb," is a symposium of sixteen contributions by both nuclear and total pacifists (Marshall Pickering, 1986).

27. *Pastoral Constitution*, para. 80.

28. *The Church and the Atom*, the report of a Church of England Commission (1948), p. 43. For a factual account of the bombing of German and Japanese cities, see Brigadier Peter Young (ed.), *The Almanac of World War II* (Hamlyn, 1981). Bishop Bell's speech in the House of Lords is recorded in Hansard (9 February 1944), vol. 130, pp. 738–46. It is also referred to in Ronald C. D. Jasper, *George Bell, Bishop of Chichester* (Oxford University Press, 1967), pp. 276–77.

29. International Institute for Strategic Studies, *Strategic Survey 1996/1997* (Oxford University Press, 1997), p. 38.

30. *Gaudium et Spes* ("The Church in the Modern World"), 1965, para. 80, in W. M. Abbott and J. Gallagher, *The Documents of Vatican II* (Geoffrey Chapman, 1966).

31. British Council of Churches resolution.

32. *The Church and the Bomb*, "Nuclear weapons and Christian conscience," an unofficial report of a Church of England working party (Hodder & Stoughton, 1982), p. 97.

33. ibid. pp. 143–44.

34. ibid. p. 162.

35. "The New Abolitionist Covenant" is printed in Jim Wallis (ed.), *Waging Peace*, "A handbook for the struggle to abolish nuclear weapons" (Harper & Row, 1982), pp. 17–21. See also Jim Wallis (ed.), *Peace-makers*, "Christian voices from the New Abolitionist Movement" (Harper & Row, 1983).

36. Quoted by William Epstein in "The ABCs of Disarmament," an article on the home page for the NGO Committee for Disarmament, at <www.igc.apc.org/disarm/>.

37. Michael Quinlan, "The Meaning of Deterrence," in Francis Bridger (ed.), *The Cross and the Bomb* (Mowbray, 1983), p. 143.

38. U.S. Bishops' Pastoral Letter, *The Challenge of Peace*, see endnote 12, pp. 43–46.

39. Paul Abrecht and Ninan Koshy (eds.), *Before It's Too Late*, "The challenge of nuclear disarmament" (WCC, 1983), p. 10.

40. Hugh Beach, "Where Does the Nuclear-Free Path Lead?," in Bridger (ed.), *The Cross and the Bomb*, p. 126.

41. Roger Ruston, OP, *Nuclear Deterrence—Right or Wrong?*, a study prepared for the Roman Catholic Commission for International Justice and Peace (Catholic Information Services, 1981), pp. 35–36, 58.

42. *Common Security* (Palme Commission Report, 1982), p. 105.

43. ibid. pp. 141, 149.

44. See, e.g., Walter Stein (ed.), *Nuclear Weapons and Christian Conscience* (Merlin Press, 1961 and 1980), and Geoffrey Goodwin (ed.), *Ethics and Nuclear Deterrence* (Croom Helm, 1982). See also Richard Harries, "The Strange Mercy of Deterrence," in John Gladwin (ed.), *Dropping the Bomb* (Hodder & Stoughton, 1985), pp. 64–73, and Richard Harries, *Christianity and War in a Nuclear Age* (Mowbray, 1986), especially pp. 134–44.

45. Ernest Lefever and Stephen Hunt (eds.), *The Apocalyptic Premise: Nuclear Arms Debated* (Ethics and Public Policy Center, Washington, DC, 1982), pp. 351–59. See also Anthony Kenny, *The Logic of Deterrence* (Firethorn Press, 1985).

46. Quoted in U.S. Bishops' Pastoral Letter, *The Challenge of Peace*. The bishops elaborated on the pope's statement, declaring that they had "arrived at a strictly conditional, moral acceptance of deterrence."

47. Bridger (ed.), *The Cross and the Bomb*, pp. 50, 60, 64–65.

48. Robert W. Gardiner, *The Cool Arm of Destruction* (Westminster, 1974), quoted by Robert G. Clouse in *War: Four Christian Views*, pp. 193–94.

49. From Dr. David Owen's introduction to *Common Security* (Palme Commission Report), p. xxi.

50. *Evangelism and Social Responsibility*, in Stott (ed.), *Making Christ Known*, p. 200.

51. See, e.g., *Defence without the Bomb, the Report of the Alternative Defence Commission* (Taylor and Francis, 1983).

6 Our Human Environment

1. Jonathon Porritt and David Winner, *The Coming of the Greens* (Fontana/Collins, 1988), pp. 267, 7.

2. Many "green" consumer guides are available in most bookshops.

3. Ghillean Prance, *The Earth Under Threat* (Wild Goose Publications, 1996), p. 31.

4. Roy McCloughry, *Population Growth and Christian Ethics*, Grove Ethical Studies No. 98 (Grove Books Ltd., 1995).

5. E. F. Schumacher, *Small is Beautiful* (1973; Abacus, 1974), pp. 11–16. The vision of unlimited growth has been pertinently criticized by Bishop Lesslie Newbigin in *Foolishness to the Greeks* (SPCK, 1986). "Growth . . . for the sake of growth," he writes, which "is not determined by an overarching social purpose," is "an exact account of the phenomenon which, when it occurs in the human body, is called cancer" (p. 114).

6. Prance, *The Earth Under Threat*, p. 45.

7. ibid.

8. ibid. p. 47. For other figures see also Jessica Tuchman Matthews, "Grasping the Concept of Environmental Insecurity," in Gwyn Prins (ed.), *Threats without Enemies* (Earthscan Publications, 1993), p. 27; and Stephen H. Schneider, *Laboratory Earth* (Weidenfeld & Nicolson, 1996), p. 112.

9. Schneider, *Laboratory Earth*, p. 107.

10. Prance, *The Earth Under Threat*, p. 41.

11. See Sir John Houghton (chairman of the Royal Commission on Environmental Pollution), *Global Warming*, "The complete briefing" (Lion, 1994).

12. World Commission on Environment and Development, *Our Common Future* (Oxford University Press, 1987), pp. 8, 43.

13. Gerhard von Rad, *Genesis* (1956; SCM, 1963), p. 58.

14. Tom Dale and Vernon Gill Carter, *Topsoil and Civilisation* (1955), quoted in Schumacher, *Small is Beautiful*, p. 84.

15. Martin Hengel, *Property and Riches in the Early Church* (1973; Fortress and SCM, 1974), p. 12.

16. *Laborem Exercens*, Pope John Paul II's Encyclical Letter on "Human Work" (Catholic Truth Society, 1981), pp. 50–51.

17. Jessica Tuchman Matthews, "Nations and Nature: A New View of Security," in Prins, *Threats without Enemies*, p. 36.

18. Prance, *The Earth Under Threat*, p. 47.

19. ibid. pp. 48–49.

20. *Man in his Living Environment*, "An ethical assessment," a report from the Board for Social Responsibility (Church Information Office, 1970), p. 61. See also *Our Responsibility for the Living Environment*, a report from the Board for Social Responsibility's Environmental Issues Reference Panel (Church House Publishing, 1986).

21. Gavin Maxwell's article appeared in *The Observer*, 13 October 1963.

22. C. F. D. Moule, *Man and Nature in the New Testament*, "Some reflections on biblical ecology" (Athlone, 1964; Fortress, 1967), p. 1. See also Andrew Linzey, *Christianity and the Rights of Animals* (SPCK, 1988).

23. Peter Singer, *Animal Liberation* (1990; 2nd ed., Pimlico Books, 1995). See also his more recent work, *Rethinking Life and Death*, "The collapse of our traditional ethics" (Oxford University Press, 1995), in which he attempts to narrow the difference between humans and animals.

24. ibid. p. 6.

25. ibid. p. 185.

26. For a good discussion of animal rights, see *Green Cross*, Winter 1996, vol. 2, no. 1. This issue is devoted to the discussion of Christian responsibility for animals. See also Richard Griffiths, *The Human Use of Animals* (Grove Booklets, 1982), and Tony Sargent, *Animal Rights and Wrongs, a Biblical Perspective* (Hodder & Stoughton, 1996).

27. From an address to the American Association for the Advancement of Science, which was published as "The Historical Roots of our Ecological Crisis," in *Science* 155 (1967), pp. 1203–7, and was reprinted as Chapter 5 of his *Machina ex Deo: Essays in the Dynamism of Western Culture* (MIT Press, Cambridge, Mass., and London, 1968).

28. Ian L. McHarg, *Design with Nature* (Doubleday, 1969), p. 26.

29. ibid. p. 197.

30. These extracts from Ian McHarg's Dunning Trust Lectures were quoted in the *Ontario Naturalist*, March 1973.

31. Keith Thomas, *Man and the Natural World* (1983; Penguin, 1984). See also Edward Echlin, *The Christian Green Heritage*, "World as creation" (Grove Ethical Studies, no. 74, 1989), and Colin A. Russell, *The Earth, Humanity and God* (UCL Press, 1994), especially pp. 86–93.

32. Thomas, *Man and the Natural* World, p. 17.

33. ibid. p. 18.

34. ibid. p. 22.

35. ibid. p. 24; cf. p. 151.

36. ibid. p. 278.

37. Barbara Ward and Rene Dubos, *Only One Earth*, "The care and maintenance of a small planet" (Penguin, 1972), p. 83.

38. ibid. p. 45.

39. ibid. p. 85.

40. Ronald Higgins, *The Seventh Enemy* (Hodder & Stoughton, 1978).

41. Klaus Bockmuhl, *Conservation and Lifestyle* (1975, translated by Bruce N. Kaye; Grove Books, 1977), pp. 23–24. For a more recent *Christian evaluation of environmental issues*, see Ron Elsdon, *Greenhouse Theology* (Monarch, 1992); Stan LeQuire (ed.), *The Best Preaching on Earth*, a collection of sermons on care for creation (Judson Press, 1996); and Colin A. Russell, *The Earth, Humanity and God* (UCL Press, 1994). See also the quarterly magazine *Green Cross*, a publication of the Christian Society of the Green Cross, a ministry of Evangelicals for Social Action—Green Cross, 10 East Lancaster Avenue, Wynnewood, PA 19096–3495, USA.

42. These organizations can be reached at the following addresses. The Evangelical Environmental Network c/o The Institute for Contemporary Christianity, St Peter's Church, Vere St, London W1M 9HP, or 10 East Lancaster Avenue, Wynnewood PA 19096–3495, USA. The Au Sable Institute at Messiah College, Grantham PA 17027, USA. The A Rocha Trust, 3 Hooper St, Cambridge CB1 2NZ, UK.

7 North–South Economic Inequality

1. *World Development Report*, 1991.

2. *North–South*, "A programme for survival," the Report of the Independent Commission on International Development Issues, pp. 7, 8.

3. Michael P. Todaro (ed.), *Economic Development* (Longman, 1997), p. 189.

4. ibid. pp. 43–44.

5. Brandt Commission, *Common Crisis*, "North-South: co-operation for world recovery" (Pan Books, 1983), pp. 9–10.

6. *Human Development Report*, 1997 (Oxford University Press, 1997), and *Economic Development*, p. 32.

7. *North–South*, p. 23.

8. The Villars Statement is included in Marvin Olasky (ed.), *Freedom, Justice and Hope*, "Towards a strategy for the poor and the oppressed" (Crossway Books, 1988), pp. 141–46.

9. Vishal Mangalwadi, *Truth and Social Reform* (Hodder & Stoughton, 1989), e.g., pp. 5–6, 25, 32, 115.

10. *North-South*, pp. 276–80.

11. ibid. p. 64.

12. ibid.

13. ibid. p. 30.

14. Griffiths, *Morality and the Market Place*, p. 127.

15. *North–South*, p. 63.

16. ibid. p. 25.

17. Griffiths, *Morality and the Market Place*, p. 143.

18. ibid. pp. 148–49.

19. "Imperatives for Economic Development," in Olasky (ed.), *Freedom, Justice and Hope*, p. 112.

20. ibid. pp. 116–17.

21. ibid. p. 145.

22. John Stott (ed.), *The Year 2000 AD* (Marshall, Morgan & Scott, 1983), pp. 72–102. Donald Hay elaborated and recast his lecture in Chapter 7, "Rich Nation, Poor Nation," of his book *Economics Today*, "A Christian critique" (Apollos, InterVarsity Press, 1989).

23. Hay, ibid. pp. 92–93.

24. ibid. p. 94.

25. ibid. p. 95.

26. Brandt Commission, *Common Crisis*. Three years later, Willy Brandt wrote another book, angry in tone and popular in appeal, entitled *World Armament and World Hunger*, "A call for action" (Pantheon, 1986). In it he drew attention to global military spending, which was estimated at $1 trillion annually, and argued that defense and development expenditure could no longer be segregated. Indeed, the former should be subordinated to the latter.

27. *Common Crisis*, p. 1.

28. See Bob Geldof with Paul Vallely, *Is That It?* (Penguin, 1986).

29. Todaro, *Economic Development*, p. 41.

30. *Human Development Report* 1996 (Oxford University Press, 1996), p. 73.

31. ibid.

32. Jubilee 2000's international petition calls for lending nations to "cancel the backlog of unpayable debts of the most impoverished nations . . . by the year 2000

... [and] to take effective steps to prevent such high levels of debt building up again." The petition will be presented to the G7 nations when they meet in 1998 and 1999. Jubilee 2000 can be reached at PO Box 100, London SE1 7RT, UK, or on the internet at <www.oneworld.org/jubilee2000>. Other development agencies share the "oneworld" site and it can be a useful site to visit for more information.

33. World Commission on Environment and Development, *Our Common Future*, pp. 8, 43.

34. Quoted in Todaro, *Economic Development*, p. 69.

35. ibid. pp. 7–19.

36. Visit <www.undp.org> for the most up-to-date information on this report as it is published each year.

37. For example, "Poverty has become feminized to a significant degree," *Christian Faith and the World Economy Today, a 1992 study document from the World Council of Churches*, p. 26.

38. See Ruth Pearson, "Gender Matters in Development," in Tim Allen and Alan Thomas (eds.), *Poverty and Development in the 1990s* (Oxford University Press, 1992), pp. 291–312; "Women in Poverty," in Todaro, *Economic Development*, pp. 156–59; and the quarterly update from June 1997 entitled *BRIDGE* (Briefings on Development and Gender), produced by the Institution of Development Studies in Sussex, on <www.ids.ac.uk/ids/research/bridge/dgb.html>.

39. Quotations extracted from press releases related to the publication of the *Human Development Report 1997*.

40. I have read that there are at least "five major and often competing development theories." See Todaro, *Economic Development*, pp. 69–95.

41. World Commission on Environment and Development, *Our Common Future*, p. 27.

42. Ward and Dubos, *Only One Earth*, an unofficial report commissioned by the Secretary-General of the United Nations Conference on the Human Environment, prepared with the assistance of a 152-member Committee of Corresponding Consultants in 58 countries.

43.. ibid. p. 298.

44. Duncan Munro, *Trade, Justice and the Wealth of Nations* (Grove Books, 1976), pp. 11, 24.

45. Barbara Ward, *Progress for a Small Planet* (Penguin, 1979), p. 277.

46. ibid. p. 257.

47. Roger D. Hansen and others, *US Foreign Policy and the Third World: Agenda 1982* (Praeger, 1982), p. 234, and the *Human Development Report 1996*, p. 199.

48. For the same Spirit, see, e.g., Romans 8:9; 1 Corinthians 12:13. For different spiritual gifts, see, e.g., Romans 12:3–8 and 1 Corinthians 12:4–31.

49. *Gospel and* Culture, the Willowbank Report, in Stott (ed.), *Making Christ Known*, pp. 77–113.

50. From a 1967 speech on the Arusha Declaration, published in *Freedom and Socialism*, uhuru na ujamaa, "A selection from the writings and speeches of Julius Nyerere 1965–1967" (Oxford University Press, Dar-es-Salaam, 1968), p. 326.

51. Todaro, *Economic Development*, p. 382.

52. *North–South*, p. 30.

8 Human Rights

1. Statistics of human rights violations are readily available from a variety of sources. I have culled mine mostly from Amnesty International's annual reports and Human Rights Watch world reports. The United Nations and U.S. government are also good sources of information.

2. Amnesty International Annual Report 1995, p. 249.

3. Gary Haugen, "Rwanda's Carnage," in *Christianity Today,* 6 February 1995, pp. 52–54.

4. "Statistics Concerning the Needs of Children Worldwide," *Action International,* January 1997.

5. Human Rights Watch World Report 1997, p. 333.

6. ibid. p. 334.

7. ibid. p. 339.

8. From the editorial by Emilio Castro in *International Review of Mission,* vol. LXVI, no. 263, devoted to "Human Rights" (July 1977), p. 218.

9. The most handy collection of these texts is Ian Brownie (ed.), *Basic Documents on Human Rights* (Clarendon, 2nd ed., 1981).

10. From Dr. Malik's introduction to O. Frederick Nolde, *Free and Equal,* "Human rights in ecumenical perspective" (WCC, 1968), p. 7.

11. Thomas Paine, *The Rights of Man* (1791), 8th ed., pp. 47–48.

12. From personal communication to the author.

13. Temple, *Citizen and Churchman,* pp. 74–75.

14. Paul Oestreicher, *Thirty Years of Human Rights* (the British Churches' Advisory Forum on Human Rights, 1980).

15. The prophetic protest against these three kings is found in 2 Samuel 11–12 (Nathan and David), 1 Kings 21 (Elijah and Ahab), and Jeremiah 22:13–19 (Jeremiah and Jehoiakim).

16. From an interview published in *Time* magazine, 24 July 1989.

17. Christopher J. H. Wright, *Human Rights: A Study in Biblical Themes,* Grove Booklet on Ethics no. 31 (Grove Books, 1979), p. 16.

18. For this renunciation of rights, see Mark 10:42–5 ("not so with you"); 1 Corinthians 13:5 (love); 1 Corinthians 6:1–8 (litigation); and 1 Peter 2:18–25 (slaves).

19. Nobel Prize speech, 1970.

20. For information about human rights violations in general, and about imprisonment and torture in general, write to Amnesty International, 1 Easton Street, London WC1X 8DJ.

21. "A Christian Witness for Justice, a Needs Assessment and Operational Outline" (November 1996, p. 1), conducted by the International Justice Mission, PO Box 58147, Washington DC, 20037–8147, USA; or on the internet at <www.ijm.org>.